"That Maker of the Home, the Open Fireplace." Page 68.

The Men of the Mountains

The Story of the Southern Mountaineer and His
Kin of the Piedmont; with an Account of
Some of the Agencies of Progress
among Them

BY
ARTHUR W. SPALDING

World rights reserved. This book or any portion thereof may not be copied or reproduced in any form or manner whatever, except as provided by law, without the written permission of the publisher, except by a reviewer who may quote brief passages in a review.

The author assumes full responsibility for the accuracy of all facts and quotations as cited in this book. The opinions expressed in this book are the author's personal views and interpretations, and do not necessarily reflect those of the publisher.

This book is provided with the understanding that the publisher is not engaged in giving spiritual, legal, medical, or other professional advice. If authoritative advice is needed, the reader should seek the counsel of a competent professional.

Facsimile Reproduction

As this book played a formative role in the development of Christian thought and the publisher feels that this book, with its candor and depth, still holds significance for the church today. Therefore the publisher has chosen to reproduce this historical classic from an original copy. Frequent variations in the quality of the print are unavoidable due to the condition of the original. Thus the print may look darker or lighter or appear to be missing detail, more in some places than in others.

Copyright © 2023 TEACH Services, Inc.
ISBN-13: 978-1-4796-1671-8 (Paperback)

Published by

TEACH Services, Inc.
P U B L I S H I N G
www.TEACHServices.com • (800) 367-1844

PREFACE

AMERICA knows least of what is most American. Melting-pot of the nations, with Europe's and Asia's dross thrown in along with their good metal, she is likely to forget, in all this conglomerate, the base of the alloy, which made the nation and which must yet preserve it. In the providence of God there has been saved to America a long wedge of that pure metal — a golden wedge of Ophir. Stretching from North to South, scarce two hundred miles inland, are the mountains that formed the frontier of English America when America became a nation. These mountains are filled with the stock of the Revolution, a race with the primitive virtues that won our liberties, that extended our borders, that preserved the ideal of freedom in its great hour of trial.

A smattering of knowledge—gained mostly from works of fiction — has the American public of this great mountaineer race, a smattering that begets more of idle wonder and vacant amusement than of honest admiration and symapthy. Yet the Southern mountaineer is, all in all, the most admirable type of American. Schooled to simplicity, not lacking in vigor, he keeps in great degree the powers that preserve nations, powers that too many of our people are losing in the nerve-racking strain of our unexampled age. What of opportunity and resource the mountaineer lacks it is the duty of more fortunate classes to supply. It is a duty of patriotism, and above all a duty of Christian brotherhood.

For an intelligent application of this aid a correct and sympathetic understanding of conditions is necessary. It has been the pleasure of a few of the mountaineer's friends to help give this understanding; yet, compared with the greater number of doubtful works that exploit chiefly his peculiarities and faults, the efforts of these friends are not too many nor too great. It is, then, with some confidence of need that this present volume is put forth, containing a brief account of the origin and history of the Southern mountaineer, of some of the most representative agencies for his development, and in particular of one widespread system that seeks to minister to the needs and to enlist more ministers.

The credit for the initiation and successful prosecution of the work on this book is due to Mrs. Ellen G. White and her son, William C. White. Their deep and practical interest in the cause of Christianity in the South, evidenced in many a phase and field, led them to propose such a work as this and to make possible the research and effort which produced it.

Acknowledgment is also gladly given of the aid rendered by the teachers of the Nashville Agricultural and Normal Institute and of the smaller schools throughout the South affiliated with them, as also of the assistance and encouragement of friends in other connections,

Preface

who have supplied information, corrected manuscripts, and given cordial support to the enterprise.

To the author the work has been a labor of love. Since, when a boy, his lot was first cast among the Southern mountaineers, his interests and affections have been closely entwined with theirs, and it is his confident hope that this book shall be a means of enlisting many more friends, both youth and those in the prime of life, in the cause of the mountaineer.   A. W. S.

Hendersonville, N. C.,
   November, 1915.

"The greatest want of the world is the want of men,—men who will not be bought or sold; men who in their inmost souls are true and honest; men who do not fear to call sin by its right name; men whose conscience is as true to duty as the needle to the pole; men who will stand for the right though the heavens fall." ELLEN G. WHITE.

CONTENTS

HIGHLANDS AND HIGHLANDERS

Chapter	Page
1. The Explorers	11
2. The Pioneers	21
3. In Times of War	32
4. Education and Religion	48
5. The Modern Mountaineer	61
6. The Heart of Appalachia	79

THE VANGUARD OF THE HELPERS

7. The Pioneer School	97
8. The Premier of Home Missions	108
9. Redeeming the Time	116
10. Coals from the Altar	129

A BROTHERHOOD OF SERVICE

11. A School of Simplicity	149
12. Learning to Teach	160
13. The Out-School Movement	166

PIONEERING

14. On an Old Frontier	177
15. Behind the Back of Mammon	187
16. Preaching by Hand	197
17. Sermons in Soil	206

THE MEDICAL MISSIONARY

18. Following the Great Physician	221
19. The Rural Sanitarium	227
20. The Nurse and the Medical Missionary	235

SCHOOL WORK

21. The Schools of God	243
22. The Mountain Child and the World	252
23. Vice and Victory	262

COOPERATION

24. Whosoever Is Not Against Us	279
25. The Times of Cheer	285

THE HELP OF THE HILLS

26. The Torch-Bearer	297
27. A Chosen People	307

ILLUSTRATIONS

	PAGE
THE MAKER OF THE HOME	*Frontispiece*
BATTLE OF KING'S MOUNTAIN	16
ON WATCH	31
BAKER MOUNTAIN SCHOOL AND CHURCH	48
RELIEF MAP OF APPALACHIA	64
OLD AND NEW	78
CROSSING THE BRANCH	93
LINCOLN MEMORIAL UNIVERSITY	94
CHAPEL, BEREA COLLEGE	97
STUDENTS AT HIGHLAND COLLEGE	112
FIRST CABIN, AND RECITATION HALL, BERRY SCHOOL	129
ONEIDA INSTITUTE	144
AN ANCIENT ART	146
ON MADISON CAMPUS	160
AT FOUNTAIN HEAD SCHOOL	168
NICKOJACK CAVE	186
SHOPS, EUFOLA ACADEMY	192
A NEW INDUSTRY	208
AT COWEE MOUNTAIN SCHOOL	216
EAGER FOR PROGRESS	226
MADISON RURAL SANITARIUM	240
PRIMITIVE MOTIVE POWER	251
GOING TO MARKET	275
IN THE SAPPHIRE COUNTRY	276
SELF-SUPPORTING WORKERS' CONVENTION	288
A KENTUCKY HOMESTEAD	294
A FAMILY REUNION	304

Highlands and Highlanders

"To THE mountains, in time to come, we may look for great men, thinkers as well as workers, leaders of religious and poetic thought, and statesmen above all." EMMA B. MILES.

I

THE EXPLORERS

THE Englishmen who set foot upon the shores of wilderness Virginia in the seventeenth century found themselves shut up against the sea by a long range of mountains in the west. Seeking a clear passage through, they might wander in vain far toward the northern confines of Penn's woods and deep into the southern recesses of the Carolina grants. Everywhere the unknown country beyond, which they sought to explore, was shut from their view by the blue, hazy, sentinel line of those mountains. They called them the Blue Ridge.

The early settlers believed that these mountains looked out upon the "South Seas." The blue haze that always surmounted them seemed proof that the ocean with its mists lay just beyond, and they thought they had only to find a convenient pass to enable them to embark upon a voyage to the Indies. It was to find such a pass that the valiant and venturesome John Smith, seven months after the landing at Jamestown in 1607, set out on that expedition which ended in his captivity to the sour-looking old Powhatan, and — perhaps — in his rescue from death by the tender-hearted Pocahontas.

Sixty miles above Jamestown, Smith's two companions were surprised and slain by Indians; and he himself, after a plucky fight, was taken captive by Opekankano, the brother of the king. He saved his life at the moment by exhibiting to his captor his mystifying compass, and following up the effect by a bewitching "discourse of the roundnes of the earth [and] the course of the sunne, moone, starres, and plannets." The savage loves no one so much as an entrancing liar, and evidently putting Smith in this catalog, the Indians carried him first to Opekankano's town, where they treated him most kindly. Thereafter he was taken about from town to town, until at last he was brought to the chief village of the Powhatans, the principal member of a confederacy of the coastal tribes. The head of this confederacy — the emperor, as Smith styles him — was also the chief of the Powhatan tribe, and was himself called, by distinction, "The Powhatan."[1]

Here for some days these two worthy representatives of the white and the red races sat exchanging their entertaining tales, each solemnly assuring himself — and with some reason — that the other believed him. John Smith informed his Indian majesty that the white men, being defeated in battle on the seas by their enemies the Spaniards, had been forced to fly for refuge into the red man's land, and then were compelled to stay there by the leaking of their ship. Further, he explained, the reason of his expedition up the river was to discover the way to the salt sea on the other side of the mountains, for there his father had had a child slain, whose death they intended to revenge.

Not to be outdone, the red man, "after good deliberation," began to describe that same country upon the salt sea, which he declared lay only just over the mountains, some five, or six, or eight days' journey. So exact was his information that he named the people who had slain Smith's supposititious brother, and told of their relations with other great peoples who sailed the seas. One of these was a man-eating nation, with

---

[1] John Fiske, *The Colonisation of the New World*, p. 246.

shaven crowns and long queues, and "Swords like Poll-axes." Another wore short coats with sleeves to the elbows, and went in great ships like the Englishmen. These were only a few of the wonders; for there were many other mighty nations, some of them having walled houses and plenty of brass. At last the king, warming to his subject, disclosed the information that his village lay but one day and a half, two days, and six days from various ports upon "the south part of the backe sea."

All this at least, along with his safe return to Jamestown, is told in "Captain John Smith's True Relation," published in 1608,[1] though his romantic story of rescue by Pocahontas he did not put forth until many years later. How much of this "relation" of the great "backe sea" just over the mountains came from the lips of Powhatan, and how much from John Smith's own fertile brain, we may not know; but the account at least explains one cause of the world's persistent faith in the western sea lapping the lower slopes of the Appalachian chain.

Smith, for the two years he remained in America, continued active in his efforts to find a passage or a path to the South Seas through those mountains. And not Smith alone; for there were many to whom not merely the wealth of the Indies, but the very real romance of discovery, appealed. In the fall of 1608 Captain Christopher Newport, who had commanded the expedition which founded Jamestown, and who had since with his ships kept up communication between England and Virginia, obeyed the injunctions of the London Company by attempting an expedition that should pierce the mountains to the seas. He succeeded, however, in doing no more than to penetrate forty miles above the village of the Powhatan, from which point

---

[1] *American History Leaflets*, No. 27, pp. 9-17; *Narratives of Early Virginia*, Tyler, pp. 41-52; *Works of John Smith*, edited by Arber, pp. 13-21.

he and his company returned worn in body and disappointed in hopes.[1]

The ambition of the London Company, far more than the desire of the sore-pressed colonists, inspired the earliest attempts to pass the mountains. The company's commands were laid upon Captain Newport, on his third voyage, never to return to England without having made at least one of three discoveries: the way to the South Seas, a lump of gold, or a white man from Raleigh's lost colony on Roanoke Island.[2]

Newport, however, was compelled to return without accomplishing any one of these three behests, and no doubt his explanation of his failure was greatly helped by John Smith's accompanying "Rude Answer" to a letter of reproach and instruction the company had sent him. In this spirited statement of conditions, Smith laid stress upon the need of establishing a firm basis for the colony by the sending of a good class of settlers, the development of agriculture, and attention to the needs and requirements of the colony, rather than to the immediate enrichment and glory of the company. For a time thereafter, while curiosity may not have lessened concerning the blue heights to the west, and what they might be hiding, the practical

---

[1] Amos Todkill and others, in "Description of Virginia and Proceedings of the Colonie," Tyler, *Narratives of Early Virginia*, pp. 151, 155, 156; *Works of John Smith*, pp. 121, 124, 125.

[2] Fiske, *Old Virginia and Her Neighbors*, p. 113; *Works of John Smith*, p. 121.

Sir Walter Raleigh was the first to attempt English colonization in America. He sent an expedition, of men only, in 1585, who settled on Roanoke Island, off the coast of North Carolina. These men, however, returned within a year. In 1587 Raleigh sent, under the command of John White, a better equipped company, which included in its number seventeen women. This company likewise settled on Roanoke Island; and here, on August 18, was born the first English white child on American soil, Virginia Dare. White returned to England for supplies, only to find himself in the midst of the Spanish war. It was two years before he could return to the infant colony in America; and when he did arrive, it was only to find a deserted place. And though search was made for many a year thereafter, no certain trace of the fate of this first and unfortunate colony was ever found.

energies of the little Virginia colony were absorbed in their local affairs.

Through the next quarter century, we catch a note now and then of interest and enterprise toward the west. In 1626 the governor and council of Virginia wrote the English government desiring that provision be made for exploring the mountain country, with the hope of finding passage to the South Seas.[1] In 1641 four prominent gentlemen of the colony applied for permission to undertake discoveries to the southwest of the Appomattox River.[2] An Indian report to the governor in 1648, of high mountains, beyond which were great rivers and a great sea to which came red-capped men in ships, almost induced an expedition thither.[3]

The governor at that time was that bluff, enterprising, grasping, ruthless British gentleman, William Berkeley. He had received from his patron, Charles I, a monopoly of the fur trade in the English colony; and as from the other side of the mountains there now began to come not only furs, but Indians with wondrous tales, Berkeley grew eager to open a route to the over-mountain country. Perhaps it would launch him upon the South Seas and the Indian trade; if not, there was profit as great in buying for a few hatchets and handfuls of beads, beaver and fox and otter furs worth thousands of dollars.

The governor, though ever upon the verge of going himself to view that good land, never really saw even the base of the mountains; but from 1650 to 1670 he dispatched or authorized several expeditions which, while they discovered no "backe sea," did open to the view of the English a broader field and a wider opportunity than the South Seas could ever have afforded them.

There lived in 1650 at Fort Henry,[4] on the York

---

[1] Alvord and Bidgood, *The First Explorations of the Trans-Allegheny Region by the Virginians*, p. 45.

[2] *Id.*, p. 28.   [3] *Id.*, p. 46.   [4] Now Petersburg, Virginia.

River, a captain and merchant of adventurous disposition by the name of Abraham Wood. A servant lad brought over from England, and indentured[1] to a planter for the payment of his journey's expense, Abraham Wood had risen step by step until he was one of the largest landowners in the colony, and a principal dealer, under Berkeley, in the fur trade.[2]

In 1650 this Captain Wood, with an English gentleman named Bland, and two others, with white servants and an Indian guide, made the first notable western exploration on record for the English. Their course led them southwesterly; but though they went some distance into Carolina, they did not reach the mountains; and their discovery, supposedly, of a "westward flowing river" helped for a brief time to encourage the belief in a near-by western sea.[3]

This view was given weight by the fictions of another explorer, who actually claimed that, in the region of what is now North Carolina, he had stood upon the shore of a sea that stretched westward beyond sight.[4]

This man was a German, John Lederer, and the statement above mentioned is from his account of his second exploring expedition. On a former trip he had won the distinction, so far as the records go, of being the first white man to ascend the mountains. In this work of exploration he was encouraged and probably sent by Governor Berkeley. Alone, except for some Indian

---

[1] An "indentured servant" was so called from the papers which bound him to a stated term of service. Such papers were usually made in duplicate, the two copies being written side by side on the same sheet, and then cut apart in a waved or indented line, for identification. Hence such papers were called "indentures."

[2] *First Explorations of the Trans-Allegheny Region*, pp. 34 ff.

[3] Id., pp. 47-51; *Discovery of New Brittaine*, by Bland, reprinted in Salley, *Narratives of Early Carolina, pp.* 5 ff.

[4] *First Explorations of Trans-Allegheny Region*, pp. 160, 161.
John Lederer's account of his southwestern travels, published in 1672, is reprinted in the above named work. It might be possible, with a little imagination, as one of his editors proves, to harmonize Lederer's accounts with geographical facts, supposing that he understates his distances and perhaps his time, and that he actually reached Florida and the Gulf; but such an interpretation is rejected by Alvord and Bidgood.

Battle of King's Mountain.
From painting in possession of North Carolina Historical Society.
"At King's Mountain was struck the critical blow." Page 39.

guides, Lederer set out in 1669, and after nine days of travel reached the foot of the Blue Ridge. It took him a whole day to climb the mountain; and then, though he imagined, from the deceiving mists to the eastward, that he could see the Atlantic Ocean, his eye searched in vain to the west; for there he beheld, instead of the great South Sea, nothing but a sea of mountains.[1]

There followed, in 1670, his second expedition to the southwest, already mentioned; and a third, in the latter part of the same year, in which he and ten other white men reached again the crest of the Blue Ridge at another point, only to view the discouraging height of the great North Mountain, far up and across the valley. Not yet was the mystery of the mountains solved.

Governor Berkeley next turned to that Captain (now Major-General) Abraham Wood whose first efforts we have seen, and commissioned him to make an attempt to "goe further in the discovry." Abraham Wood responded, not by personally heading an expedition — for he was now, perhaps, too greatly busied with his growing affairs — but by fitting out a party under Captain Thomas Batts, with Robert Fallam, two other white men, and an Appomattox chief named Perecute. They were later joined by several other Indians of the same tribe. It is possible that Abraham Wood himself had before this crossed the mountains, but the evidence thereof is too vague to make it certain,[2] and so far as records go, Batts and Fallam have the distinction of being the first to reach the waters of the Ohio.[3]

Captain Batts and his party crossed the Blue Ridge, and entered the upper part of the Shenandoah Valley near the site of the present city of Roanoke. A few miles

---

[1] *Id.*, pp. 64, 145 ff.

[2] See *First Explorations of Trans-Allegheny Region*, pp. 52-55; Collins, *History of Kentucky*, p. 805; Shaler, *History of Kentucky*, p. 59.

[3] This expedition of Captain Batts and his party has received scant notice in American histories. If not in extent, at least in significance, it should rank with the journeys of La Salle and Marquette; for by it the

south of this they crossed the divide, and entered the valley of a river flowing northward, which they followed to the present borders of the State of Virginia, at Peters Falls.[1] At this point, their provisions having all been spent for some days, and game being hard to get, their Indian guides insisted on turning back. They were also doubtless influenced by the nearness to a great and fierce tribe of Indians living to the north and west, "on the Great Water, and [who] made salt."[2] These were probably the Shawnees, and their salt works were at the numerous "salt licks" plentiful in Kentucky, though the Shawnees lived north of the Ohio River, and only made short forays into Kentucky.

Batts and Fallam, before they retreated, made simple but solemn proclamation that King Charles of England owned these waters and the lands wherethrough they flowed, and they branded five trees with the initials and signs of Charles, Berkeley, Wood, and themselves. As they lingered upon a height, and cast their eyes westward, they were persuaded that they saw, "westerly, over a certain delightful hill, a fog arise, and a glimmering light as from water," and "supposed there to be a great bay." Not yet had the myth of the "backe sea" lost its charm. It was considerably later, no doubt, before the reports of the Indians, the investigations

---

English were given such right as discovery bestows to claim the overmountain country for their king and nation. But so little known have been the sources of this history, and so garbled the account by some early historians, that the foremost American authorities have either ignored it or mentioned it only to dismiss it as unreliable. Even Captain Thomas Batts' name has undergone wondrous transformations in the pages of his few chroniclers, from "Henry Batte" (his brother) in Beverly's "*Virginia*," p. 62, to "Bolt" in Shaler's "*Kentucky*," p. 59, and "Bolton" in Parkman's "*La Salle and the Discovery of the Great West*," p. 5. In a recent and most valuable work, the sources for the history of this expedition, as of other early English explorations, have been gathered and placed in the hands of the public: "*First Explorations of the Trans-Allegheny Region*," by C. W. Alvord and Lee Bidgood, Arthur Clark Company, Cleveland, 1912.

[1] *First Explorations of the Allegheny Region*, p. 192, footnote.
By them this river was named Wood River. It is now known in the upper part as New River, and in the lower as the Kanawha.
[2] *Id.*, p. 198.

of farther-going explorers, and the accounts of the French upon the Mississippi and the western plains made clear the immense distance at which lay the Pacific, that great "backe sea."

When Batts and Fallam returned, Governor Berkeley, excited by their report, renewed at once his oft-thwarted intention of heading an expedition to the mountains. But he was just at this time given sufficient employment nearer home by a discontented people, who, under a certain well-remembered Nathaniel Bacon, rose up in the first insurrection of an America that would be free. The exciting cause of Bacon's Rebellion was the unpunished outrages of the Indians, who had grown hostile. Their attitude shut off the West for a time from the Englishmen; and while it is possible that there were some venturesome hunters and traders who penetrated the mountains, yet, so far as records go, the matter of western exploration rested for half a century.

In 1716 Alexander Spottswood, then the energetic governor of Virginia, roused both by love of adventure and the fear of the encroaching Frenchman in the West, determined to take a step toward occupying that rampart of the mountains which separated his people from their foes. With a gay cavalcade of fifty Virginia gentlemen, as many black servants, an unknown number of "rangers, pioneers, and Indians," and a train of pack horses to carry his equipage and his wines, the governor set out from Williamsburg, the capital, and in late August or early September crossed the Blue Ridge at Swift Run Gap.

With due formality, Spottswood, arriving at the bank of the Shenandoah River, took possession of the valley in the name of his king, burying there in an empty flask a paper witnessing thereto. Then the happy party of gentlemen went back home, to boast to their descendants of this doughty and inspiring deed, and of their entrance thereby into "The Order of the Horseshoe." Their horses, accustomed to bare feet on the soft soil of the lowlands, had been shod as a protection against the rocky ground of the mountains; and to commemorate the lesser with the greater fact, Spottswood presented to each of his gentlemen companions a golden horseshoe, set with precious stones for nailheads, and bearing the legend, "*Sic juvat transcendere montes*": "Thus it is a pleasure to cross the mountains."

But Spottswood's expedition, agreeable as it was made to be, was not merely a pleasure jaunt. The clear-sighted and enterprising governor had been looking with troubled eyes at the progress of the French along the Great Lakes and southward. The English were as yet but a little fringe along the seacoast. More inclined to build solidly than to venture daringly, they were allowing French influence to outrun them in the Mississippi Basin; and, as Spottswood clearly saw, unless they should at least occupy the mountain passes before the French should reach them, their seaboard colonies would be at the mercy of their rivals. The governor pointed out these facts to the king's court, and offered to conduct an expedition, not only to secure the mountains, but to establish a post upon Lake Erie. While his suggestion was not acted upon, English minds were from this time on more fully occupied with securing first the mountains and afterwards the over-mountain country.

The Appalachian system had done a very distinct service to the English, by shutting them up against the sea. It kept them close enough together to grow strong and capable, while the French were stretching their thin line from the St. Lawrence to the Gulf. And when the struggle for America began in good earnest, the English had the advantage of a good base from which to launch their attacks upon the exposed French territory. Other and greater causes there were for the English successes, which made America Anglo-Saxon and Protestant instead of Latin and Catholic, yet the mountains had no small part to play in that great drama.

II

THE PIONEERS

IT WAS sixteen years after Spottswood's expedition before there came permanent settlers to the mountain country. Where the torrent of the Potomac breaks through the Blue Ridge at Harper's Ferry, there is formed a natural passage that leads into one of the most beautiful and fertile valleys in America, the famous Shenandoah, or valley of Virginia. This valley lies between the Blue Ridge and the ranges of the Alleghenies. Its lower end is bounded by the Potomac, though its counterpart on the northern side of the river runs up through Maryland into Pennsylvania. The valley is drained by the Shenandoah River, a principal affluent of the Potomac.

In 1832 sixteen families from Pennsylvania, whose names indicate that they pretty well represented the mixed character of the population the valley was to receive,[1] hewed their way through the woods to the Potomac, and about two miles above Harper's Ferry passed over as the first settlers to enter the valley of Virginia.[2] The next few years saw a rapid increase in the number of emigrants, chiefly from Pennsylvania, though tidewater Virginia, Maryland, New Jersey, New

---

[1] The names given are Joist Hite, George Bowman, Jacob Chrisman, Paul Froman, Robert McKay, Robert Green, William Duff, and Peter Stephens.

[2] Kercheval, *History of the Valley of Virginia*, p. 45.

York, and various countries of Europe helped not a little to swell the tide. The great majority of these first immigrants were Germans, or "Pennsylvania Dutch," who in religion were chiefly Lutherans, Calvinists, and Mennonites, with a few Dunkers, the last two being Baptist bodies.[1] Many Quakers also entered the valley; and English Baptists, when they began to arrive, about 1745, were so zealous in spreading their doctrines that, with the later Methodists,[2] they became in time the predominant religious influence.

Of all nationalities, however, the Scotch-Irish were most deeply to influence the character of the valley and the mountain population. These people with the compound name were in blood almost pure Scotch. The last part of their name was derived from the residence of their people for two or three generations in the north of Ireland, during which time they received but very slight infusion of Irish blood, but not a little of Irish influence.[3] They were Presbyterian in religion, democratic in spirit, enterprising and thrifty in business; and these qualities subjected them to the opposition of the bishops, the king, and the merchants of England. In the early years of the eighteenth century, the difficulties of their situation in Ireland began to drive them from their homes there, to seek liberty in the New World. They came by the tens of thousands, some to Boston, more to Charleston, but most of all to Philadelphia. From this latter place they were dispersed throughout the back parts of Pennsylvania; then, following southwestward the trend of the mountains, they poured into the valley of Virginia, the piedmont and highlands of North Carolina, and the valley of the Tennessee. From thence they filled the moun-

---

[1] *Id.*, p. 56.

[2] The first Methodist preachers came into the valley in 1775.— *Id.*, p. 62.

[3] Fiske, *Old Virginia and her Neighbors*, pp. 391, 392; Bolton, *Scotch-Irish Pioneers*, pp. 1-4, 294-300; Henry Cabot Lodge, art. "Distribution of Ability in the United States," *Century Magazine*, September, 1891.

tains and poured over upon the western plains. They soon greatly outnumbered the Germans, and for a long time, if not always, exceeded the settlers of English extraction. It is estimated that one-third of all the Scotch-Irish in Ireland emigrated to America.[1] Besides the Scotch-Irish, there were, it seems, not a few of the true Irish and of Scotch from Scotland, who were easily mixed and easily confounded with the Scotch-Irish, all of them being Celts.

In the valley of Virginia there was for a generation a lively state of things between the sturdy Germans and the Irish, the latter assisted, little doubt, by the Scotch-Irish and the English. No one could deny the thrift and ability of the "Dutch," with their fine big barns, their fat flocks and herds, their overflowing garners, and their heaped-up feather beds. And though their more lively Celtic neighbors might find a narrow toe-hold for ridicule of their slow-witted men and their broad-waisted, barefooted women, they could not do better than imitate the steadfastness of the one and the housewifely virtues of the other.

But when these races came together in the first town of the valley, Winchester, their "national prejudices," says the old historian, "promised much disorder and many riots. It was customary for the Dutch on St. Patrick's Day to exhibit the effigy of the saint with a string of Irish potatoes around his neck, and his wife Sheeley with her apron loaded also with potatoes. This was always followed by a riot. The Irish resented the indignity offered to their saint and his holy spouse, and a battle followed. On St. Michael's Day the Irish would retort, and exhibit the saint with a rope of sauerkraut about his neck." Then the Germans would take up the challenge, "and many a black eye, bloody nose, and broken head was the result."[2]

At first the settlers were peacefully received by the

---

[1] Bolton, *Scotch-Irish Pioneers*, p. 7.
[2] Kercheval, *History of the Valley of Virginia*, p. 179.

Indians. The reputation of William Penn was high, and the red man supposed that whoever came from Penn's colony must be of the same character as himself. They therefore welcomed the immigrants from the north. But of the Virginians, whom they called the "Long Knives," they held a very different opinion. Their race had been exterminated in the land of the "Long Knives," and it was fortunate for the mountain settlements that the Indians saw the majority of the invaders coming from the land of the Quaker rather than of the Cavalier.

When at last the Indians, after the defeat of Braddock in 1755, determined to make war on the mountain settlers, they found them too well entrenched to be driven out. And though the usual horrors of frontier warfare were endured by the whites, they succeeded in keeping their place in the country.

Here George Washington received some of his earliest training in command and warfare. This young man, just past his majority, had become famous in the operations against the French in the West, and he was now placed in charge of the defense of the frontier. In spite of the terror and confusion of the valley dwellers, and in spite of official delay and neglect, Washington succeeded in meeting the necessities of the case, and crowned his efforts in the autumn of 1758 by entering at the head of his men the nesting place of the French and Indian terror, Fort Duquesne.

Thus was "the father of his country" identified with the early history of the mountain people. Several years before this, he had become well acquainted with their country, when, at the age of sixteen, he was employed by Lord Thomas Fairfax to survey his extensive holdings in the valley. That world-weary old English nobleman had settled here in the wilderness as a refuge from disappointed love and hopes. His haughty temper and his immense holdings, which sometimes conflicted with his neighbor's rights, made him none too popular with them. But he brought around him a very considerable settlement of English from tidewater Virginia, and in his manor of Greenway Court held a sort of feudal authority that made the chief distinction and almost the chief discontent of the democratic valley.

Lord Fairfax formed a deep attachment to the young Washington, and bestowed upon him as the reward of his surveying, a large tract of land, to which Washington in later years added much by purchase. Through the interest thus created, Washington became deeply responsible for the later development of this mountain country.

As the lower part of the Shenandoah became settled the later immigrants passed on to the southwest, the upper part of the valley, which there grows higher and more broken. These immigrants, mostly Scotch-Irish, formed what was known as the Backwater Settlements; that is, the settlements on the back- or headwaters of the streams. Though this part of the depression between the Blue Ridge and the western ranges is crossed and broken by ridges and hills, it does not lose wholly the character of a valley, and after the divide is passed, south of the present city of Roanoke, the country again rapidly broadens into the valley of the Tennessee. It was through this natural gateway that the western part of the mountain country was chiefly settled.

While the Shenandoah Valley was filling up with settlers and pouring the surplus over into the Tennessee, another source of population was forming near the mountains in North Carolina. This colony received the most of her population, not from her seacoast (for she had no good ports), but from Virginia on the one side and South Carolina on the other. From the latter colony there came up into North Carolina not a few settlers, some English and Scotch-Irish and many Huguenots — French Protestants who had fled from the persecutions of Louis XIV. On the other side, from

Virginia, partly through the valley and partly from the lowlands, there poured into the middle part of North Carolina a stream of the sturdiest kind of settlers, men of little wealth for the most part, but of good bone and sinew and of independent mind. Virginia's landed aristocracy, with their slaves, left small place in the lowlands for the poor man, and the back counties of North Carolina offered such men a refuge and an opportunity. The settlers were largely Scotch-Irish Presbyterians, English Quakers, and German Baptists. Forsythe, Rowan, and Mecklenburg counties, stretching north and south across the State, midway east and west, came by the middle of the eighteenth century to hold that independent class of citizens that first resisted British tyranny and both in word and deed preceded the Massachusetts and Virginia patriots in striking for liberty.[1]

The larger part of the mountains and plateaus in western North Carolina was held by the Cherokee Indians, the fiercest of the Southern tribes, and that country was late in being settled. But some venturesome pioneers began to settle in the northernmost parts. Here, in what is now Watauga County, there came to live, in 1750, a family of Quakers by the name of Boone. There is still standing, near the county-seat, the blackened stone chimney of the cabin of one of the sons, Daniel Boone, best known and most worthy representative of the hunters, explorers, and frontiersmen of that day. He well deserves the fame that has come down with his name. Though one of the most enterprising and tireless of frontiersmen, Daniel Boone, true to his

---

[1] The Mecklenburg Declaration, adopted by a midnight convention in Charlotte, N. C., May 20, 1775, preceded the national Declaration of Independence by over a year. It declared the people of Mecklenburg County free and independent from the British crown. It was inspired by the same causes that were stirring the whole country, but its early boldness shows the influence of the free frontier life.

Even earlier than the Mecklenburg Declaration was a similar pronouncement made by the men of the Virginia backwater districts, at Abingdon, Va., in January, 1775.

Quaker training, was a peace-loving man. Daring oftentimes, but never reckless, modest and peaceable, but restless and enterprising, he kept ever in the van of the western settlers, until he died, at the age of eighty-six, on the other side of the Mississippi, still on the western border of civilization.

At the age of eighteen, Daniel Boone married his seventeen-year-old bride, and for seven years, pressed with the cares of a growing family, he played the perfect part of a quiet Quaker farmer, a life varied only by an occasional trip to the coastal towns as a wagoner and by the annual hunt that replenished the winter larder. But in 1759 the Cherokee Indians, who had watched with jealous eyes the steady encroachments of the whites upon their mountain lands, broke in upon the border settlements with tomahawk and torch, and the times of blood, of unrest, and of adventure began.

Two years of war, in which Daniel Boone bore his part, bought peace from the conquered Cherokees. Boone had during this time become somewhat acquainted with the upper part of the Tennessee River country, and had made several hunting trips thither from his North Carolina home. It was on one of these trips, while gazing from a mountaintop upon a herd of buffalo beneath, that he is said to have exclaimed, "I am richer than the man mentioned in Scripture, who owned the cattle on a thousand hills: I own the wild beasts of more than a thousand valleys!" It is safe to say that, despite his Quaker training, he was unacquainted with the identity of the "man mentioned in Scripture," or he would scarcely have made such a boast; but the exclamation reveals his delight in the wild and wide freedom which the wilderness gave him.

In May, 1769, Boone, with five neighbors and a trapper guide, John Finley, undertook the journey to Kentucky through Cumberland Gap, famed as the great gateway for Indian war and hunting parties, and for settlers' caravans and armies yet to come.

Then begins the most romantic portion of Boone's life. Sometimes alone, sometimes with but one companion, sometimes with more, hunting, watching, dodging Indian war parties, once captured and hardly escaping with life, after two years he returned home to bring his family from the Yadkin to the Blue-grass country. In 1773 a company started with him, including his own and several other families, among them the first women to dare the dangers of the journey to the plains of Kentucky. But the party was stopped by an Indian attack in the upper valley of the Tennessee, a circumstance which decided his more timid companions to remain for a while where they were, in the midst of the mountain settlements. It was nearly two years before Boone saw his family, with some others, settled in the Blue-grass of Kentucky. With this event he passes for the most part out of the life of the mountains.[1]

Another man there was who came to the valley of the Tennessee as soon as Boone, and who bore a large part in the development, first of the mountain country, and later of middle Tennessee. This was James Robertson, who in 1769 traveled with Boone from the settlements on the Yadkin over the mountains to the Watauga Old Fields, in the northeastern corner of what is now Tennessee. He found there the cabins of William Bean, the first settler in the Tennessee Valley,[2] and of one Honeycut, with whom he stayed during the summer and raised a crop of corn. In the autumn, Robertson started back alone to bring his family and friends. He carried his provisions on his horse's back — a sack of parched corn mixed with maple syrup, to be supplemented by the game he might find along the way. There was no road, not even a trail, and he must keep his course by the sun and the woodman's signs. But for days the

---

[1] See *Life of Boone*, Bruce, Ellis, Thwaites, and others.
[2] Ramsey, *The Annals of Tennessee*, p. 94.

sky was overcast, and he lost his way in the Iron Mountains. Coming to a precipice down which he could not lead his horse, he was compelled to turn him loose. His provisions were at last all gone, and his powder was spoiled. For fourteen days he wandered without food, until, completely exhausted, he fell at the foot of some cliffs in a dying condition. He was roused from his stupor at last by the sound of voices, as, guided by an unseen hand, two hunters — the only persons, perhaps, in all that trackless wilderness — came directly to where he lay. They revived him, nursed him for several days, and then, giving him some of their provisions, they set him upon his way, and he reached his home on the Yadkin in safety.[1] A few weeks later he led a considerable body of settlers over the mountains to the Watauga settlement, with which he was for ten years identified as a leader and counselor, before going on into the West. He was much like Boone in character, peaceable and humble, but he had less of the roving spirit and was far more practical and capable. As the Tennessee Valley became more thickly populated, he relinquished to his abler friend, John Sevier, the leadership of the colony, and in the midst of the American Revolution headed an expedition farther to the west, where on the Cumberland River he became the founder of Nashville, the present capital of the State of Tennessee.[2] With John Sevier he is counted the chief founder of Tennessee, as Boone and the Shelbys are of Kentucky, and Clark of Indiana and Illinois.

---

[1] Gilmore, *Rear Guard of the Revolution*, p. 41; Ramsey, *Annals of Tennessee*, p. 104.

[2] The visitor in Nashville today, as he waits for his car in the transfer station of the street railway, may observe a dim record on the opposite wall, a record that transports his mind from the rush and thunder of the busy city back to the quiet of the river's reedy banks by the old French Lick, the site of Nashville:

From 1784 to 1807
The site of this building
was owned by
James Robertson
Founder of Nashville.

From the population of the broad valleys the mountains received their scantier portion. In the midst of the various ranges there are many beautiful little valleys and smaller gorges, or "coves," and the plateaus often make rolling table-lands which invite first the woodman and then the farmer. When and how all these little valleys, plateaus, hills, and mountainsides received their population there is little of chronicle to tell us. Some, doubtless, of those who started from the eastern lands to go to the far West, were stopped by weariness or accident in some fair spot that promised a home to a heartsick woman or a broken man. Others came back into the mountains when the valleys, crowding fuller, offered less of opportunity, because of high-priced land or because of the hateful presence of slavery, which in a way bore harder on the poor white man than it did on the negro. Here in the beautiful free mountain country they reared their families and sent forth their sons and daughters to conquer the harder fields and hills that always remained. And so the mountains were filled, until today, from the Ohio and the Susquehanna in the North to the brows of Kennesaw and Lookout in the South, the mountaineers muster four million souls.

They make a distinct and a notable class. They are the Highlanders of America, in environment, in habit, in disposition, and largely in blood. For they remain, as they began, America's purest stock of the British Isles, Scotch and English and Irish, with some infusion from the best blood of Germany and France. If we were to judge from the family names in the mountains today, we should say that the majority of the people are of Scotch and Irish descent, with the English element almost as great, a very respectable percentage of Huguenot blood, and the German almost lost.[1] The speech

---

[1] Without doubt there are many Anglicized German names which pass for English, and by this means it is impossible correctly to measure the amount of German blood among the mountaineers. But, in every way, the impress of the German is scarcely to be seen upon the mountain people, except in the lower Shenandoah.

is eighteenth-century English, with some Scotticisms thrown in. The great valleys, of course, have more nearly kept pace with the progress and the decadence of the rest of the world, but the people of the more isolated mountain sections well deserve, in all that the phrase implies of honor and respect as well as of sympathy, the term which has been applied to them, "our contemporary ancestors."

After photo by Scadin.

III

IN TIMES OF WAR

THERE was never a more fearless people than the men of the mountains. In their forward march they faced not only the discomforts and dangers of the wilderness, but a savage people who had no mind to be dispossessed of their hunting grounds.

About midway in the Southern lands there stretched from the ocean to the Mississippi a group of Indian tribes remarkable for their courage, independence, and high-hearted resistance to the encroachment of the whites. On the eastern side of the mountains, in North Carolina, lived the powerful tribe of Tuscaroras, kin to the Iroquois of New York, the most advanced and the most powerful of all the native peoples. In 1711 the Tuscaroras began a terrific assault upon the infant settlements of eastern North Carolina. They were finally subdued, and in making peace the remnant of the tribe agreed to remove to the land of their brethren in New York. There they joined the confederacy of the Five Nations of the Iroquois, which was thereafter known as the Six Nations.

Inhabiting the mountains to the west, from the Blue Ridge to the Cumberlands in Tennessee, were the Cherokees, who were divided into two sections, the mountain Indians, or Otari, who lived in the highlands of North Carolina, and the Erati, or valley Indians, who held the valley of the Tennessee and adjacent parts. They were noted as the most spirited and warlike of all the Southern tribes.[1]

There was an offshoot of this tribe dwelling in towns near the present city of Chattanooga, and afterwards inhabiting the gorges of the river below, in Alabama, known as the Chickamaugas. They were at first composed wholly of Cherokees, but afterwards received many renegade white men and runaway negroes, as well as outlaws from other Indian tribes, and by this infusion of bad blood, added to the already great ferocity of the tribe, they became the most bloodthirsty, treacherous, and vindictive Indians with whom the settlers had to deal.[2]

Lying south and west of the Cherokees was the great Creek nation, a people of high intelligence and great ability. They did not so delight in war as the Cherokees, but they were a very powerful tribe, and possessed of courage in the defense of their rights. Beyond them, and reaching to the Mississippi, were the Chickasaws, similar in character to the Creeks, though partaking more fully of the warlike nature of the Cherokees. South of the Chickasaws, and often joining with them, were the Choctaws, a tribe of less importance both in peace and in war.

These Indian tribes faced the settlers on their southern and western frontiers, and long contested the ground with them. Kentucky was uninhabited by any set-

---

[1] The fighting qualities of the Cherokees have been depreciated by a modern writer, who quotes a tidewater Virginian as authority. But writers nearer to the Cherokees in point both of time and place, bear a very different record. They represent them as warlike and courageous, with a haughtiness born of almost invariable victory over neighboring tribes. When in 1730 the white people tried to induce the Cherokees to make peace with the Tuscaroras, with whom they were habitually at war, the reply was, "We cannot live without war. Should we make peace with the Tuscaroras, we must immediately look out for some other with whom we can be engaged; for war is our life." When the Tuscaroras left, the Cherokees faced the whites. See Ramsey, *Annals of Tennessee*, p. 83; Turner, *Life of John Sevier*, pp. 24-26.

[2] Ramsey, *Annals of Tennessee*, pp. 183-186.

tled bands of Indians. It was the common hunting ground of the Northern and Southern tribes, never in the peaceable possession of either, but always the scene of hostile encounters whenever opposing hunting parties chanced there to meet. The Shawnees, to the north of the Ohio, mingled with the fierce Iroquois, and their bands were the most troublesome that harrassed Daniel Boone and his companions in Kentucky.

It was with the Cherokees and Chickamaugas, however, that the greatest difficulties were experienced. Treaties were made with them by the English and the colonial governments at different times, by which they ceded lands to the settlers; but the treaties were illy kept. Some of the Indians protested against them; and the settlers, as they grew more numerous, stepped over the boundaries and took up lands which did not belong to them. Various other grievances, as thefts and murders committed by white outlaws at different times, enraged the Indians, and their natural thirst for blood prompted them to assail the lonely cabins and even the log forts.

The Tennessee Valley dwellers were fortunate in having a leader capable of meeting this savage foe. John Sevier, a Virginian of Huguenot descent, in 1772 settled in the Watauga country, on the Nolichucky River, and by his gallantry and his genial and hospitable nature soon became, as he always remained, the most noted and the most popular man in the Tennessee Valley.

Oconostota, the far-seeing head of the Cherokee people, and Atta-culla-culla, the vice-king, fought fiercely against the whites, until, their towns in ashes, their fields and orchards destroyed, and many of their warriors slain, they were fain to purchase a peace of their conquerors.

John Sevier's method of Indian warfare was harsh and seemingly cruel, but it was the only kind that would impress the Indian mind. After he had carried fire and sword remorselessly through the midst of their country, until they sued for peace, he was ever ready to extend to them his friendship, upon their promises of good behavior, and no one was trusted so much by them as this same "Nolichucky Jack," as Sevier was familiarly called by both Indians and settlers. To his own people he was a tower of strength, to whom they turned in every hour of danger. He was a copy, on a ruder stage, of his gallant and glorious fellow-countryman and fellow-religionist, King Henry of Navarre. He never lost a battle, and though always at the head of his men, he never had a wound. He was the idol of the frontiersmen of Tennessee, who followed him unquestioningly into the haunts of the bloody Chickamaugas and the fastnesses of the mountain Cherokees, or after the marauding Tory and British bands in the East.

Forty miles to the north of Sevier's home lived Evan Shelby and his son, Isaac, who were, almost equally with Sevier and Robertson, the leaders of the men of the valley. Under the Shelbys, the Watauga men joined the Virginia and Pennsylvania forces that won the great battle of the Kanawha against the Shawnees and Iroquois in 1774; and they were among the leaders who marched over-mountain in 1780 to fight the British at King's Mountain. Isaac Shelby became the first governor of Kentucky, as did John Sevier of Tennessee.

When the Revolutionary War came, it found the Tennessee Valley with about three thousand settlers—men, women, and children—while the valley of Virginia had a much larger population, probably fifteen or twenty thousand. The valley of Virginia bore its full part in filling the Continental armies, for it was close to the scene of action, and was felt to be an integral part of the colony. One of its sons, General Daniel Morgan, raised in the valley his famous rifle corps, which won fame in both Northern and Southern campaigns, contributing in great measure to the victory of Saratoga and to Greene's successes in the South.

But the Tennessee Valley people, and with them the Backwater Settlements, were more distant, and with the great mountain mass between them and the coast, they were more shut up to their own problems and difficulties, and were also protected from invasion. But they had no unimportant part to play as "the rear-guard of the Revolution."

The British had agents of influence among the Cherokees, and in 1778 they persuaded these Indians to plan an attack upon the over-mountain settlers, at the same time that the Shawnees and British were to march down from above the Ohio, and the British were to sweep the country east of the mountains from Savannah and Charleston to the Potomac.

The plot was well laid and carefully concealed. Savannah and Charleston had fallen into the hands of the British, and all of Georgia and South Carolina were under their control. This opened the road to the Indian country, and the British thereupon sent a pack-train with large supplies of ammunition and money up through Georgia to the Cherokees, who for safe keeping bestowed the treasure in the towns of the Chickamaugas. British officers were among the Cherokees, carefully planning every detail of the plot, which was to be suddenly and secretly sprung, and was to wipe out the over-mountain settlements in a day. If it had succeeded, there is little question that the British would have held everything south of Virginia, and very likely have won all America. For with the Tennessee Valley smitten, there would have been no one to fight King's Mountain, no King's Mountain to turn back the tide of Cornwallis' success, and finally no Cornwallis cooped up in Yorktown to surrender British hopes with his sword.

But God was watching over the fortunes of America. The plan of the British and Indians was defeated by the impatience of Dragging Canoe, the Chickamauga chief, to begin the war. He could not see so much powder and shot lying idle those long weeks, while the Cherokees were getting thoroughly ready, and so he started with some of his braves on a raid. James Robertson, who had been appointed commissioner of Indian affairs for North Carolina, and who had taken up his residence at the Indian town of Chota, heard of the threatening storm, and informed the settlements. In consequence, only a few of the outlying, lonely homes were surprised.

The Tennessee men determined to make a counter stroke which should effectually stop these preparations. A force of several hundred men were gathered on the upper waters of Clinch River, and under the command of Evan Shelby they went swiftly down the river to the Chickamauga towns. Falling upon the Indians without warning, Shelby defeated them in detail, burned several of their towns, and destroyed the stores placed among them by the British.

This disaster cooled the ardor of the Chickamaugas for a time, and their war party suddenly returned home. But yet they and their Cherokee brethren brooded sullenly for some months, and before long broke out again. This time the whites, aroused and on their guard, and with Sevier and Shelby at their head, so thoroughly reduced their savage foe that the Indians were glad to purchase a peace of "Nolichucky Jack," and promise to live in love with their white brothers.[1]

Thus the terrible storm that was to have burst on the rear-guard of America was dispelled. Sevier returned to his home on the Nolichucky, Shelby to his in the Holston district, but now, with all their fellow-settlers, alert for danger and stirred to fiery indignation by this revelation of the fiendish plot against them.

While in this state of mind, they received a message across the mountains from Ferguson, a British officer whom Cornwallis, advancing up into North Carolina,

---

[1] Ramsey, *Annals of Tennessee*, pp. 186-190; Roosevelt, *Winning of the West*, Vol. II, pp. 114-120.

had sent out toward the mountains to gather what Tories he could to his ranks, and to overawe the patriots. Ferguson had encountered a company of four hundred over-mountain men who had been sent over too late to help save Charleston. Stirred to wrath against these strange, long-haired, buckskin-shirted men whose aim with the rifle was so unerring, he sent a letter by a liberated prisoner to the Tennessee settlers, warning them that unless they ceased fighting the British, he would march over the mountains and burn them out. It was an idle threat, but it had an unexpected answer. The letter was sent to Shelby, who had headed some of the four hundred, but who had now returned to his home. He rode at once to Sevier's, and together they resolved to answer Ferguson's threat in person.

They sent word to William Campbell, sheriff of the Backwater Settlements, who marched to join them with four hundred men from Virginia. The rendezvous was at Sycamore Shoals on the Watauga, and here the men of the mountains gathered to the number of nearly a thousand. Practically the whole military strength of the Tennessee settlements was present, and lots were drawn to determine who should remain at home to defend the settlements. Then the little army, after being dedicated to their work in a prayer by the old Presbyterian minister, Parson Doak, took up their line of march, most of them on horseback, single-filing over the mountains. Being joined east of the mountains by a force from that section, till they numbered fifteen hundred, they set out in rapid search of Ferguson, who, when he heard of their coming, began a hasty retreat. They overtook him, however, at the border line of North and South Carolina, after so rapid a march that they left all but nine hundred of their men behind.

With about one thousand British and Tories, Ferguson entrenched himself on the top of a wooded hill, which he named King's Mountain. The nine hundred and ten mountaineers surrounded him and began their assault, which lasted all day. As the British would charge down one side with the bayonet, the mountaineers, who had none, would retreat on that side, but on the other they would be creeping higher, and when the British returned to their entrenchments, they were followed by the foe they had so lately driven. Slowly the British were hemmed into a compact mass at the very crown of the hill, where they were mowed down by the terrific rifle fire. The end was the death of Ferguson and the surrender of his army.

The following day the mountaineers started on their return march. Some of them remained to fight in the army of General Greene, but the majority, fearful for their homes which they had left so scantily guarded, returned at once across the mountains.

At King's Mountain, however, had been struck the critical blow of the Revolution. At the time of that battle, the Carolinas and Georgia were wholly in the hands of the British, and Cornwallis was just about to invade Virginia. On hearing of the disaster to Ferguson, Cornwallis hastily retreated toward Charleston, followed by Greene, who during the next year played the game of war so well that he manipulated Cornwallis into Virginia, finally to fall into the hands of Washington at Yorktown. The victory of King's Mountain was the turning point of the Revolution, a victory won by the sudden and unexpected forward movement of the "rear-guard," the men of the mountains.

There were no British to meet in Kentucky, and no organized and determined Indian foe as in Tennessee. But Virginians, mainly mountain men, under George Rogers Clark, were the heroes in wresting Illinois and Indiana from the English, in 1778-79. With a dwindling force, in the depths of winter, Clark successively took Kaskaskia, Illinois, and Vincennes, Indiana, surprising the British garrisons and cajoling the French inhabitants. His march from Kaskaskia to Vincennes, a distance of two hundred miles, was made in the time of the spring floods, when for days his men had to march through waters often up to their necks.[1] But he and his Virginians took and held the Northwest Territory.

After independence was secured, the western tide of emigration rapidly increased, and Kentucky especially filled rapidly with settlers. She was the first State west of the mountains to be admitted to the Union. This was in 1792, and Tennessee followed in 1796. The after development of those States was chiefly in the lowlands. The mountains between Kentucky and Virginia were only gradually filled, and the same is true of the Cumberlands in Tennessee. The North Carolina plateau, lying between the Blue Ridge and the Great Smoky chain, for the most part continued to be held by the Cherokees, until their removal by treaty to Indian Territory in 1838. The northern part of this plateau had, however, received not a few settlers, and the more southern part, especially the wide, rolling French Broad Valley, was speedily occupied upon the removal of the Indians. Only a fragment of the tribe now remains upon a small reservation in the Great Smoky Mountains.

As has been said, it was largely the encroachments of slavery that filled the mountains with its population of the poorer or more conscientious or more race-conscious of the white people. Though such comparatively level country as the Shenandoah and Tennessee valleys and parts of the North Carolina plateau had not a few slave-holders, the vastly great majority of the mountaineers were without slaves, and were haters of slavery, the most of them not so much from a moral as from an economic point of view. One of the strongest champions of the Union in East Tennessee was "Parson" Brownlow, of Knoxville. In his paper, *The Knoxville Whig*, he fiercely and fearlessly lashed secession and secessionists; yet just as fiercely he turned

---

[1] Roosevelt, *Winning of the West*, Vol. II, p. 221.

his scorn upon the slave-carriers of the North.¹ But while he entered a plea for slave-owners, he cursed secession, and used all his powers to preserve the Union. In this attitude he was representative of a certain class of his fellow-mountaineers. The negro was no charge of theirs. If they must see him at all, they preferred to see him a slave. But they loved the Union. They felt the heart-throb of the nation more than the pulse-beat of the section. They had a State pride, but their pride in the nation was greater. They had grasped and borne aloft the "Stars and Stripes" wavering in the fierce strife of the Revolution, they had in great numbers fought under the folds of "Old Glory" in the wars of 1812 and 1846; and with the fierce loyalty of the mountaineer they exclaimed in 1861 that the old flag should not go down.

Yet another and perhaps a larger number put their hatred of slavery in the forefront. From the foothills of North Carolina came forth the challenge of the free-soilers of the South to the slave-holders: "Our motto — and we would have you to understand it — is the abolition of slavery and the perpetuation of the American Union. If by any means you . . . take the South out of the Union today, we will bring it back tomorrow. If she goes away with you, she will return without you. . . . If . . . the oligarchs do not quietly submit to the will of a constitutional majority of the people, as expressed at the ballot-box, the first battle between freedom and slavery will be fought at home — and may God defend the right!"²

---

[1] "The States of this Union north of Mason and Dixon's line, commonly called the New England States, alias the Free States, were never to any great extent *slave-holding*. No Sir-ee! Their virtuous and pious minds were chiefly exercised in slave-stealing and slave-selling. To Old England, the mother country, our Pilgrim Fathers of the New England States are indebted for their knowledge of the art of slave-stealing; and to the pious, God-fearing and liberty-loving New England States are we of the South wholly indebted for our slaves!"— *Brownlow, quoted in* "A History of Tennessee and the Tennesseans," *Will T. Hale, p. 455.*

[2] Hinton R. Helper, *The Impending Crisis*, pp. 186, 413. Helper was born in Davie County, North Carolina, near the mountains, and

It is to be remembered that the men of the tidewater section and the men of the mountains were in great part from different peoples. The coastal region was settled chiefly by Englishmen, who had been used, either in themselves or in their superiors, to pleasant lives of wealth and culture. The mountain population, while it included the more daring spirits from among the English, and to a lesser degree the sprightly Huguenot and the stolid German, was chiefly composed of and influenced by the Celtish blood of the Scotch and Scotch-Irish, lovers of wild liberty and haters of oppression. There was always antagonism between the mountains and the lowlands in the politics of Virginia and the Carolinas, with slavery as a predisposing cause. As for the western parts of Tennessee and Kentucky, they were peopled by the same men who filled the mountains, and it took time for the differences of location, soil, and social conditions to create antagonism between them. Thus it came about that when slavery was drawing near its crisis, there was a sharper distinction between the mountaineers and the lowlanders in Virginia and North Carolina than in Kentucky and Tennessee. Yet when it came to war, there was a curious twist in the situation: of the two Northern States, Virginia, the easternmost, felt the sharpest cleavage in its population; of the two Southern, Tennessee, the westernmost, had the most decided division. Kentucky's Union sentiment was widely distributed throughout the State; Virginia's was so greatly localized that the western counties split off and formed the new commonwealth of West Virginia in 1863. North Carolina,

---

was a representative of the non-slave-holding class so greatly in the majority in the South. His book, addressed to the South, made a masterful appeal for the abolition of slavery, based upon unanswerable economic, historical, and moral arguments. But, coming as it did at the very climax of the struggle, and stinting no words in its arraignment of the slave-holding aristocracy, it had less influence in the black belt than in free-soil regions. It had great influence in the campaign that resulted in the election of Lincoln, and it greatly helped in shaping the attitude of the mountain country. As for the author, he was driven out of the South, to find a refuge in the nation's capital.

though its mountains held many Union sympathizers who in State politics were opposed to the slave-holding oligarchy, yet felt the surge of Southern sentiment deeply to the very walls of its western line; but East Tennessee, despite outside influences which strenuously sought to win her to the Confederacy, remained chiefly Unionist to the last.

And when it came to fighting—"I reckon y'all had the draft in your country," said a Kentucky mountaineer to a Northerner after the war.

"Yes, we had the draft."

"We didn't have no draft in our country," said the Kentuckian.

"Why not?"

"Because we 'listed so fast the draft couldn't catch us," was the proud reply.

Kentucky gave seventy-five thousand men to the Union armies from all parts of the State; and the gift of Virginia's mountains was thirty-seven thousand. Tennessee furnished over fifty thousand soldiers to the Federal armies, thirty-five thousand of whom were from the mountain section. The mountains of North Carolina, Georgia, and Alabama, though largely Unionist in sentiment, had not Tennessee's advantage of being next to Union territory; and so their Union men were either compelled to enter the Confederate army or take the uncertain chances of the lier-out and the refugee.[1]

These were the *men* of the mountains; what of the women? In the story of the war between the States, the women of the South have right to the high praise given them for the spirit with which they cheered their men and the courage with which they endured the pain of privation and the anguish of loss. And none were there more spirited than those daughters of Huguenot and Covenanter who dwelt in the mountains.

---

[1] Anderson, *Fighting by Southern Federals*, p. 10.

They saw their men swept away to fill the ranks of the Union and the Confederate armies. Alone with their children, they tilled the fields and garnered the harvest, often but to see it vanish in the raid of the soldier or the guerilla. Often they escaped to the laurel only in time to save themselves from death at the hands of marauders who set their homes in flames. Many a time did they go on scout and courier duty when men were lacking or their peril greater.

A great poet has chanted the praises of Paul Revere, who rode twelve miles to warn the Concord men that the redcoats were coming. But who has sung the fame of Mary Love, who rode in winter weather thirty-five miles by road and trail, and through the enemy's lines, to carry word from General Grant to the beleaguered army at Knoxville? or of the mother of the little John Brown who seized the dispatches from the hand of the fainting girl, and piloted her little son at night through the hostile pickets till he was safely on his way with the news of relief to Burnside?[1]

But not in daring merely — more in watching, waiting, enduring, succoring, are written the annals of the women of the mountains. Yet sometimes their spirit shamed even brave men who had faced a thousand dangers, but quailed before a sudden assault. Of all the Union leaders in east Tennessee, few were better known than "Parson" Brownlow, then the editor of the fiercely partizan *Whig*, and after the war the governor of the State. None were more bitterly hated by Secessionists or more fully trusted by Unionists. His courage had been tried and proved in debate, in plot, in prison, and in exile, and to the people of East Tennessee his giving way before their enemy was almost unbelievable. But when Burnside retreated before Longstreet, word was sent to the most prominent noncombatants of Knoxville that it would be wise for them to leave. Accord-

---

[1] Temple, *East Tennessee and the Civil War*, pp. 521-523.

ingly some of the chief Unionists whose place was not in the army left, under cavalry escort, for Kentucky. Among them was Brownlow.

Through the miry roads, in a heavy downpour of rain, the melancholy procession went on its way toward the North, everywhere being greeted with startled inquiries as to the state of things at the front. Just over the first county line they came, early in the night, upon a cabin out of which swarmed a host of children, with their stout mother at their head, holding high a pine torch.

"What in the name of God," she said, "does all this mean? Where are you men going? Is Burnside retreating? Who are you, anyhow?"

One of the party thus roughly challenged answered mildly that General Burnside, so far from being able to retreat, was probably now a prisoner with all his army.

"And you are running," she exclaimed, "without firing a gun!"

"Oh, no," said an ironic old gentleman, "we are simply retiring in good order, to save the country."

"Yes!" she returned, waving her torch in their faces with a patriotic fierceness, "and I expect the next thing I'll hear will be that old Bill Brownlow is running too!"

At this point that doughty hero, concealed in the midst of his party, remarked in a subdued but fervent tone of voice: "Gentlemen, this is no place to make a stand. I think I'd rather encounter Longstreet's army or Vaughn's cavalry than that woman!"[1]

It was the strong element of the mountaineers, allied to the very considerable Unionist party in the lowlands, that made all but the most southern States doubtful to the Confederacy. North Carolina at first voted down secession; Tennessee voted it down once and almost the second time, and was out of the Union but three months; Virginia at first voted against secession, and

---

[1] Humes, *The Loyal Mountaineers of Tennessee*, p. 382.

when it at last went with the Confederacy, it lost to the Union its northwestern portion. Kentucky never left the Union.

It has been said by competent authorities that if it had not been for the mountains and the hostile mountaineers, the South, despite the odds against her, might well have won in the Civil War. She was fighting a defensive war, always an advantage in itself. Her armies were composed of men than whom none could have been more brave and enduring, more hopeful and persistent. But the South was cut into three parts. In the west the Mississippi clove between the western South and the main body. More important still, in the east the mountains formed a barrier between the coastal States and the middle States, in which sections the main part of the war was fought. And neither armies nor supplies could well be transported without a long detour around the mountains. The difficulties of transportation across the mountains might have been surmounted, but an indifferent or hostile population made the perils of the passage too great, and, moreover, forbade to the South the strategic advantages the mountains naturally afforded. And therefore to the mountaineers is due in great part the credit for the preservation of the Union, first, through their hostility to slavery and to the State supremacy which was the bulwark of slavery; second, through the disproportionately large number of soldiers they furnished the Union armies; and third, through their holding for the Union that long wedge of territory that cleft the South in two.

On themselves, however, the effects of the great Civil War were in large measure disastrous. While the rest of the South received a terrible destruction of property and life, the mountains, especially in the parts less open to the influences of civilization, received the most terrible destruction of peace and peace ideals. For it was largely in the quarrels of the Civil War, when brother fought brother and clan fought clan, that the perpetual feuds of today had their origin. It is true that the feud was transplanted from Scotland with the immigration of the first settlers, and it is a form of punishment or vengeance naturally fostered by the conditions of mountain isolation; but it is a matter of record that many of the Kentucky feuds (where almost all the feuds are) were born in the Civil War. Not all the mountaineers were Unionists, and the most horrible effects of war were to be witnessed, not where great armies fought pitched battles, but where the bushwhacker lay in wait in the mountain thicket to shoot his neighbor, or where a party of guerrillas, rendered as savage by their irregular life and warfare as the Indian foes of their fathers, had passed from house to house, pillaging, and murdering helpless women and children. And when one man of a family was murdered, his brothers or his sons felt it their privilege and their duty to murder the murderer, for which in turn they must be murdered.

"War," said General Sherman, "is hell," and he who carried sword and torch through the heart of the South should know what he was talking about. But nowhere were the horrors of war so apparent as in those nightly raids that left bloody corpses and blazing homes, those dastardly ambushes and fierce encounters as of wild beasts, which left the scars of war not merely upon the face of the land but upon the hearts of men to generations then unborn.

The mountaineer has shown his prowess in battle through the whole history of our country, from the days of the Indian wilderness to the last great struggle between the brothers of the Union. But let us be glad that the qualities of loyalty, courage, endurance, and force which he has manifested in the wars of his people, can now be called to nobler warfare and put to the test in a conflict that may glorify rather than debase him.

IV

EDUCATION AND RELIGION

THE settlers who filled the mountains were Protestant in religion, and Protestant they remain today. Indeed, there is much of eighteenth-century intolerance inherited by the present generation from their popery-hating fathers. With good cause, doubtless, yet without knowing the cause, the mountaineer, pent within the narrow limits of his knowledge and experience, holds in abhorrence the very name of Catholic, and even looks with aversion upon the Episcopalian, who, in the Highlander's traditions, is tarred with the same stick. For it was English Dissenter and Scotch Presbyterian that chiefly filled the valleys and settled among the hills, and to them, who had fought episcopacy along with tyranny in the old country, the Church of England was only the papacy transferred to English soil. Something more of contempt than of ignorance is manifest in this story current in the mountains, of the old woman who was visited by a missionary in clerical garb.

"Mother," he asked, "do you know of any Episcopalians hereabout?"

She chewed a few meditative moments on her snuff-stick.

"Hain't never seed none," she replied at length, "but my old man's hung up yander the skins of all the varmints he's kilt. Ye might go thar an' look!"

Baker Mountain School and Church, North Carolina.
"Its people believe in religion and long for education." Page 60.

It might be expected from the large Scotch element that peopled the mountains that the church of greatest numbers and influence would be the Presbyterian. And indeed in the early history this was true. Presbyterianism was the prevailing creed, where there was any, not only in the mountains but in the western part of Kentucky and Tennessee, into which the mountain population overflowed.

Into the valley of the Tennessee, in 1780, came Samuel Doak, the first Presbyterian minister of whom we have record as crossing the mountains.[1] He settled first in Sullivan County, near the northeastern boundary, and later in Washington County, on the Nolichucky. He was teacher as well as preacher, and to him belongs the honor of establishing, in 1783, Martin Academy, the first school west of the mountains. Here he supported himself on his farm while at the same time preaching and teaching.

It was at once the strength and the weakness of the Presbyterian Church that it demanded an educated ministry. It was its strength because it thus maintained a high standard of service and of worship; it was its weakness in this western country because it could not supply ministers enough to reach the rapidly growing and scattered population. Thus the mountaineers were left largely without the help of ministers and teachers, and too frequently large communities lapsed into irreligion and ignorance.

Education was by no means so widely diffused in the eighteenth century as at present, and it must not be supposed that the majority of the western settlers, whether they came from the seaboard or from Britain, were able to read and write. Of Daniel Boone, in many respects the superior of his fellow frontiersmen, one of his biographers states that he was the worst speller he ever knew, a fact attested by a short record left by

[1] Wilson, *The Southern Mountaineer*, p. 80; Phelan, *History of Tennessee*, p. 218.

Boone on a beech tree until recently standing near Jonesboro, Tennessee:

```
            D. Boon
  CillED    A BAR         On
                          Tree
    in       ThE
  yEAR
            1760
```

Even those who could read, in the more isolated districts, often lacked books for their children, who grew up with no learning but that of the woods and fields. Naturally, these rough frontiersmen, free of thought and rude of manner, grew impatient with the formal and polished Presbyterian service, which they had only infrequent opportunity to attend, and Presbyterianism then tended either to become modified in form or to be driven from the field by the simpler Baptist and Methodist forms of worship.

The Presbyterians, however, maintained their hold in the larger and more settled communities, and especially did they do great service in the establishment of schools. Samuel Doak was not the only one who founded a school. Before the nineteenth century was fairly upon its way, there were several educational institutions in the valley of Virginia, and at least four academies in the valley of the Tennessee. One of the former was Washington College, afterwards famous as Washington and Lee University. And one of the latter was the Southern and Western Theological Seminary, or Maryville College, as it was afterwards called, out of which came hundreds of devoted ministers and educators for the mountain country. Maryville College was founded in 1802 by Rev. Isaac Anderson, a young Presbyterian minister located in east Tennessee, after a fruitless journey on horseback to Princeton University to beg for help for his mountaineers. Indeed, education was almost wholly in the hands of the Presbyterians in those early days, and the efforts of their educators, self-sacrificing and to a great degree self-supporting men, are not belittled by the heroic labors of their Methodist brethren who displaced them in the outlying districts.

The only Methodist school of the early days was Bethel Academy, established in 1790 in Jessamine County, Kentucky, in the edge of the Blue-grass. It was a daring venture at a time when Indian massacres were common and pioneer minds were more engaged with bullets than with books. But it flourished for a time, only to become neglected and forsaken after a few years.[1]

But education, in the sense of book learning and scholastic training, was clearly out of the question for the mountaineers in isolated sections. Not infrequently parents of some education left their children, for lack of opportunity and for stress of living conditions, wholly illiterate. There was no system of free public schools, and the community schoolhouse could not flourish where neighbors were five to fifty miles apart; and the parents themselves were too much occupied with the struggle for existence to give much attention to the personal instruction of their children. Thus it came about that the mountain country, except the valleys, was largely left without schools or any means of instruction.

This did not mean, however, that mental life was dead. There was an education in the strenuous and sometimes precarious life of the wilderness, an education that made sharp eyes, skilful hands, and shrewd minds. The independence and the hard life gave an education in frugality, sturdiness, and shrewdness, that did but await a wider opportunity to show a wider power.

Methodism entered the mountains almost as soon as it appeared in America. It thrived far more in the Southern and Middle States than in the Northern, the Methodist General Conference in 1781 reporting 9,666

---

[1] Redford, *Methodism in Kentucky*, p. 69; McFerrin, *Methodism in Tennessee*, pp. 271-273.

members south of Pennsylvania, and but 873 north of Maryland.[1] The valley of Virginia was well within the field of the earliest laborers, but the over-mountain country was later in being reached. Yet it was only the year 1783 when Jeremiah Lambert was appointed to the Holston Circuit, which meant the valley of the Tennessee, and there in that year he found sixty members, the result, doubtless, of the work of some nameless lay preacher.

Carried by the undaunted and tireless circuit-rider, Methodism spread with marvelous rapidity through the western country. The circuit-rider was a minister who had several churches or preaching places in his charge, around to which he went, usually on horseback, sometimes on foot, on a circuit that was often a hundred miles in extent, and not infrequently more. The pioneer preachers are more properly called itinerant, or traveling ministers, than circuit-riders, since there was no regular circuit established until some churches or companies were formed.

These itinerants and circuit-riders were often men of little learning, but of mighty zeal. They endured privations and persecutions that would have daunted ordinary men, braving the terrors of the wilderness and the even more terrible vengeance of lawless opposers, who did not hesitate to beat and stone them. We read concerning one of these, of his "breakfasting on a frozen turnip; sleeping at night in a wretched cabin, with his head in the chimney-corner; fording streams; living on the poorest fare; preaching in cabins, sometimes with part of the congregation drunk, at others with children about him bawling louder than he could speak; and receiving, for the four months of his toil, three dollars and fourteen cents." Yet he writes, "Though the life of a Methodist preacher is very laborious and fatiguing, it is what I glory in!"[2]

---

[1] Stevens, *History of the Methodist Episcopal Church*, p. 164.
[2] *Id.* p. 300.

These Methodist itinerants received little pay, often none. Bishop Asbury, himself the head of the church in America in its earliest days, and who set the example of arduous and untiring labor, continually traveling from Maine to Georgia and from the seacoast to the western frontier, one year received, we read, but sixty dollars in money. Often worn and sick in body, this great leader of the circuit-riding brotherhood pushed himself on by sheer force of will and fervor of love. Almost every year after 1784, Asbury rode over the mountains to visit and strengthen the valley churches, ministering on the way to the few settlers scattered along the French Broad River in North Carolina, down the gorge of which lay his way to the Tennessee settlements. He records that he was "strangely outdone" for want of sleep, having been greatly deprived of it through the wilderness, "which is like being at sea in some respects, and in others worse. Our way is over mountains, steep hills, deep rivers, and muddy creeks; a thick growth of reeds for miles together, and no inhabitants but wild beasts and savage men."

The freer expression of religious emotion which the Methodist preachers brought into their services appealed to the nature of the frontiersmen, who without doubt added something of their own wildness to the character of the western meetings. What is known as "the Great Revival" began in 1800. While it originated and was carried on most fully in middle Tennessee and Kentucky, its influence quickly spread into the valleys and mountains, and in time into the Eastern States.

The state of religion among the mountaineers and the western settlers at that time was melancholy. What churches existed were for the most part cold and formal, with ministers of the same character. The doctrine of predestination, held by both the Presbyterian and the Baptist churches, was little calculated to win men from that life of wild license and sin which the frontier conditions so easily induced.[1]

---
[1] See Blake, *The Old Log House*, pp. 14-18.

Located in Logan County, Kentucky, just north of the Nashville settlements, was a Presbyterian minister named James McGready. Early in his life, he confesses, he had entered the ministry without being converted. His ministry, naturally, had little power. One night he overheard two friends talking over his case, with the expressed conviction that he was an unconverted man. This set him to thinking and closely examining himself, and the result was, a little later, his thorough conversion.

A few years later, in 1796, he removed from North Carolina to Kentucky, where he took charge of three small Presbyterian congregations. Abandoning the Calvinistic view, he preached a gospel of free salvation to every man who would take it. Then he made a covenant with his believers to spend one Saturday of every month for a year praying for the conversion of sinners. Within a year a work of revival began, but it was stopped by the opposition of other ministers.[1] In the summer of 1799, under the earnest work of Mr. McGready, the revival began again. "But," he writes, "the year 1800 exceeds all that my eyes ever beheld upon earth. All that I have related is only, as it were, an introduction. Although many souls in these congregations during the three preceding years have been savingly converted, and now give living evidences of their union to Christ, yet all that work is only like a few drops before a mighty rain, when compared with the wonders of Almighty grace that took place in the year 1800."[2]

The occasion was that of a sacramental meeting (the Lord's supper) held at the Red River church. Two brothers, William and John McGee, the former a Presbyterian and the latter a Methodist minister, started from the Nashville country on a preaching tour toward

---
[1] *Id.*, p. 25; McDonald, *History of the Cumberland Presbyterian Church*, pp. 39 ff.

[2] *The Old Log House*, p. 28.

Ohio, and they stopped at Red River for the communion.¹ In the preaching that followed, especially on Monday, hardened sinners, some of them church-members, were broken down. There came a tremendous power upon ministers and people. In the midst of an intense silence, when no man in the pulpit could find voice to speak, a woman in the far end of the house cried out for mercy. Soon nearly the whole congregation was tremendously exercised, and scores were converted. From this time and place "The Great Revival" spread.

This first meeting was continued for some days. One man brought his family in his covered wagon, and camped on the ground. Soon after, a meeting was held at Muddy River, not far distant, and a number followed the example of this man, some camping in the open, some in their wagons, and a few beginning to use tents, or else making shelters of brush. Thus began the camp-meetings of America, soon to spread in every direction, even back into the Eastern States.

This "Great Revival" spread with wonderful power and rapidity. It was especially fostered by the Methodists, whose ideas were not opposed to its somewhat extreme manifestations. The Baptists were also considerably affected by it, and great revivals took place in their churches. Among the Presbyterians, the opposition of church authorities led to the secession of the revivalists, who formed the separate church known as the Cumberland Presbyterians.² The two chief differences were one of doctrine and one of policy. In the first case, the new church differed from its parent by believing in a general rather than a limited atonement. In the second case, it accepted as ministers men who had not received the finished classical education required by the Presbyterian Church. The con-

---

[1] Redford, *Methodism in Kentucky*, p. 265.

[2] McDonald, *History of the Cumberland Presbyterian Church*, pp. 39 ff.

ditions of the frontier, and the feeling of some men of limited education that they were impelled to preach the gospel, seemed to these revivalists to be a call from God for more liberal views. And so there went out to preach the gospel men often lacking in outward polish, but filled with fire for the salvation of souls.

This character, indeed, came to be typical of western preachers in all denominations, but particularly among the Methodists. Some of the men most powerful in their mission were neither scholars nor great students, except of their Bibles. "Brother Gwin," said an educated young minister from the East to one of these men, "how is it that you are ever prepared to preach? You seem to be seldom in your study, and scarcely ever read."

"Oh, my son," replied the frontier giant, "you do not understand it: you preachers of your class have to read and study books to master your subjects, but I know what the books are made of before they are printed!"

Many were the famous characters produced on the circuits of those days, men fearless in danger, unwearying in labor, enduring in privation, powerful in exhortation, ready in wit, and often prepared to use physical as well as spiritual muscle in their combats with the devil and his human agents.

Among the most eccentric and most successful was Lorenzo Dow, a roving preacher whose work was not confined to the mountains nor the frontier; for though he labored from among the high peaks of North Carolina to the banks of the Mississippi, and from Georgia to Canada, he was well known also along the Atlantic coast and even in England and Ireland. Restless and eager, he continually traveled, nor would he marry until he had found a young woman who would cheerfully promise that she would spare him from home twelve months out of thirteen.[1]

---

[1] His proposal of marriage ran as follows: "If I am preserved, about a year and a half from now I am in hopes of seeing this northern country

Education and Religion

Lorenzo Dow journeyed, sometimes on horseback, often on foot, sometimes well tricked out in new clothing by his friends, only to return from a journey of hundreds of miles in rags, and with everything of value either stolen or pawned, but feeling successful in that he had preached the gospel to those who would otherwise never have heard it — settlers, desperadoes, Indians. Many a time he was offered money or other valuables which he would not take, lest he be called, as he says, "an impostor" who loved money rather than souls. Later, he himself made hundreds of dollars by the sale of some of his books, which he would frequently give for the building of meeting-houses or other purposes of the church.

His sermons were often eccentric in form and matter, yet always powerful. Though endeared to the rough people of the mountains and backwoods, he not infrequently scandalized the more conventional of his Methodist brethren, as when he one day announced to an impenitent crowd that having just preached from the Word of the Lord, which they rejected, he would the next day preach to them from the word of the devil — and did so from Luke 4: 6, 7.

He traveled to the most out-of-the-way places to carry the gospel, crossing the North Carolina mountains into Tennessee for the sole purpose of preaching to the one lone settlement in those mountains, Buncombe Court-house (now Asheville); and delving with equal zeal into the mazes of West Virginia, where he made an appointment to return and preach in exactly thirteen months, on such a day and at such an hour, an appoint-

---

again; and if during this time you live and remain single, and find no one that you like better than you do me, and would be willing to give me up twelve months out of thirteen, or three years out of four, to travel, and that in foreign lands, and never say, Do not go to your appointment, etc.— for if you should stand in the way, I should pray to God to remove you, which I believe he would answer — and if I find no one that I like better than I do you, perhaps something further may be said upon the subject."—*The Life of Lorenzo Dow*, by himself, p. 152.

ment which he filled most punctually. It was his custom, indeed, to give out a string of appointments a year or more ahead, and to meet them scrupulously on time, though he might have to travel from Canada to Mississippi to do it, sometimes in a pinch traveling for several days and nights in succession, through mud, rain, and cold, going from carriage to horse and then to foot, in order to be at the appointed place on time.

He was constantly dreaming dreams that forecast events for him, and he believed he had what the Scotch call "second sight," and that he could sometimes foretell events for others, and even read the secrets of their lives. But despite his oddities, he was a most thoroughly consecrated and successful Christian laborer, and thousands were reclaimed to the Master whose *sheriff* he proclaimed himself to be, and in whose name he offered a great reward for the "runaways whose marks he would now describe."

It was in this southwestern country, especially in the great camp-meetings, under the powerful exhortations of such famous preachers as James B. Finley, Jesse Walker, and Peter Cartwright, that the peculiar physical manifestations known as "the jerks" began to appear. In the midst of his discourse the preacher was apt to see various ones begin nodding or jumping or jerking more and more vigorously, and the infection was likely to spread until almost the whole congregation would be affected. Sometimes the head was snapped backward and forward so rapidly that it would seem the neck must be dislocated; or the limbs and even the whole body would be jerked so violently that the person could keep his feet only by grasping a tree or some other object and holding on desperately. No uncommon sight was a clearing next the log church, in which everything had been removed except saplings cut breast-high, to which the victims might resort to jerk. Or sometimes the seizure would set a person to dancing, slowly, it is said, and with grace.

"The jerks" affected the converted as well as the impenitent, but with different effects. Those who yielded themselves to it felt no discomfort, even though their contortions were alarming to the onlookers, but those who resisted it would experience much pain, and even at times be injured by the exercise. Often by this means scoffers and hardened sinners were brought to the penitent seat.

The strange phenomenon was doubtless due to extreme nervous excitement in simple, uncontrolled natures. It was not consciously induced by the preachers, who at first looked upon it with suspicion and aversion, but who came finally to accept it as something beyond their control and often of value in their work for the people. Its manifestation passed away within a few years.

The solid work of the circuit-riding minister was manifested in the religious character given to the western country, which in the middle of the nineteenth century was found, on the whole, much more open to religious influences and to the reception of truth than was the more staid and settled East. To this day the South, and especially the mountain country, is remarkable for its religious spirit.

The great mass of the mountaineers today belong to either the Baptist or the Methodist Church, and their religion is the fervid, soul-storming religion of the pioneer days. To them and to their preachers, hell and heaven are very real places, and the way to avoid the one and secure the other is through the process of regeneration, preferably, because most easily, at the semi-annual protracted meeting. The fervor of their proceedings in these meetings — shouting, crying, moaning, stamping, and clapping, is apt to strike harshly upon the more staid religionist, but the sincerity of the worshipers is not to be questioned.

Yet there are many, in the more isolated sections, who have not even the benefit of these services. Thousands there are who seldom hear the voice of prayer, who have never seen a Bible, and who could not read it if they had it. The story is told of a minister visiting for the first time one of these homes far back in the mountains, and there to a little family telling the story of the Cross. They followed him with rapt faces; and when he had concluded, the mother, leaning toward him, whispered hoarsely:

"Stranger, you say all this happened a long time ago?"

"Yes," he said, "almost two thousand years ago."

"And they nailed him to that thar tree when he hadn't done nothing to hurt 'em; only jest loved 'em?"

"Yes."

She leaned farther and placed her hand impressively upon his knee. "Wal, stranger," she said, the tears standing in her eyes, "let's hope hit ain't so!"[1]

There is no more promising field, both for true religion and for education, than in the mountains of the South. Its people believe in religion and long for education. Their heritage of body and mind is the best of earth's; and they need but the help it should delight Christians to give, to make of them the most worthy recruits for Christian service.

---

[1] John Fox, Jr., *Blue-Grass and Rhododendron*, p. 23.

V

THE MODERN MOUNTAINEER

THE conditions of colonial life persist today in a very considerable part of the mountains. This is particularly true of the southern Appalachians. Those portions of the Appalachian system which lie in the Northern States are less isolated and have partaken more of the life about them; but from Virginia to Georgia and Alabama the broad extent of mountain and plateau have conspired with political and social causes to keep the mountaineer separate and to keep him back, until he has come to represent a distinct type of American.

The southern mountain country embraces an area of 101,880 square miles, this reckoning including 35 counties of West Virginia, 4 of Maryland, 42 of Virginia, 28 of Kentucky, 46 of Tennessee, 24 of North Carolina, 4 of South Carolina, 26 of Georgia, and 17 of Alabama. This section is about 600 miles long and averages 200 miles in breadth. It is twice as large as the State of New York; it would cover New England, New Jersey, Delaware, and two Marylands; and is much larger than England, Wales, and Scotland together. Its population is somewhat over four million, more than twice as many as the thirteen colonies held at the time of the Revolution, yet little more today than the State of Ohio (which has an area of less than half that of the mountains), and it is less than the city of Greater New York.

Four million souls are too many to neglect, and their value and importance to American and Christian life are enhanced, not lessened, by their scattered state. The closer men crowd together, the less power does the individual have, both because of his environment and because of his education; but a people spread out until every man has room for development of thought and resource, is a people of whom "one of the least is over a hundred, and the greatest over a thousand."

It is not to be understood, however, that all these four million are ignorant or poverty-stricken or helpless. This enumeration includes the valley-dwellers as well as those on the mountain tops, and as they range from owners of rich bottom lands to those of thin, rocky peaks, so in practically the same order they range from prosperous and cultured modern citizens to ill-nourished and backward men who need help.

For convenience the mountaineers may be divided into three classes, though this is a rather arbitrary arrangement, since the types and classes are much more varied, shading almost imperceptibly into one another.

In the first class are the prosperous valley-dwellers, descendants for the most part of those early settlers who had the first choice of the best locations. The valleys of Virginia and Tennessee contain not only fertile farms, but cities like Staunton, Roanoke, Bristol, Knoxville, and Chattanooga. In the same class may be put such a broad and accessible section as the French Broad Plateau in North Carolina, with Asheville, its metropolis, and other prosperous cities.

The people who constitute this class are abreast of other thriving sections of the United States. They have the same comforts, the same educational, social, and wealth-producing opportunities, and they constitute one of the most important elements in the progress of the South and of the nation. Their ability, enterprise, and prosperity are a promise of what other mountain classes may become with equal opportunities. Upon the corn and wheat lands of the valleys and the river bottoms may be seen the latest farm machinery, drawn by big Percheron horses or heavy mules. Here and there, even, is seen the traction engine, pulling gang-plows and harrows. Large dairy barns and silos are no unusual sight, and in some sections fine herds and flocks or beautiful orchards and vineyards proclaim the cause of the prosperity typified in roomy, comfortable, and up-to-date dwellings.

Besides agriculture, which remains the chief industry, there are other important interests — mining, lumbering, and manufacturing. The economic advantages of this section are being more fully realized and exploited every day, not always to the moral nor even the financial advantage of the mountaineer.

As a rule, these prosperous mountaineers are interested in their poorer and less fortunate neighbors, who, while more abundant in isolated regions, are yet to a considerable degree scattered among them.

"Foreign missions!" exclaimed a bank president and church deacon who was no Missionary Baptist, "talk to me of sending my dollars along with your preachers to the heathen, when every day I deal with men who can't write their names, who can't scratch together enough hog and hominy to keep their children, and whose only prayers are cuss words! Start a work to teach these men and their children how to live like Christians in this Christian land, and you have my support. That's my foreign mission!"

The mountaineer employer, be he small or great, generally has in him not so much a philanthropy as a benevolence toward the people he employs. His sympathies go out to the individual rather than the group. He may in times of stress exclaim against the shiftlessness or the small necessities of his employees, which permit them to knock off work at a critical time. He may rage against the independence and the sensitiveness of a race who will hardly stoop to service and never to anything they count humiliation or insult. But when it comes to dealing with the individual, he is lenient to faults and generous to needs.

Take, for example, Mr. George, the manager of a well equipped plant in the North Carolina mountains, whose workmen not infrequently felt the need of something more diverting than humdrum labor, and whose sprees and escapades were a matter of constant exasperation to their long-suffering employer.

"There's that Zeb Bean," he confided one evening to a visitor in his home. "Got a wife and six children. Sick for two months this fall, and the company carried him along through it all. But when he gets well and earning again, what do you think he does?— Buys little gewgaws to hang round his children's necks when they're needing shoes, and runs an account at the company store for corn-meal and bacon, while, if he gets a dollar, he dives straight for a blind tiger. And I told him, 'Now, Zeb, you've got to let liquor alone, and you've got to walk straight if you don't want to get fired.'

"Comes Christmas, and Zeb pipes up for a dollar. 'What for?' I says. 'Want to celebrate,' he says, 'it's Christmas, and I got to celebrate, ain't I?' 'You'll celebrate by keeping sober and reducing your account,' I told him. But what does the fellow do? Somewhere or other he gets hold of a dime, buys that much black powder, and fills an old wagon-skein with it. His slow match proves a fast one, and he blows two fingers off his right hand, and lays himself up for another six weeks. And now who's going to take care of him this time, I'd like to know."

"Oh, you are, of course!" said his wife, with a quiet little laugh. Mr George's wrath collapsed into a mellow chuckle, that bespoke repentance for his indignation, indulgence for his erring employee. "I reckon I am," he said.

Next morning, over the frozen ground, there came

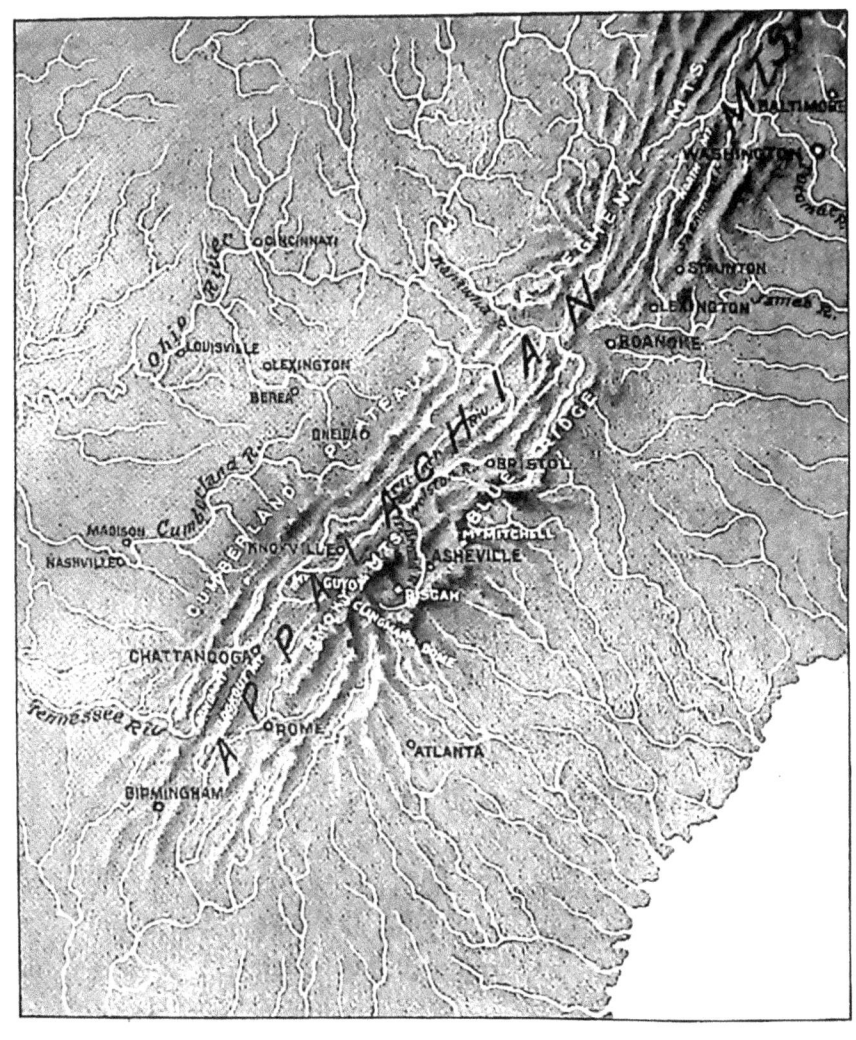

Relief Map of Appalachia.

"The mountains of Appalachia run in two great parallel ranges." Page 79.

to the door a barefooted little boy whose ostensible errand was a transparent excuse. He was brought in to the fire, and warmed and fed and talked with, and laden for home with a basket packed by the good lady of the house with substantials and delicacies.

"How's your papa, son? Tell him to hurry up and get well. Tell him, 'Don't worry, everything will be all right,'" cooed the stern magnate of last evening. The barefooted boy was a son of Zeb.

Such charity as a practise may not be according to the modern theories of scientific philanthropy, wherein a departmented bureau lists cases, investigates appeals, sifts evidences, collects gifts, distributes bundles, and presides over mass dinners. Undiscerning personal charity, we hear, robs the giver and pauperizes the recipient. It may have that effect among those huddles of humanity that are the dregs of civilization; and, despite the natural independence of the highlander, it may have that tendency in the mountains. But one thing is certain, it accords more nearly with the letter, and — our hearts tell us — with the spirit of the Master's teachings; and its prevalence in the mountains among both rich and poor makes an atmosphere of brotherhood that may possibly count for more than scientific exactness. Efforts for the betterment of the poorer mountain classes, be they free-handed or card-cataloged, will find among the prosperous mountaineers a strong support.

In the second class may be put those who occupy sections less accessible, and yet of fair natural advantages. There are people in little valleys and considerable plateaus who, if they had access to good markets and to the advantages of a broader life, would be not at all behind the rest of the world, but who, because they have not such access, live to a great extent in their own world, comfortable, easy, though usually hard-working, shut in to a live but rather narrow world that has little knowledge of things outside, and not much concern for them.

Many of this class are fairly well-to-do, but their standards of living correspond more fully to those of the eighteenth century than to those of the twentieth. They are content with poor housing, meager equipment, and unenterprising methods of work.

With others, this condition, irrespective of choice, is the necessity of their poverty. They may own a "beast," which means a horse or a mule, but just as likely their dependence for plowing and hauling is on a "jinny" or an ox. The one-horse wagon is coming to be very common, yet beyond the land of good roads the home-made sled, with runners hewn from the tough sourwood, is made to bear the burdens too heavy for bent shoulders. The one-horse turning plow, preferably the reversible hillside plow, has taken the place of our grandfather's wooden share (discarded specimens of which may still be found in the mountains), but it is far from having driven out the "bull-tongue," which may be described as a single-toothed cultivator with wide-flaring wings. With many men, this plow is their sole horse tool, being used first to scrabble the ground two or three inches deep for the planting, and afterwards, along with the heavy iron hand hoe, to cultivate the crop. Add to these implements the ax and the gun, and you have fairly represented the complete mechanical equipment of the far-back mountaineer.

There are fields, indeed, too steep for any plow to cultivate or any beast to work upon, and there the soil is never touched except with the hoe. John Fox is not to be accused of hyperbole when he tells of one who broke his neck by falling out of his own cornfield. Such fields are usually good for only one or two seasons of cultivation after having been cleared of their forest growth. By that time their fertility has mostly disappeared, half of it upward into the corn, half downward into the creek. If the owner can afford to seed it, he may keep his field as a permanent pasture, but he will do better to let it grow up to natural grass and brush.

Such fields, it goes without saying, are not the mountaineer's preference, nor are they any large part of the farm lands. "Hobson's choice" they are to the man whose level land consists of a few irregular square rods of "branch bottom."

The typical home is the log cabin. Year by year, as the capital and enterprise of the outside world push farther back, eating up the resources of the mountains, some of that world's fashions and a little of its money come to change the standards of living. So, where yesterday the frame dwelling, when it appeared at all, was the mark of the great man of the community, today it is elbowing and shoving its humble log neighbor back into the coves and through the gaps. Yet the latter is still so greatly in the majority that it has right to give its name to its land —"The log-cabin country."

The log house is of all sizes and of all degrees of excellence, but its unit is the single room, rough-floored and ceiled, with a big stone chimney at one end, a door at front and one at back, and possibly a window or two. A narrow front porch of plank, and a lean-to of the same material at the back, represent the first improvements.[1] As prosperity attends him, the mountaineer may add another log room or two alongside the first, covering them with one roof, and usually leaving an open passageway between them.

The stone chimney, when carefully and conscientiously made, is a thing of beauty and a joy forever. Often composed of hewn stone, and hiding a great part of the cabin's end with its broad base, it stands the symbol of stability and massive beauty. Within, as you face its flaming, glowing depths, the abode of warmth and cheer and savory cooking, you speedily become as much its devotee as the veriest child of the land.

"I ain't no use," declares Uncle John Andrews, "for

---

[1] In the mountains the sawed "boards" of the North, no matter how thin, are "plank," while "boards" are the hand-rived shingles that cover the roof.

these here little ginky black sheet-iron contraptions they calls *stoves*. I cain't git proper heat lessen I kin *see* fire. Set up a stove, and y're in a black hell. They ain't no place to set, and they ain't no place to luk, and they ain't no place to spit! Gi' me a fireplace, er turn me out o' doors." And in this land of forests, certainly there can be no excuse for abolishing just yet that maker of the home, the open fireplace.

The house itself is almost certain to be of hewn logs; that is, hewn on two sides, one to face inward for a somewhat smooth wall, and one to face outward to give an appearance of finish to the building. Few take the trouble to square the log on all four sides. The round sides are turned toward each other, and the cracks made by their failure to meet are chinked with wedges of wood and wet clay or mortar. Important crevices which appear in time may be plugged up; unimportant chinks help in the ventilation, in which the wide fireplace and the open door are the most important factors.

The habit of open-door is a daytime habit, born both of hospitality and of desire for light and air. At night the door is shut and fastened, doubtless a precaution that dates from the days of Indian warfare, and yet one not unmixed many times with a fear of night air. If the beds be in the room with the fireplace, however, as some of them usually are, there can be no complete stoppage of ventilation; for there are bound to be cracks somewhere, and a wide and warm chimney throat to take the draft up and out.

Hospitality is a cardinal virtue of the mountaineer. He usually has a spare bed for company. If not, and he knows you cannot fare better at a neighbor's, he will make sure that you are accommodated, though the children or his wife and himself have to sleep upon the floor. The farther back in the mountains, the truer this is; nearness to cities and the railroads and the incoming "furriner" have made the mountaineer both more suspicious of his ability to please the tastes of the stranger, and more greedy of the stranger's money. It is indeed rather uncommon now-a-days, except in some of the most out-of-the-way places, to receive accommodation free. A quarter or a half-dollar is usually expected for a night's lodging with meals. But for all that, the log cabin wears no air of the hostelry. If the stranger knows how to fit in with his fellow-men, he gets from his stay in the log-cabin home a warmth of welcome, a freedom of spirit, but slightly bitten by the tinge of barter that comes with the passing of silver.

The traveler fresh from the pampering homes and restaurants of the cities, may find the mountain fare meager. It is at least the habit of the mountaineer — primed, perhaps, by experience — to offer his hospitality with an apology for its plainness: "You-all are sure welcome ef you can eq'al our fare." Yet in season one may find at many a table a surprizing variety and in superabundance. What the mountaineer eats, for the most part he raises on his own land, "hog and hominy" being the most common staples, supplemented by a greater or smaller variety of vegetables, grains, and fruits, according to the enterprise of the individual.

Though the cook-stove is a not uncommon possession, even of the far back mountaineer, the fireplace is the standby of perhaps the majority of the cooks. The iron pot of our great grandmothers yet swings on the crane in the mountain fireplace, and the "Dutch oven", or "bake kettle," as it is most commonly called in the mountains, still does its duty amidst the glowing coals on the hearth. Have you ever eaten real corn pone — white corn meal, cold water, and salt, patted into a long, thick cake, and deposited with its twin in the bake kettle, to remain till it comes out a golden brown, crisp, crumbly, nutty, and altogether sweet with the natural sweetness of the corn? Such corn pone is first cousin, at least, with the cakes that angels ate in the hospitable pilgrims' tent on the plains of Mamre. Not so tempting is the fried pork or the grease-soaked beans that usually accompany it; but the stranger of simple habits may, if his mind agree, fare sumptuously every day and grow fat with corn pone and sweet milk or buttermilk. Moreover, nearly everywhere in the mountains, and nearly always, he may be "comforted with apples."

In the corner or on the porch of many a home stands the spinning-wheel. Its hours of duty today are not so many as in generations past; for though occasionally a loom may be found to weave its welcome threads into linsey-woolsey and jeans, homespun has for the most part retreated before the cheap "store goods"; and carding and spinning have more regard to the need of socks and mittens than of shirts and dresses. Buckskin and coonskin also have surrendered to the shoe and hat industries of the lowlanders. Yet still the mountaineer keeps much of the skill and ingenuity which characterized our independent forefathers, and with his ax and knife makes himself the chief part of America's waning guild of home arts and crafts.

The educational and religious advantages of these mountaineers are not overgreat. The mountain school may run three or four months in the year; the circuit-rider comes once or twice a month to the little log church. Protracted meeting in spring and fall (neighborhood equivalent for the old-time camp-meeting) is the great emotional outlet of natures at other times pent within the barriers of a stern self-control or a wistful shame.

Also, there is the singing-school, attended mostly by the young people. The singing-master, that modern successor of the old-time bard, goes peripateting from settlement to settlement, calling together at the schoolhouse or church such musical souls as have been stirred at the country dance with "Old Dan Tucker," or at the revival with "I Feel Like Traveling On." High, sweet voices have many of these lasses, though unfortunately sometimes spoiled by the effort to shout in singing.

And as for the boys, if it were not for the tobacco which makes some of their voices husky, there could be no clearer, sweeter, farther-carrying melody than the singing and the yodeling that come out of the early and sometimes the late night.

The singing-master holds perhaps a ten days' school, and with his shaped notes[1] and his rousing time and his very real enthusiasm, he does no little service in fitting the class of Bethany Church for the singing contest next winter with North Star Church over in Wildcat Holler.

As for the school, that fares according to public sentiment. The state furnishes a three or four, or even six months' term of school, and the districts are usually small enough to make the farthest home but two or three miles distant. Yet in some places the population is so sparse that the distances must be far greater, and if you go far enough into the recesses of the hills, you will find plenty of children who never have gone to school and bid fair never to go. Yet the parents are almost always eager for their children to go to school; that is, after "laying-by time" and outside "fodder-pulling time," and when it is not too cold. The temperature rarely reaches zero in the Southern mountains for even one night, but thin clothing and sometimes entire absence of shoes and stockings make a 20° or 30° mark forbidding weather to careful parents. To avoid the severest parts of the winter, school usually is begun in July or August, and closed before Christmas. But this time must be broken into by the older boys and girls when the fodder is ready to strip and the corn to pull.

---

[1] "Shaped notes" are written the same as ordinary notes, except that their shapes denote the syllables of the scale; thus:

do △, re ▽, mi ◇, fa ◣, sol ○, la □, ti ○

Obviously, the art of note-reading is made easy by this method, but those who learn to sing by shaped notes, though they see them on the staff, are usually helpless before ordinary written music.

This breaking of time is disastrous to scholarship, and it must be admitted that the commonest arts of reading and writing are but shoddy accomplishments with all but a favored few. Arithmetic, especially "head figuring," is more in line with common pursuits, and finds more than one adept where he would be least suspected.

As for the teachers, they are a devoted but scarcely a peerless class. With less than half a year's term, and that on small pay, the teacher secured is seldom all that could be desired. Of the men teachers, who are disproportionately common in the mountains, practically all depend upon farming or some other support for the most of the year, and have but little chance to improve their talents by further training. And as for the women, they follow the world-wide custom of teaching until they get a good offer of marriage. Yet there are some who are trained and capable teachers — invariably those who for shorter or longer time have been won to the work by love rather than by money.

Let one of these, who, of all the interpreters of the mountains, has written the most illuminating and faithful account, paint for us a closing picture of the mountain school:

"Our log church stands in the forest. There is scarce enough space cleared around it for a playground. Woodpeckers drum on its roof in the daytime, and whippoorwills sing there at night. Acorns drop upon it in October, with resounding taps that startle all the little ones within. Its walls are laid of heavy pine timbers, squared roughly and well matched together, the cracks chinked with chips driven in slantwise, and daubed with native clay. There is no belfry. The door is at one end, and the high pulpit at the other.

"At one side is a stone chimney, massive as a door, whose fireplace on cold days seems about to swallow the huddled school. It requires the strength of all the larger boys together to bring in a backlog. When I was a child, I remember a number of us, on the heels of some prank, once hid in its sooty depths from the rod of a teacher, much as the Indians took shelter in Nickojack from the pursuing forces of Sevier. How could we have kept school without the aid of that hospitable cavern? We roasted nuts in it, and potatoes, and apples, and pigs' tails brought from home. We even boiled eggs there in a tin bucket when Mis' Robbins' old blue hen obligingly stole her nest under the floor. We watched the sparks fly up the chimney when we should have been studying. We told fortunes, making and naming marks in the ashes. And oh, the visions we saw in its smoke, the futures we painted in its ruddy coals!

"Still it stands, the mighty chimney, and now it is I who must sometimes chase the little fellows, laughing and squealing, into its dark recesses and out again. With so few pupils, little discipline is necessary, and we often spend the hot afternoons of September outside with our books — old McGuffey readers, blue-back spellers, Testaments, or whatever comes to hand, scattered about on the ground. If the young minds wander afield with the scampering and flitting of little brothers of treetop and burrow, what matter? Perhaps they learn at such times something not to be found between the covers of Webster.

"As for that, our study is never confined to the text-book long. The first hour of our day is devoted to reading in four classes of different grades, the second to arithmetic in three. Then we spend about thirty minutes in drawing maps and talking about the country represented, a primitive method of studying geography, but the best possible in default of more expensive books. Next we write either a spelling lesson or a composition on some out-door subject, until it is time for the noon 'ree-cess.' Dinner, eaten in the shade outside, is over in a few minutes, and then playtime scatters the little folks through the woods, making playhouses and bending down saplings for 'ridey-hosses,' until it is time to recall them by rapping on the door with a stick, as if the hollow house were a giant drum.

"The afternoon is very much like the morning, except that there is a class in such grammar as we can manage without a text-book. Last of all, I give them something to take home with them to think over and dream about — an object-lesson, a story, a poem, or a simple talk on some bit of natural science."[1]

This second class, who make up the bulk of the true mountain people — distinct from the valley dwellers — are among the most valuable elements in America's population. They best represent that dauntless, daring race, Saxon and Celt, that not only conquered the mountains, but that has been foremost in the winning of the West. Elsewhere in America, East, North, and West, the blood of Britain has mingled with that of the Teuton, the Latin, and the Slav. Here alone dwells the triple-welded American — English, Irish, and Scotch, with an Elizabethan language and a Cromwellian temper, speaking his thoughts with an unconventional force, and doing his deeds with a resolute directness. He is not lawless, but he is a lord of the law. In an abstract sense "the law" — a phrase frequently on his tongue — is the personification of justice, order, and dignity of government, to which he is ardently attached. But concretely, his intimate contact with the state's statutes has taught him that "the law" is a great game in which he whose wits are sharpest and whose pocket-book is longest, may win. Sometimes, therefore, his reason tells him, it is more to his advantage and satisfaction to settle his troubles by more primitive law. There are very few grown men in the mountains who have not had some contact with "the law," either as principal or accessory or witness. Court day finds the county-seat crowded; and trials and decisions hold at least equal value as mental food with sermons and revivals.

[1] Emma B. Miles, *The Spirit of the Mountains*, pp. 3-6.

There is a third class, consisting of the poorest men of the mountains, those living in the distant gorges or "coves," on the mountain sides or mountain tops, and in the rough hill land. They are also to be found scattered all through the other communities, infrequently landowners, more often renters, sometimes little more than paupers. They are usually housed in a ragged relative of the log cabin, though sometimes more forlornly in a slatternly plank hut. In such a house the chimney has degenerated into a cobblestone-and-mud daub, or even perhaps, into a stick chimney, sometimes carried little above the height of the fireplace, so that "you can sit in the chimbly and spit outdoors." Cracks in the walls, in the floors, and often between the curled "boards" of the roof, invite the weather, and the "sage broom"— a bundle of broom-sedge or "sage grass"— restricts its sphere of usefulness to the uneven, rock hearth. A patch of corn and beans, a hog or two, make most of their worldly wealth. Down in the "settlemints" the men will work, perhaps, when occasion and necessity agree, at odd jobs of crop-tending or wood-chopping or road-mending, which will yield them seventy-five cents or a dollar. In sections where no such opportunities are found, the abundant leisure time is spent hunting or sunning or "jest waitin'."

It is really unfair to the best of this class to count them under the same head as the worst, and it is only their economic condition that invites it. For while some, from mere lack of opportunity, or perhaps of worldly-wiseness, are wofully poor in material things, they are possessed of much moral and no little mental power, and are capable, if given instruction and opportunity, of rising into the second class. On the other hand, some of them are degenerates and the sons of degenerates — a class that is by no means confined to the mountains. They can be known and classified only by a personal and individual acquaintance. But a natural distinction will at first sight be made between those who are poor because they live in the most inaccessible and isolated regions and those who remain poor though in the midst of more prosperous communities.

It is chiefly from this third class, though partly also from the second, that the popular conception of the mountaineer is gained. He makes the most picturesque character in fiction; and fiction is the road by which the average American travels outside his own narrow neighborhood bounds. The ideas of the mountaineer which he thus gains are about as correct as the ideas of the life of Indian, cowboy, soldier, and jolly tar, gained by the boy who reads the Henty and Alger type of book.

While, because of his long isolation, the backward type of mountaineer may have peculiarities of speech habit, and idea, he will, upon thorough acquaintance, be found as human and as natural as any other neighbor, with the same faults of temper, prejudice, and self-interest, and the same virtues — a little emphasized — of curiosity, hospitality, and brotherly kindness, to which all the world is heir.

There are besides, within the mountain country, some sectional differences of character, according with the same general laws of isolation or accessibility. Roughly speaking, the mountain regions of Virginia, North Carolina, and Georgia are more accessible than those of Kentucky, Tennessee, and Alabama. Partly in consequence of this, it is in Kentucky that the blood feuds occur which have unjustly branded the whole mountain people in the popular mind; and it is on the broad Cumberland plateau of the more southern States, alongside the prosperous Tennessee Valley, that the densest ignorance and most hopeless economic conditions exist. "There are places on S— Mountain," is a phrase with which other mountaineers are wont to begin stories of conditions below their own. The other States have these conditions, or conditions approaching these, in plenty, but they are not so typical of large sections, for the simple reason that the eastern mountains are penetrated more fully by means of communication with the outside world. These facts make each State and each community in each State a separate problem by itself, corresponding only in general features to the great whole, and requiring study and peculiar treatment each for itself.

Beyond the mountains, in the piedmont, or foothill sections, there is a people kin somewhat to the mountaineer, and having the same needs. Indeed, throughout the rural South the state of society is practically that of the mountains, with the addition, however, of the upper crust of the aristocracy and the bottom crust — now more or less upheaved — of the negro. It was under slavery that the poorer or less successful white man was forced away from the richest lands of the South and up into the foothills. He lacked, and lacks today, the same advantages that the mountaineer lacks, without all the compensating advantages of the mountaineer, in the inspiring life of the great heights, the far views, and the healthfulness of his elevated region. Some writers declare, also, that a greater proportion of outlaws and degenerates mingled with the inhabitants of the foothills than with those of the mountains. However that may be, the esteem of the wealthy lowlander was given more to the mountaineer than to the foothiller, his contempt for the latter being preserved today in the various opprobrious terms used for the hillsmen, from Carolina around through Georgia and Alabama to Tennessee, such as, "redneck," "sandhiller," "corn cracker," "mudsill," and "hill billie."

Nevertheless, that the foothiller lacked opportunity more than ability has been proved since the upheaval of the Civil War, by his increasing activity in the public life of the South. For two generations he has been coming more and more to the front in politics and education; and many of the leaders in public life in the South are from this class. The mountaineer and the foothiller together may boast that slavery gave them only a temporary eclipse; for in the early days of the nation they were the producers of such national figures as Jackson and Clay; even in the death throes of slavery they brought forth such men as Lincoln; and today the voices of their sons are heard in State and national councils more fully than is generally realized. Dry soil of wonderful promise, they await only the living streams of education and social and economic opportunity to bear the fruits of civilization and culture. And out of their ranks, deeply spiritual as they are by nature and training, may the church gain for itself, for the world, and for God, heroes of faith and action to stand in the ranks of the last great battle for truth.

THE OLD AND THE NEW

VI

THE HEART OF APPALACHIA

THE Potomac marks the northern boundary of Appalachia. This is the ancient application of the term. To the earliest settlers the Indians to the southwest were known as the Appalachians, and from them the mountains gained their name. While today the term is made to cover the whole system of the eastern highlands, in a distinctive sense it applies only to the Southern mountains. Appalachia is set off by its heights, its climate, its products, and its people, from the lands surrounding it. It may perhaps be allowed to extend as far as the Alleghanies take it into Pennsylvania, but it has no kinship with the Catskills, the Adirondacks, the Green or the White Mountains, much less with the plains. They belong to another world.

The mountains of Appalachia run in two great parallel ranges, beginning in Pennsylvania and trending southwest. The one is the Blue Ridge, the other is the Allegheny and Cumberland system. Between these two ranges lies a great trough-like valley, cut into three parts. The northernmost is in Pennsylvania and Maryland, where it is known as the Cumberland Valley. With this, in our study of the Southern mountaineers, we will not deal. There remain, then, two great divisions of the valley south of the Potomac. The first is the Shenandoah, or more broadly, the valley of Virginia, under which name it continues to near the southwestern corner of the State. Here the valley is broken by cross ridges, in the midst of which the New River flows from the highlands of North Carolina across the Great Valley and northward through the Alleghanies. But continuing southwestwardly, the Great Valley quickly slides down into the valley of the Tennessee, the upper part of which is divided, according to its several head-streams which flow therein, into the Holston, the Clinch, and the Powell valleys.

This great Appalachian Valley divides the mountains into two grand divisions, which, by the transverse ridges in lower Virginia and between Tennessee and Kentucky, are made into four. In the northern section, the valley of Virginia lies in the eastern part of the mountain mass, there being only the Blue Ridge between it and the lowlands, while the great body of the mountains is to the west, in Kentucky and West Virginia. In the southern division, on the contrary, the Tennessee Valley leaves to the east the wider stretch of mountain country, where the Blue Ridge broadens out, making an elevated plateau in western North Carolina, between the Blue Ridge proper and the Great Smoky Mountains. To the west of the Tennessee Valley lie the somewhat narrower Cumberland Mountains or Plateau. The general character of the ranges to the east is that of true mountains, with rounded peaks that mark their individuality by rising above their connecting ridges; while those to the west, in Kentucky and Tennessee, are in the nature of elevated plateaus, their faces making abrupt cliffs and their tops broad, rolling country.

Below this mountain system, especially on the east and the south, which look toward the sea, is the gradual descent known as the piedmont or foothills. Next to the mountains the piedmont is rough and heaped with high hills, and the population is practically the same as that of the mountains. Farther toward the coastal plain the piedmont settles down into rolling or almost level country; and in this section, generally speaking, is found the highest development of agriculture and of manufactures.

To the west of the mountains the character of the country is slightly different. In Tennessee the Cumberland Plateau gradually descends toward the west and, except where the great river basins cut it deeply, glides almost imperceptibly into the lowlands. In Kentucky and West Virginia, the rough, hilly, mountainous land west of the main ranges is of a character to make it popularly included among the mountains. The Bluegrass country, which lies just outside the westernmost of the Kentucky hills or mountains, is an undulating plain stretching away toward the Mississippi.

If, now, we would see more particularly the domain of the American highlanders, let us follow the trail of their fathers, that long trail that leads from the gorge of the Potomac at Harper's Ferry up to the backwater districts, and there divides, running one way into the mountains of West Virginia, another into the tablelands of Carolina, and yet another — the chiefest trail —down into the valley of the Tennessee and through Cumberland Gap into Kentucky.

Upon our left, as we go up the beautiful valley of the Shenandoah, lie the walls of the Blue Ridge, whose forbidding heights daunted so many generations of our English forebears. Yet the Blue Ridge, for all its half a dozen parallel ridges within its sixteen miles' breadth, is not impassable, and through its water-gaps and passes the English did finally sweep in to join the steady current of Scotch-Irish that soon began to settle the valley.

But across the valley to the west rise abruptly the limestone cliffs of the Alleghanies. Small wonder that the pioneers grew discouraged before these forbidding ramparts; for the Alleghanies oppose to western progress not one height only, but ridge after ridge of perpendicular walls carved out of its limestone bed. If, as the settlers entered the Great Valley at its lowest point, by the Potomac, they turned their eyes to the westward, they saw their way barred by that first outpost of the Alleghanies, the great North Mountain, whose lines faded out to the southward only to reveal the Shenandoah Mountains behind. And if through such a water-gap as that of the James at Clifton Forge, two hundred miles and better up the valley, they should win their way through the Shenandoahs to the valley of the mineral springs, it was but to be faced at last by the still unbroken battle-line of the main Alleghanies, with a hundred miles of like country behind it.

So the pioneer, who had no need to seek the hardship and danger which were always seeking him, kept his face still turned up the easier way of the valley, finding his home therein whenever he could, or pressing on to the fair lands of Tennessee and the Kentucky Blue-grass.

Well might the homeseeker choose his home in the valley of Virginia while there remained homes to be preempted; for that lap of the mountains was the fairest land in all Virginia; and till today it keeps its boast. Twenty miles apart, the Blue Ridge and the Alleghanies stand to guard it with their heights; and in the midst, running in the long hollows of the hills, flow the streams of the Shenandoah. The soils of this valley, formed from decaying limestone, are the richest in the State. At an average altitude of 1,200 feet, its climate misses the heat of the lowlands, and its products are those of the northern temperate section. With its wheat and other small grains, as well as corn, the valley has ever been the granary of the State, and it is no less famous for its production of fruits, especially of apples.

Strictly speaking, the valley can be called the Shenandoah no more than two hundred miles from the Potomac, for there the headwaters of the northward flowing Shenandoah begin. Within these bounds, the three chief cities are Winchester at the lower end, the first town of the valley; Lexington, the seat of Washington and Lee University; and Staunton, at the upper end, a city of some fifteen thousand inhabitants, the center and shipping-point of a wide agricultural district, and the seat of growing manufactures.

Above Staunton the Great Valley, while keeping still its trough-like character between the chief ranges, becomes for another two hundred miles the debatable land of the great water systems. As the fingers of the Shenandoah leave off clutching at the hills, the James River, through its many wide-spreading tributaries, takes possession, and gathering the waters of the mountains, rushes them through the Blue Ridge eastward to the lower end of the Chesapeake. Then, as we pass Roanoke, the metropolis of the valley of Virginia, with its 30,000 inhabitants, its railroad shops, and its manufactures, we come to the height of land that marks off the domain of the New River, whose course Batts followed in his efforts to reach the limits of the mountains. The New River turns its back upon the East, and, cleaving a way through the Alleghanies, rushes down through West Virginia, under the name of Kanawha, to join the Ohio.

Here, on the heights overlooking the narrow valley of the New, let us pause to take a survey; for now we have reached the divide, the "Backwater Settlements" whence went the Campbells and their followers, in the days of the Revolution, to join the Tennessee men for the great stroke at King's Mountain.

Here the Great Trail divided. While the chief division kept on its course to the southwest, into the valley of the Holston and the Tennessee, two ways branched off, one up, the other down, the waters of the New. To the right lay the northwest trail into western Virginia, the nearest way to the Ohio; and by this way went many emigrants to fill the limestone valleys between the Alleghany ridges, and later the thin-soiled, flat tops of those same ridges, while others continued down to the richer bottoms and the hills below.

On the other hand, to the south ran the trail up to the sources of the New River, in what is now the northwestern corner of North Carolina. From there lay the way south among the mountains, or east into the piedmont along the Yadkin and the Catawba. This was one of the main routes for the settlers of Carolina's hinterland, though another and perhaps a greater stream of immigrants flowed east of the Blue Ridge.

The New River occupies no unimportant place in the geography of the mountains. It marks the height of land that divides the Great Valley into its northern and its southern parts. And, more than this, it does its will with the mountains. The place where it cuts through the western ranges marks the point where the Alleghanies stop on the north and the Cumberlands begin on the south. Higher up its course, it plays with the eastern mountains. To the north of the New's course, the Blue Ridge is a single chain, with several parallel ridges, but compact. But when it comes to the New River, it straddles that stream, and running south, spreads out into the Carolina Plateau, with the Blue Ridge proper on the east, and the Unakas (the Iron and Smoky Mountains) on the west.

Thus, where the New River crosses the Great Valley, we stand, physically speaking, in the heart of Appalachia. It is near the geographical center — a little high up and a little to the left, as the heart should be. It marks approximately the meeting place of the four great divisions of the Appalachians. The fertile valley of Virginia, with its mountains, is to the northeast. To the south is the beautiful Carolina Plateau, "the Land of the Sky," with its charming valleys and hills and its hundred towering peaks, highest of all the eastern mountains. To the northwest are the Alleghanies and the rough lands of West Virginia and Kentucky, isolated and long forgotten. Separated from them by cross-ridges — a little farther to the south, along the State line — is the southwestern country of the Tennessee Valley and the Cumberland Plateau. Far to the south, with their two feet on the sandy piedmont of Georgia and Alabama, end the Blue Ridge and the Cumberlands.

From our height of land whence we have taken this rapid glance, let us turn first toward the west and north. Here lie the mountain lands of Kentucky and West Virginia. The real mountain country consists of the Alleghany and the Cumberland ranges. These ranges consist of a plateau of limestone and sandstone foundation which has been cut by the forces of nature into long, narrow table-lands with almost unscalable sides. The narrow valleys between these ridges, which hold the greater part of the population, have little communication with one another. It not infrequently happens that the inhabitants of one valley know less of those in the valley but a few miles across the mountain than they know of those scores of miles away down the more level path of their streams. The valleys contain the best land, some of it — above limestone formation — of excellent quality. The table-lands have generally thin, sandy soils.

After the Alleghany ridges have been passed, there comes a wide extent of broken, hilly, or even mountainous land, almost all of it, however, being of much lower altitude. This covers the greater extent of the mountain country of Kentucky, and at least half that of West Virginia. Heading usually in the Alleghanies, and running through the lower mountains and foothills, are a number of important streams like the Monongahela, the Kanawha, the Big Sandy, the Kentucky, and the Cumberland. Rapids and falls hinder their navigation very far up into the mountains, and while some improvements have been made upon some of them, the value of their commerce has not warranted great expenditures. The most of their navigation within the mountains consists of the rafting of logs by the mountaineers in the time of the spring floods.

These mountains, lying between the great arteries of travel on east and west, have had at least an equal share of isolation with the Cumberlands of Tennessee. The measure of the world's life that has been brought in to them has come almost wholly through the development of their mineral and forest resources, and in this matter to the present time West Virginia has shared much more fully than Kentucky. In consequence, this broad expanse of mountain country, containing more than a quarter of the mountain population, has furnished the world its chief examples of a stagnant civilization, with all its spectacular features of blood feuds, moonshining, and ignorance, along with the pleasanter qualities of loyalty and free-handed hospitality.

Retracing our steps to the Virginian valley, we now turn southward into the region of the great mountains. In the north there are but few high mountains, but as we enter at its acute apex the long triangle of the Carolina Plateau, we find the mountains piling up in great masses. It is along the inner chain, the Iron and Smoky Mountains, or in the transverse ranges that connect it with the eastern Blue Ridge, that we find the greatest heights. From the piedmont of North Carolina the Blue Ridge rises abruptly, yet seldom above three thousand feet, and on its western side its top in some places is scarcely above the level of the plateau. But in the ridges that cross and cut this plateau are found more than eighty mountains which can claim between five and six thousand feet altitude, besides thirty-two that rise above the six-thousand-foot mark. Among these is Mount Mitchell, in the Black Mountains, a little west of the Blue Ridge, which, with its 6,711 feet above sea level, overtops every other mountain east of the Rockies. It is closely followed, however, by many peaks in the Black and the Smoky Mountains, one of which, Clingman's Dome, still disputes honors in the opinions of some authorities, with Mitchell.

These mountains, like all the eastern Appalachians, have few cliffs or rocky peaks. Their full, rounded outlines swell up from their surrounding valleys like the ancient mountains of Eden. And indeed, the eyes of Adam may have rested upon these mountains somewhat in their present form; for we know from the story of their granite framework that they are among the most ancient of earth's hills. As you gaze from some height out upon the billowy ranges, clothed to the top with forest and grasses, or as you wander along its trails and streams among the azaleas and the rhododendrons in spring and early summer, it is not difficult to believe that you stand in a part of earth's prime domain, as unspoiled as may be by the ravages of the Deluge. "The Land of the Sky" it was named long ago by one of its admirers, and in loveliness of scenery and climate it deserves the name.

The climate of this "Land of the Sky" may with slight variations fairly represent that of the whole Blue Ridge country, and, with somewhat greater modifications, that of the whole mountain land. The summers are cool, and the winters but slightly more severe than those of the lowlands in the same latitude. For comparison three cities may be taken: Asheville, North Carolina, in the mountains, at an altitude of 2,250 feet; Lynchburg, Virginia, in the piedmont, at an altitude of 685 feet; and Nashville, Tennessee, at an altitude of 405 feet. The average mean temperature for summer is, in Asheville 70.9°, in Lynchburg 77°, in Nashville 80.4°. In winter Asheville stands at 35°, Lynchburg at 36°, and Nashville at 39.2°. The highest temperature ever recorded at Asheville was 92°.

From Asheville we turn down the gorge of the French Broad River into the valley of the Tennessee. From the altitude of the plateau, 2,200 feet, we drop rapidly into the plain, the lowest part of the Appalachian country. At Knoxville we are scarcely a thousand feet above the sea; at Chattanooga, but 668. The fertile soil of this valley rivals that of its northern sister, the Shenandoah. Besides the value of its agriculture, the valley has within its hills and mountainsides incalculable wealth in coal and iron deposits, as well as other metals in scantier proportions, all of which are rapidly being more and more fully exploited. Its chief cities are Bristol, Morristown, Knoxville, Cleveland, and Chattanooga.

Below Chattanooga, at the southern border of the State, the Tennessee River begins its long, sweeping curve through northern Alabama, to turn northward into the Ohio. In this course it cuts a sharp gorge through the Cumberland Plateau, the gorge which in Sevier's time became the haunts of the Chickamaugas.

Southeast of Chattanooga, the Georgia highlands rise gradually, the Blue Ridge system extending into that State in the last of its southwestern trend. The general depression of the Great Valley continues, however, between the Cumberland systems, through the northwestern corner of Georgia, until it ends in the lowlands of Alabama. That part of the Cumberlands cut off to the south by the Tennessee River forms the two well-known narrow table-lands of Lookout Mountain and Sand Mountain, the former running but eighty miles to an abrupt end in northeastern Alabama, the latter continuing farther and gradually shelving down into the piedmont in the region of Birmingham. The same name in the plural, Sand Mountains, is generally used also to cover the irregular lower highlands that stretch westward nearly across the State, below the Tennessee.

Now, facing northward and crossing the Tennessee, we come into the chief portion of the Cumberlands, the wide table-land that stretches from the eastern valley across to the Tennessee in the west. Abrupt and high it is on its eastern face, rising to an average altitude of 2,200 feet, but gradually it shelves off to the westward, until its Highland Rim, in the middle part of the State, is but a thousand feet or less above the sea level, and still lower when it reaches the Tennessee.

The plateau is cut and gullied by many streams into valleys and gorges, and the Cumberland River, sweeping down from Kentucky in the north, narrows its western part into a long tongue that passes south of Nashville westward to the Tennessee. These western highlands, however, with their gradually lessening altitude, are not generally regarded as a part of the mountain system, the technical western edge of the Cumberland Plateau running some sixty miles east of Nashville.

The Cumberland Plateau, built up largely of sandstone, though in places with limestone formation, is, generally speaking, of far less value agriculturally than the lands farther east. This fact, more than its topography, has made it less open to communication with the outside world. While two or three railroads run up its narrow valleys from the south, and one crosses it from east to west, it is, on the whole, far from possessing good facilities for transportation. A few flourishing towns there are within its bounds, but its greater part is almost as undeveloped as when the "Long Hunters" crossed its wilderness, more than a century ago.

Still northward bound, we are now to come to one of the most interesting places in the mountain country. Just at the meeting point of the three States, Tennessee, Virginia, and Kentucky, is the famous Cumberland Gap. From the Tennessee Valley we make our way toward it through the valleys of the Clinch and Powell rivers, the ancient path of the Indian, the pioneer, and the soldier. For Cumberland Gap has gathered within its constricting embrace much of the history of two races and untold generations. Its narrow pass, cut through the cliffs that tower up on either side a thousand feet, afforded the most direct and the easiest way out of the mountain country into the plains. And this way the forces of war, of adventure, and of civilization turned.

The Cumberland Ridge at this point is 2,500 feet high, and 1,200 to 1,500 feet above the land about it. The Gap cuts this altitude down to 1,675 feet, but still there is a climb of some hundreds of feet from the eastern side and more of a descent upon the western. The old road that led over and through the Gap was the despair and the curse of the adventurers who dared it in their quest for the land of promise beyond. Rocky, miry, narrow, and gullied, whether it led in or out of the mountains, it typified the barriers of the mountaineer's best alliance with the world. When over such roads must come the products of an outside civilization, the mountaineer would perforce be content with his own products and his own civilization. He hewed him out his home from the forest; he raised the corn and the meat that supplied his board; he grew the wool and flax that his own spinning-wheel and loom made into the homespun that covered his meager form. He remembered or he forgot what religion and culture his fathers had brought in, and where the teacher and the circuit-rider failed him, the Scripture, the story, and the ballad of his traditions made spice for the mental food that lay about him in field and forest and hill. Shut in by the mountains, he kept the legacy of his fathers in speech and thought and habit; and as the great world outside made to itself wealth of mind and matter, he was left upon his heights the living monument of a by-gone age. Only where, as in the great valleys, the lines of communication were open and wide, there the pulse-beat of the nation and the larger world struck rhythmically and full. But up on the mountains, beyond the cliffs of the tableland, behind the rampart of the forbidding hills, there the mountaineer remained "our contemporary ancestor."

But today the scene is changing. Cumberland Gap is no longer a solitary wilderness pass. The railroad pierces it, cities lie on either side of it, the hum and roar and movement of busy industry strike its gray old walls. The stores of wealth the hills contain have called out the forces of industrialism to subdue it. Shafts and tunnels, furnaces and forges and factories have invaded this vestibule of the mountains. Hotels and palaces are taking the place of the log cabin, and with them come the kindergarten and the college. Here where the first explorers threaded their cautious way amidst the forest, and where the later settler built his stockaded and loopholed home, here where so long brooded the stillness of the backwoods and where dreamed the slow-moving thought of a belated people, here has sprung to life at last the dominant, insistent, driving civilization of the twentieth century.

This is the manifest destiny of the mountain country everywhere, whether for more good or for more evil, let them say who can see. Elements there are in the new civilization that make for good; others there are which tend to evil. The forces of religion and of education are at work in the midst of the dominant industrialism. Whether the happy ideals of this last century —which are the age-old ideals of Christianity— shall prevail over the loud business of Mammon, depends upon the devotion and the diligence of those who minister them. Before the inflowing of this new culture the mountaineers are changing. Some there are who readily assimilate the standards and methods of their teachers, and become merged in the new life. Some, troubled and resentful at the invasion, are retiring into the yet untouched wilderness where they can continue their traditional mode of life. But more there are who remain under the influence of the new conditions, becoming not its masters but its slaves. Poor in goods they were, and poor in goods they remain. Contented in their station they were, sometimes with a despairing content; but now, seeing a new and more expensive standard of living, they are discontented with a deeper despair. Independent and proud of spirit they were in their single-class society; now, a lower stratum in a complex world, they are learning to bow and cringe to the superior power. The break-up of the primitive society of the mountains by the industrial invasion, without a more than equal educational and religious uplift, means nothing but a reduction to the lower terms of a class society.

The industrial exploitation of a great part of the mountains is inevitable. When it begins, it works with far greater rapidity than the philanthropic forces work; because it is able to command greater capital and it attracts a larger force of agents. It has its psychical as well as its economic value, but it carries with it a menace as well as a promise.

Yet after all, the new life, wherever it reaches, offers to the mountaineer the same choice of selection that the rest of the world have long had. Does he choose, and is he able, he may join the pushing, jostling crowd of money-seekers, and with a shrewdness no whit inferior, run a fair race with all the rest. Is he content with meat and drink, and nothing of higher life, he can find the plane of the wage-earner, with a freer spending ability than he ever yet has known. But does he look for a broader vision, a higher life, a deeper power, there too lie at his hand, or near enough to invite effort, the instruments for culture and development. Thank God that the heart of Christianity has not entirely forgotten the mountains. The school is being put within the reach of the needy; and though yet inadequate to the great needs, it is reaching forth with one hand to help the aspiring child of the mountains, and with the other stretched for the bounty of Christianity that shall make its aid more effective.

As we stand in the Gap, and watch, far over the hills, the receding form of a romantic isolation, and nearer at hand, in the valley, the clamoring, pulsing forces of a new era, our eyes stray up the slope until they rest upon the form of a mediator between these old and these new forces. The school has entered the

Gap.[1] It stands between the startled, bewildered mountain child and the life that is either to serve him or to crush him. The school is the hope of the mountaineer. Through it he may be adjusted to this more strenuous life that threatens to undo him. By it his strong, simple, enduring powers may be shaped to a service unequaled among America's workmen. With deepest interest, then, may we turn to a study of the forces that have been at work for this preparation and direction of the men of the mountains.

---

[1] The representative of the school at Cumberland Gap is Lincoln Memorial University, founded by Gen. O. O. Howard, and now presided over by Dr. George A. Hubbell.

Crossing the Branch

Lincoln Memorial University, Cumberland Gap.

The Vanguard of the Helpers

"ALL around us we behold the sounds of a coming educational revival. It is topping our mountains with life and glory; it is spreading a verdure green over the broad plains; and it is rustling like sweetest music the leaves of the forest. Let it come and let it come quickly." HENRY S. HARTZOG.

Chapel, Berea College.
"Berea never can be rich so long as anybody in the mountains is poor."   Page 107.

VII

THE PIONEER SCHOOL

IF WE should follow Daniel Boone in seeking a way to the Blue-grass through Cumberland Gap, we should trace a trail through the mountains for near a hundred miles northwestward, before ever we should see our desire. Then, as through a narrow gap there shows a promise of the plains, we should climb upon our right the bold, rocky headland of West Pinnacle, and there stand long to gaze out upon the beauty of Kentucky's fairest land. For there stood Daniel Boone when first his eyes rested upon the Blue-grass. So says, at least, the local tradition.

But today, instead of an untamed wilderness of forest and meadow, the feeding-grounds of herds of elk and buffalo, with not so much as a log house or even a skin tent to claim sovereignty, today we shall behold a land of homes and pastures and cultivated fields. And just below us, scarcely three miles across the valley of Silver Creek, we shall point out — with what quickening of the pulse if we be sons of the mountains — we shall point out upon a little hill the clustered buildings of Berea. For Berea is in the van of the helpers of the mountains: the first discoverer, the earliest advocate, the keenest student, the broadest teacher, of the mountaineer.

Berea was in the making before the mountaineer

was recognized as a people. The hand-clasp of the highlander and the lowlander had so slowly loosened, from the day of the Revolution to that of the Civil War, that neither well knew they had lost touch. The nation, clamorous in debate, had forgotten the mountaineer. The North drew a line from east to west, and began to speak of the Solid South. The South, seaboard and inland, if it thought of the mountains at all, thought of them as its back yard, neglected, perhaps, but inalienable.

Then the mountains began to awake, and Berea was there to witness the awakening. About the year 1846, a young Kentuckian, John G. Fee, began preaching in his native State. He did not confine his preaching to platitudes: he had a message, and he spoke it in no uncertain terms. Although the son of a slave-owner, he had, through the influence of his grandmother and his later studies, become convinced that slavery was sinful, and he said so, emphatically, insistently, and with courage. His father disinherited him, his church rebuked him, and his fellow-citizens mobbed him; but none of those things moved him. So common was his experience of violence, in which his family sometimes suffered with him, that his daughter, then a little girl, said in later life that they were never disturbed by the dangers: "They were to us like thunder-storms, things to be expected. We supposed everybody had mobs!"

There was another fighter among Kentucky's anti-slavery men in those days, not a preacher, but a statesman, Cassius M. Clay. Fearless and fiery, he faced his composite audiences with a message for every party. "This," he announced as he stepped upon the platform and held up a bound volume, "this is a copy of the Holy Scriptures, which enjoins us to prove all things and hold fast that which is good. For the benefit of those of you who revere the ordinances of God, I will read from it. And this"— lifting another volume —"is a copy of the constitution of the commonwealth of Kentucky, which guarantees to every citizen the right of free speech. For those who fear not God, but have respect for the laws of men, I lay it here beside the Scriptures. For those who fear neither God nor man, if there be any such present, I have still another argument." And reaching down into his capacious hip pocket, he produced a wicked-looking army revolver, and laying it beside the constitution and the Bible he entered upon his arraignment of slavery.

Of the same stock as the men of the mountains, Clay found his chief supporters, or rather his most solid support, among Kentucky's mountaineers, freeholders and free-soilers, men who owned land, but who neither held nor wished to hold slaves. Clay owned land in Madison County, a border country, part Blue-grass and part mountain. Attracted by Fee's stout-hearted stand, he invited him to come and settle in Madison County, and build up an antislavery church. Fee came, and in 1854 housed his family in a cabin he had built in a thick scrub of blackjack pine, on a ten-acre tract Clay gave him.

Around him gathered a band of "more noble" spirits, whom he organized into a church and named Berea. They were in the border land, the highlands behind them, the lowlands in front. Now came with increasing frequency those threats and raids and houseburnings and whippings that gave the little Miss Fee her impressions of normal life. The mountain men were largely in sympathy with Fee and his fellows, but the Blue-grass was mostly hostile, and did not hesitate to show it.

John G. Fee was not content with preaching and writing and printing. Looking to the future, he hoped to see a generation produced that should hate slavery. To this end there must be schools. So he built a schoolhouse, called in teachers from Oberlin College, and in 1855 Berea School began.

Three years later, Rev. John A. R. Rogers, an Oberlin man, received his inward call to adventurous service and came to Berea. After earnest prayer, Fee and Rogers and their companions decided that God wanted a college established here in the shadow of the mountains; whereupon, "in order to promote the cause of Christ," Berea College was chartered in 1858.

The questions of the nation were beginning to stir the highlanders. Berea's advent at this door of the mountains brought home to these freeman the questions that were threatening to split the nation; and they, in proud memory of Vincennes, King's Mountain, and New Orleans, of Clark, and Shelby, and "Old Hickory," silently took their stand for a Union one and inseparable.

These mountain people, so steadily backing the ideals of Berea, attracted the closer attention of Rogers. He perceived that in the mountaineer, a child yet unweaned from the ideas that came with the birth of the nation, there was a force to be reckoned with, and this he began to tell the nation. His first social studies of the mountaineer were published in the New York *Independent* in 1858. Thus at the very beginning of Berea, her mission to the mountains began to take form.

But upon the heels of this event came John Brown's raid and a succeeding time of trouble for two years, until the Civil War broke out in earnest. In the strife of parties and the surge of armies, Berea was tossed like a ship upon the waves. Driven from home, Fee, Rogers, and others of the Berea company came back again and again. During the time of their exile they continued to make payments upon their land, confident in the hope of seeing Berea fulfil their vision. Though they made more than one attempt, it was not until the first of the year 1866 that the school could be reopened.

Then began a period of development, the fruit of heroic effort. Berea was yet in the wilderness, no railroad within half a hundred miles. Yet in that wilderness, with material hewn from the hills or hauled from

Lexington and Cincinnati, were erected two threestory buildings that were an astonishment not only to the mountaineer, but to the stray visitor from the outside world. When, a dozen years later, the surveyor for the incoming railroad emerged from the wilderness to catch sight of Ladies' Hall upon the oak-crowned hill, he exclaimed, "Great Scott! Whoever put up a building like that in this far-off country must have had faith!"

Though Mr. Rogers retired from the headship of the school upon the accession of President Fairchild in 1869, he remained as a professor for many years, and was a trustee, with heart and soul devoted to his work, until his death in 1906. The three patriarchs, Fee, Rogers, and Fairchild, were united in calling to the presidency in 1892 the present head of Berea, William Goodell Frost.

With President Frost's accession began a new life in the school, a new era for the mountaineer. From Oberlin, like his predecessors, he came with a heart prepared to catch the spirit of Berea's founders, and a mind broadened to the great problems involved in bringing the mountains and the world together. To him has been due, more than to any other, the great expansion of Berea's work, the deeper insight into the conditions of the mountains, the new awakening of the isolated mountaineer, and the response, in some measure, of philanthropists and public men to the silent appeal of Appalachian America.

President Frost went up into the mountains to learn at first hand what were the conditions that Berea must help. And out of these investigations have come the social studies which have helped to systematize the work among the mountaineers. In "the land of saddle-bags" his horse carried him from cabin to courthouse, from river bottom to stony mountain farm, fording streams, climbing cliffs, winding in and up by narrow trails, and being entertained in homes of every description up to the second grade. As he went, he questioned with eyes and tongue.

What were their resources?— The steep slopes and the narrow bottoms clustered around the log house gave their scant inventory of corn patch, of cow and hog and sheep, of a few apple-trees and a tangle of wild blackberries.

Who were their fathers?— When they remembered, there came tales of Union soldiers, of earlier volunteers for Buena Vista and New Orleans and Tallapoosa, and dim memories of great-great-grandfathers who fought at Kanawha and King's Mountain, and who with Boone had traced their earlier line back to North Carolina and Pennsylvania and Old England.

What were their ambitions?— Where ambition rose, mostly in the young and artless, it was to be strongest of arm, surest of eye, most skilful of hand, most faithful to blood, perchance to become, through shrewd trade and honest skill, the man of property and the recognized leader of clan and country.

What were their accomplishments?— To split a twig at a hundred yards with the rifle-ball, to fashion with ax and knife the needs of their civilization, from hewn log house to cord-bed and dulcimer, to wring from a niggardly soil the sustenance of life in bread and shoe and linsey-woolsey.

Not too many were there who felt free to boast of superior "book-larnin'." The boy he met out "gunnin' for b'ar" rested his rifle pacifically in the hollow of his arm, while his bright eyes searched the face of the questioner. Could he write numbers?

"Reckon I can write *some* numbers," was his guarded reply.

A strip of smooth bark made an examination paper on which Dr. Frost wrote the nine digits, which were promptly called by the young hunter. Then came combinations, among them the year 1897.

"I don't guess I can tell that thar."

The teacher explained, and then asked, "Do you know what '1897' means?"

"Hit's the year, haint it?"

"Yes; but why is the year called 1897? It is 1897 years since what?"

"I never heard tell."

But he wanted to know; and when he had learned that, there rose other questions in his mind, beginnings of questions broad, deep, uncomprehended, but clamoring for settlement. Bear-hunting fell from its pedestal among the mighty things of earth, and the wider knowledge, the nobler activity, to which Berea was the gateway, became the aspiration of the mountain youth.

These tours of inquiry have developed into the institution of Berea's Extension Service. Today the library and farm demonstration wagons of the college go forth, accompanied by teachers and advanced students, to carry a gospel of broader living and widening opportunity to the mountaineer. Still farther go the rider on the sure-footed mule, or the more independent pedestrian, peering into the secrets of the mountains as he gives glimpses of the mysteries without. Every summer sends forth these missionaries, delivering lectures, lending books, distributing leaflets, exhibiting stereopticon pictures — a work that touches five States, helping those who cannot come to school and inspiring those who have not yet wanted to come.

Berea starts with the child. Through its Preparatory School it takes the youngest and sets his feet on the path toward higher things. But is it a youth already entered into his twenties who first feels the impulse to go to school, and yet who fears himself too late a beginner ever to reach the top? There is waiting for him the Foundation School, in which special help is given those whose years but not whose attainments place them beyond the common grades. And then he may be encouraged to enter the Vocational School, where the young man is trained for efficiency as farmer, carpenter, smith, printer, and the young woman as nurse and home-maker.

Does he become aroused by this experience to master more, despite his early handicap? Or does he bring his younger brother and sister? Is the spirit of helpfulness aroused in the mountain youth and the determination to become teachers of the broader life to their home communities?—There is waiting for them the Normal School, with its broad training not only for the schoolroom but for the garden, the farm, and the forest, for cooking, dressmaking, and nursing. And above, for the few whose time and talents permit, is the College. Berea is really a small university adapted to the practical needs of the mountain people.

At such a school the mountain boy and girl put their fingers on the pulse of the wider world. Not only are they received by teachers, men and women of broad sympathies and deep understanding of their nature, whose help is consciously given toward their right development; but they also meet students from the lowland South and from the North, of whom Berea has more than a sprinkling. In their society they find the truest index of their relations to the wide world. They touch here, in the higher life, the same forces with which their parents wrestle on the lower plane of industrialism.

They find the necessity of adjusting themselves in some way to the rush and tension of twentieth-century America. With his earnings from the lumber camp in his jeans, the boy has walked, perhaps, a hundred miles from an interior county down here to "the Settlemints," where he gets his first sight of a railway train, his first view of big buildings, his first impression of a complex society. The girl, side-seated on the mule her "pappy" has given her, has ridden an equal distance, now to turn her beast into the cash that may be converted into learning; and with her mountain training of greater self-effacement than her brother, she meets these new conditions with more evident shyness than does he. What a type of the whole life is to them the limited express that rushes with flash and roar past their faces at the station. Alone in their mountains, unhelped, they would gaze from their ox-cart in dull wonderment or resentment at the motor-car that flashes past on the new county road, with its raucous voice and its terrifying haste, to disappear speedily in its cloud of dust. And, with their father, they would shrink from the intrusion and withdraw farther into the silence of their mountains and their souls.

But here at the school they feel that they can grasp the wand that will open before them and their people their Red Sea. Though inclination and duty keep them to their own people, though they may not seize the chariots of the Pharaoh that so closely pursue them, they may have a mightier power. Through the Almighty's furrow in the sea they may march upon dry ground, lighted by a pillar of fire, to a victory that triumphs over chariots and armor. Well will it be for the mountain people if in their progress toward Sinai and the Promised Land, there mingle with them but few of the mixed multitude.

Back into the mountains go the trained man and woman from Berea, and there follow them, slowly but persistently, the evidences of order, enlightenment, and progress. Teachers and home-makers, they are carrying with them neatness, knowledge, skill, and patience. The young man develops his father's farm, rebuilds his mother's home, turns the "blab school" finally into a better-housed, truly disciplined, and progressive institution whose power is not to be measured by its size. The young woman makes a home where there was only a house, brings in hygiene of dress and diet and personal habit; and she runs no whit behind the man in the courage and energy with which she lifts communities by that mightiest lever, the school.

The problem in the school is not of the pupils alone: it is of the community. For generations which have received the traditions of the "old field school," its carelessness, its crudity, and its rough and coarse ideals, finding pleasure more in its omissions and irruptions than in its regularities, accustomed to idling and absences and trouncings of the teacher—such generations have instilled into the young manhood of the mountains the idea that the school is meant as the butt of horseplay. This spirit must many times be reckoned with by the girl teacher as well as the man teacher. Of the way she meets it, an appreciative old man of the mountains testifies:

"I tell yeou hit teks a moughty resolute gal ter do what that thar gal has done. She got I reckon about the toughest deestric in the county, which is sayin' a good deal. An' then fer a boardin' place — well, thar warn't much choice. Thar was one house with one room. But she kep' right on, an' yeou would hev thought she was havin' the finest kind of a time ter look at her. An' then the last day, when they was sayin' their pieces an' sich, some sorry fellers come in thar full o' moonshine, an' shot ther revolvers. I'm a-tellin' ye hit teks a moughty resolute gal."

The mountaineer and his well-wishers look with affection and hope toward that pioneer of the mountain schools, Berea. Others have taken up the work, nobly daring and enduring and succeeding, but there can be none of them that will refuse today the salute of respect and love to the living monument planted and shaped by Fee and Rogers, Fairchild and Frost. Its birth half a century ago was in a log cabin, with a score of students; today, with piles of brick and stone it houses seventeen hundred children of the mountains, seeking to fit them to meet the duties of the new age as their fathers nobly met the old. Is there not hope that, as the periods of the Revolution, the expansion, and the Rebellion found the mountaineer meeting the emergencies with leaders and following, so the present era, with its more dazzling opportunities and its more subtle dangers, may find in him, if opportunity serve, a bulwark of the freedom and virtue of America? Says President Frost:

"The whole case of the mountaineer may be summed up in the story of Abraham Lincoln. His great career hinged upon the fact that his mother had six books. In that circumstance he differed from the other boys of the region. Is it too much to say that but for that ray of light, his great soul would have been strangled in the birth?"

To such institutions as Berea College the mountains owe a debt. And the mountains are paying it in trained and resolute men and women who are giving their all to the uplift of their fellows who may yet make the backbone of America's liberty. To such institutions as Berea America owes a debt; for they are making to America a bequest more precious than the treasures of the mines, the wealth of the plains, and the commerce of the city marts. And America has but in small part discharged its debt. Some coins have day by day been dropped into the treasury by the rich men, some little equipment, some wider facilities have been added now and again to the tremendous investment due to Appalachia; but still the army of the mountain helpers may say of their work as Berea says: "Berea never can be rich as long as anybody in the mountains is poor!"

VIII

THE PREMIER OF HOME MISSIONS

IT IS a fact little known that up to 1830 the greatest strength of the antislavery forces in America lay in the Southern States. The Northeast had shuffled off its soiled garments of slavery, the Northwest had never put them on, and thus they had largely escaped the discomfort of mind and the tortures of soul that went with the slavery question.

But the South was struggling with a conscience. Its rice and cane and cotton fields were teeming with slaves whose labor a wrong-headed philosophy declared profitable. Yet the great majority of Southern white men were not slave-owners. Where there was one who owned slaves, there were perhaps ten who owned none;[1] and from among these ten there were many who spoke out against slavery, who demanded its abolition. Of the one hundred twenty antislavery societies in the United States in 1830, eighty were in the South. Of the forty in the North, Pennsylvania claimed twenty and Ohio sixteen.[2]

---

[1] Hart, *Slavery and Abolition*, pp. 67, 68. Hart states that only one in thirty-three of the population of the South held slaves. As he reckons each of these to be the head of a family, however, he thinks the true proportion of the slave-holding class to the nonslave-holding class was one to four or five. But this seems a very high estimate; for there were many slave-owners with no family, and there were many families in which not only the father but the mother and some of the children owned slaves. One in ten would be a safer estimate.

[2] Adams, *The Neglected Period of Antislavery*, p. 154.

But in 1830 came Garrison, the firebrand of abolition, declaring slavery to be a sectional sin rather than a national or a class wrong. He and his followers began to array the North against the South. They were men of one idea, of one aim, and they shot straight. Unfortunately, their single-mindedness took no account of the fact that the main forces of their antislavery army were on the battle-front toward which they were pointing their straight-shooting guns. They took their friends in the rear; the abolition army of the South crumpled up, broke, scattered. Its outposts disappeared from the Gulf States, its strong battle line retreated from North Carolina, Tennessee, Virginia, Maryland. Only in one State of Dixie still thundered the guns of an antislavery force.

That State was Kentucky. There the mountain statesman, Cassius M. Clay, pressed the demands of the free-soilers for the abolition of slavery. There the Bluegrass preacher, John G. Fee, in the face of terrorism, insult, abuse, and mobbing, held forth from his pulpit the doctrine of liberty. Kentucky was the last contested ground between slavery and freedom before the case was taken from the court of logic to the field of arms.

And there the battle was bitter. Fee, deserted by his relatives, discountenanced by his church, estranged even from Clay at last by his advocacy of a "higher law" than the Constitution, and finding it impossible to support his work on what his poor friends of the mountains and the border were able to give him, at last turned his eyes to the North for help.

There was little there to encourage him; for the first fruits of Garrison's propaganda had been the arousing of the neutral North to a violent opposition. Abolitionists — Garrisonians and Moderates alike — were hated, denounced, and mobbed. Abolition, which had been driven from the South and was hard pressed on the border, was also beleaguered in its new Northern stronghold.

But in one quarter Fee found help. Two years before Fee's appeal, there had been organized, in 1846, at Albany, N. Y., the American Missionary Association, a body called into existence by the zeal of men who "would sustain missions for the propagation of a pure and free Christianity," and "institute arrangements for gathering and sustaining churches in heathen lands from which the sins of caste, polygamy, slave-holding, and the like shall be excluded." This organization was a protest against the attitude of other missionary societies then existing which refused to take a definite stand against slavery. The American Missionary Association at first took over and conducted some foreign mission stations which had been independently established by its supporters, but its "Home Department," which was soon formed to carry on work among the Indians, negroes, and other foreign peoples in American possessions, became in time its only work.

Fee's appeal did not go unheeded, and in the fall of 1848 the association sent him its commission, and promised its financial and moral support. This was continued until near the time of the Civil War. Thus, in that earliest work which Fee and his colaborers of Berea College began for the Kentucky mountaineer, the American Missionary Association had its place and part.

Its attention thus turned to the mountaineer by Fee's stand before the mountain wall, the association began to seek an alliance with the highlander in other parts. Into the mountains and foothills of North Carolina, whence came in 1857 Helper's clarion challenge to slavery, the association sent Daniel Worth, a man of fearless courage and commanding eloquence, who there played well the part of Fee in Kentucky. Several stations were established in Kentucky and North Carolina, destined however, to a short life; for when in 1859, John Brown raided Harper's Ferry, the shudder of fear that shook the South sent all the Association missions, along with Berea, into exile. This closed for twenty-five years the work of the American Missionary Association among the mountaineers. Invited by Berea's founder, it had been the first of missionary organizations to turn toward a helping of the mountain people; and though immediately after the Civil War its energies were chiefly absorbed in the great task thrown upon the nation by the needs of the freedmen, it was again among the first to take up work for the mountaineer.

In 1884, when the stress of the work for the freedman had begun to slacken, and when the mountains had begun to open to outside capital their wealth of iron and coal and timber, then also their spiritual treasures began to call again for the developing forces of Christianity. An appeal was made to the American Missionary Association to establish schools for the mountaineer, and the association, responding, picked up the work it had been compelled a quarter of a century before to abandon. Williamsburg, Kentucky, a county-seat in the midst of mountains, which had lived its sixty-seven years without a church building and with scarce a school for itself or its county, was selected as the first point of occupancy. Here was erected Williamsburg Academy, the first of ten institutions of higher grade, besides many primary schools, to be established from Kentucky to Georgia as the response of the American Missionary Association to the needs of the mountains.

Industrial education was a feature of the program of this Association in its first school among the Mendi people in Africa. And the industrial feature has continued to be a part of its work in its schools among the mountaineers as well as among the negroes and other peoples. The nature of this industrial work has been such as the needs of the schools and their communities demanded. It may be a splendid achievement to train a young man as a civil engineer, but if the immediate needs of his home point to the woodpile and the sawmill, it shows a more profound understanding of pedagogy to put the ax and the cant-hook into his hands.

The character of the industrial training the Association has provided may be illustrated by an extract from a paper by the principal of Pleasant Hill Academy on the Cumberland Plateau in Tennessee:

"We were fortunate in the first five years of my principalship in having in Pleasant Hill our dear Father Dodge, who had the happy faculty of getting at Northern pocketbooks, so that many young people were given an opportunity to be in school who would not otherwise have been able to do so.

"As the young men and young women were given the opportunity to enter school, it was felt that, to make our help wise, we must require them to give some equivalent for their chances. It was not difficult to provide housework — dish-washing, sweeping, cooking, and ironing, for girls; and we could use several boys in the heavier work of the boarding department and as janitors, but it was more difficult to provide for still others.

"The first fall we added sheds to our very small barn, cut considerable wood, and did some repairing. During our first vacation two student young men built a cottage for friends of the principal, and in the following autumn a storeroom was added to the girls' hall, and a bath-room was fitted up.

"Father Dodge conceived the plan of buying out an old mill property near at hand and fitting it up with modern machinery. In this he was successful, so we have the mill. Thus we count our mill a great factor in the enlargement of our whole work, as well as the industrial department. Only one man has been employed regularly in the mill, the rest of the work being done mainly by the student boys.

"Through this instrumentality twenty homes have been erected in Pleasant Hill in the last three years, thus affording increasing opportunities for families to avail themselves of the privileges of the school; and besides this, forty or fifty homes have been built, improved, or repaired within a radius of twenty miles.

Students at Highland College, America Inland Mission.
"If you cannot afford to pay for schools for the poor Highlanders, God can pay for them." Page 127.

"Three years ago we were very much crowded for dormitory room for the boys. Dodge Hall was erected, a brick building, three stories in front and four behind, eighty feet long and forty feet wide. Brick would have cost twenty-five dollars a thousand if brought from their place of manufacture, so we called in some of our boys, secured a brick-maker to direct, and soon had 150,000 brick ready for use at the cost of five or six dollars per thousand.

"When it came to laying the brick, the lime would have cost forty cents a bushel, delivered, so we built a lime-kiln on the side of the mountain, about seven miles away, and secured our lime at half that rate. We bought the standing timber at one dollar a thousand, hauled it to the mill — much of it with our own academy team — and prepared it for the inside work.

"Our own boys and parents of our girls and boys did nearly all the carpentry work. All the finishing material for stairway, molding, ceiling and flooring was prepared at our mill. We kept down expenses so well that we called on Northern friends for only $2,500, and did not call on the Association treasury for a penny, yet fair Northern judges state that it would cost, completed, $8,000 or $10,000 there. This hall contains rooms for sixty boys, besides rooms for principal, boys' reading-room, guest-room, and basement for shop and woodhouse.

"Since the erection of Dodge Hall various forms of work have been done. Hundreds of rods of fencing have been built, hundreds of feet of sidewalk, work in blacksmithing and wagon repairing, repairing and making of furniture — wardrobes, dining-room tables, wash-stands, small tables and book-cases, picture-frames and so forth; ground cleared for cultivation, and last year twelve or fifteen acres cultivated; several tons of hay, as a result, put into the new barn."

The American Missionary Association was organized as a non-sectarian agency, and for many years received support from various of the great religious bodies. After the war, however, as these churches developed particular work and organizations within their own constituencies, the American Missionary Association was left more and more fully to the care of the Congregational Church, members of which were largely instrumental in its founding; and today this church stands chief sponsor for the Association.

The work of the American Missionary Association is not confined to the mountaineers among the white people of the South, but through its schools and missionaries extends into the lowlands. Its highest school for whites is Atlanta Theological Seminary, located in the capital city of Georgia. The association is one of the chief agencies, as it was the earliest, at work among both negro and white elements in the South, and while at the present time it is not the largest society operating in these fields, its thin skirmish line is stretched over a wider space, and its outlook is therefore perhaps the more comprehensive.

The policy of this Association, in distinction from that of many other agencies, has been to diffuse its benefits among the people through many small schools, rather than to concentrate them in a few large centers. Says one of its spokesmen:

"From the standpoint of financial support this has required courage. Experienced money-raisers testify that they can more easily secure funds for one or two big schools than for many smaller ones. Such is the tendency of present-day philanthropy. It likes great show and to settle upon large institutions: to the school that hath shall be given. The American is peculiarly under the spell of bigness. A single one of the larger institutions of the Association might well absorb its entire current income. Such an institution would then be able to dominate the imagination of the public along with the one or two which now monopolize it.

"In spite of all this the policy of diffusion is the deliberate choice. The most distinctive American school is the small college, in intimate relations with its community and with a constituency chiefly local. As a type it is more widely useful than a great university ever can be. Not only is the education of the smaller school apt to be sounder and its administration invariably more economic—but it remains closer to the people."[1]

The force of these words, the value of this policy, will be recognized by every one who has been in position to make a comparative study of the results of the small and the large school, and who remembers, furthermore, that God's model of the school is the home, not the monastery.

Of the position of this Christian missionary body, Dr. A. D. Mayo says:

"The first, and still the most notable, of the several great missionary associations . . . in the Southern States, through schools of every grade and the ordinary methods of mission work employed by the evangelical Protestant churches in the Northern United States, was the American Missionary Association."

The American Missionary Association is today, in its history as well as its spirit of evangelism and education, the premier home mission society of America.

---
[1] Douglass, *Christian Reconstruction in the South*, pp. 210, 211.

IX

REDEEMING THE TIME

ONCE, in the early days of the nation, the churches of America were roused to a sense of duty to the mountains and the country just beyond. The frontier, so came the report, was sinking in iniquity and godlessness. Then the Methodists sent in their circuit-riders, the Baptists followed hard upon their heels, and the Presbyterians awoke to a new power among the forgetful children of their kirk. So came the "Great Revival" of 1800. The West, from being godless, became the wellspring of a new life in America's religion.

But then, the deed done, the gift bestowed, the church forgot the mountain people, and left them to themselves. The momentum of the "Great Revival" carried them far. It reopened and made to flow freely the springs of reverence which had become choked with worldliness and ignorance. And even today the rough clearing of that great movement shows its traces in the religion of the mountains.

But that was not sufficient. That did not end the mission of the church. Elsewhere the spiritual and the mental life have been developed, shaped, polished, by contact with the world's life current. But here in the mountains, without schools, without broad intercourse, it swirled in its little eddy, stationary, and ever more faint. For more than three quarters of a century the church forgot the mountaineer, and the nation remembered him only to require service, not to give it. The mountaineer had entered his lot abreast of the world. It was at a time when the railroad was yet unknown, the printing press a luxury, the school a costly privilege. Without the railroad or canals or good roads, there was little trade, little travel. Without the newspaper, with practically no books, there was little exchange of thought or community of purpose. Without schools, with reading and writing the distinction of the great, there could be no progress. Thus the mountaineer became a fixed type, the type of that pioneer life of his beginnings.

And that was at a time when the world was just beginning that marvelous leaping march which has crowded the progress of a thousand centuries into one. Who could foretell, when the mountains wove their people into their chrysalis, what ink and steam and electricity were about to do to the world? or how far behind its advance was to leave those who were made to stand still? Busied with their own race, the world and the church forgot the sleeper in the hills.

When, therefore, after eighty years of neglect, the church felt the tug of the mountaineer upon her skirts, and turned to reach a helping hand, she found that a mighty pull was needed to bring him to her side. There was more than a century of time to redeem.

The religious movement of the early nineteenth century left the mountain church Baptist and Methodist, more largely Baptist.[1] What was more natural than that these churches should regard the field as occupied and competent to meet its own needs? The detached congregational system of the Baptists made local responsibility the greater, while by the split in the Metho-

---

[1] Baptists in the mountains make forty-eight per cent of the total church-membership. Thirty-one per cent are Methodists, six per cent Presbyterians, and five per cent Disciples. Episcopalians have about seven-tenths of one per cent, mostly in the towns. Roman Catholics are practically unknown, except among the foreign populations of the mining districts and in the few cities.

dist Church over slavery, the mountain churches—spiritual kin to the North but living in the South—were left orphans.

Among themselves, the Baptists and Methodists of the mountains did provide such facilities for education as their resources permitted, and a considerable number of academies, seminaries, and colleges attest their zeal for education. Yet these have touched but a small proportion of even their ministers, the class for which they are specially designed. The Northern branches of these two churches have left the problem of the mountains to the Southern divisions, and these have in comparatively recent times taken up the work of reenforcement of their forces in the mountains.

In 1898 the Southern Baptist Home Mission Board turned its attention to the development of the mountain people by assisting in the establishment and support of mission schools. In six mountain States they now have thirty-three schools of academic grade and one college, in which are five thousand youth under training. Several of these schools are located upon small farms, and the board is encouraging the beginning of industrial education.

Work among the mountaineers on the part of Southern Methodists, under charge of the Home Department of the Woman's Missionary Council, was inaugurated in 1897, as the result of one woman's determination to "illumine some dark corner." Miss Bennett's longing to see a permanent educational work established in the Kentucky mountains was not gratified before her early death, but today the Sue Bennett Memorial School at London, Kentucky, with an enrolment of over three hundred students, is the monument to her devotion. The Home Department has one other school, Brevard Institute, in the beautiful upper valley of the French Broad in North Carolina; and the department stands behind the movement, now gaining momentum among Southern Methodists, to widen the opportunities and develop the talents of their mountain constituency.

Over in Virginia, the patrimony of the Episcopal Church, there had never been anything done for the Blue Ridge mountaineers. "If it be asked," says one of its spokesmen, "why have these mountaineers been neglected and allowed to sink to the low level on which we find them today, when the church has been at work in Virginia for so long a time?— the answer is, that after the Revolutionary War, the church was at such a low ebb that its life was nearly extinguished. After its revival under Bishop Meade, the Civil War came on, which swept away the wealth and property of the churchmen, and from this impoverished condition they have only lately begun to recover. In addition to this it must be remembered that the church in Virginia has inherited a large number of country parishes from old colonial times, and the great problem for many years has been how to keep these parishes going, and the churches open."

But the time of action had come. The church sent a young worker, Archdeacon Neve, to a parish that touched the Blue Ridge. In his visits among the people, he soon came into touch with some of the backward communities who had no church, no school, no wide view nor high ideals of life. His sympathies were aroused. He drew first his parishioners, and then others, into his work of uplift.

It was not exactly a sympathetic subject that received their first ministrations. A friendly visit in the log home, a prayer, a sermon — these were very well and quite proper, no doubt, as the work of a churchman; and here and there a soul hungering for spiritual food broke through the barriers to respond to the advances of the minister. But any step beyond the narrow limits of the Episcopal service was met with suspicion. Was land wanted on which to establish a mission?— the owner suspected the presence of undiscovered mineral wealth, and refused to sell. Was a school proposed?— the object (echoes of 1812!) was to get hold of children, to ship them over to England, and put them into the British army. Was a building at last in process of erection?— it was a railroad station to serve the yet undiscovered designs of the "furriners."

Such an attitude could be met only by patient living and ministry. A party of young students one summer camped out on top of the Blue Ridge, and anxious to do some good while there, they visited the homes of the people about and read to them from the Bible. Among a class many of whom had never heard a sermon nor Scripture reading, they found some who were delighted at this service, and they were begged to stay there with them always. They could do no less than promise to come back or send some one in their place.

The first step was to find a Christian teacher who should make her home in such a neglected community, and through visiting, nursing, and teaching carry a concrete gospel to the needy. This first movement was developed into a large day school, with two or three teachers. Then a workers' home was proposed, for the sake both of better preserving the health and strength of the workers and of making a model for better homes and home life. This Workers' Home has proved a model for others, from out of which go forth Bible readers, evangelists, nurses, and teachers, who are helping to raise the standard of living in every practical way.

The Episcopal Church has three special missions: this, the Blue Ridge Archdeaconry in Virginia, another in Kentucky, and a third in the foothills of North Carolina. In the Blue Ridge Mission are four homes for workers, each of which is the center for several schools. On the other side of the mountains, in Kentucky, Archdeacon Wentworth is in charge of seven missions and twenty-six mission stations in the mountain districts, besides eight missions and twenty-two mission stations in the foothills. There are two schools, one at Beattyville and the other, St. John's Collegiate Institute, at Corbin; but with or without school buildings the whole work is educational, in how great and varied degrees an extract from one narrative will partially show:

"Everywhere, in each department, we find more response than we hoped for. We were warned that the children would not care for reading, but nowhere have I seen more appreciative audiences to stories read or told. Friends were kind to us this year in sending some books and many magazines, and the children were delighted with our well-stored book press in the kindergarten rooms. The magazines we carried to the outlying points were seized upon with shy eagerness. 'The best book a man ever read,' said one old man to me, 'is this here *Areny*, and next to hit is the *Reeview of Reeviews*.' As for our Proctor children, they spent happy hours in the grassy yard while one of us read aloud stories from *St. Nicholas*. The boys giggled gleefully over 'We Boys' at League meetings. On the singing evenings we read aloud to quiet but interested and responsive audiences of children and grown people, 'Rab and His Friends,' 'Patience and Experience,' and other stories of high literary quality.

"Before we went up this year, Mr. Barnes and Dr. Wood sent us a well-stored medicine chest, with salves and ointments, lotions for burns and bruises, talcum powder and castile soap. It would have repaid these friends, as it a thousand-fold repaid the labors of an amateur nurse with more good will than knowledge, to see the comfort this simple outfit brought to tormented babies, and cut and bruised small boys and fever patients, to whom talcum powder was a new luxury. Miss Mahan wrote a month later: 'It would do you good to see the bare brown legs I am watching in the school yard, with never a sore or a scar in sight.' For the last week of our stay Miss Cook was with us and taught a cutting and fitting class, heroically finding time and strength for a course of ten lessons in that short time, and winning the lasting gratitude of mothers, whose problem is to make one yard do the work of two, and whose want of training often wastes the one. . . .

"On this evening Mrs. Scott sang for us, and next day, early in the afternoon, dear old Uncle Frank Dougherty came by, and, sitting on the step, he said: 'Hag and the girls tell me there's a lady here that sings to beat all the sweetness a body ever heard.' And so Mrs. Scott, undiscouraged by the kindergarten piano, sang some of the ballads he loved, and the tears rained down the old man's cheeks. 'I'm that kind of an old fool,' he said. 'But, faith, ef she'd kape it up forever, I'd niver want to see hiven!' And then the old Irishman added: 'For the mather o' that, I'd as lief stay here onyway — I'm acquainted here, ye knaw.' That morning, in the blazing sun, Miss Couchman rode off with Mr. Patterson to help a family above Duck Fork o'Sturgeon, where were five cases of typhoid fever in a one-room windowless cabin, and where a ten-year-old girl lay dead. We sent some flowers and white ribbon, and Miss Couchman helped dress the little maid. When we were there a year ago we had grieved over a doll tied up on the wall — too good to play with. Miss Couchman tells us they put it into the little mother's arms at last when she was asleep. . . .

"I have no time to tell you of the mothers' meeting, nor of the League's work, nor even of the final erection of the Page fence, to which the kindergarten babies begged to sing 'Good Morning,' to the great joy of the League adviser; nor of the League's good use of the set of tools sent them by Smith, Watkins, and Company; nor of the delightful 'play party' at the home of the fourteen-year-old girl of whom I told you; nor of all the kindness shown us by the people; of invitations to their homes, a few of which we made time to accept; of the boat which Mr. Martin loaned us, and Mr. Bailey's promise to help the carpentry class make us a boat of our own next year; of all the help and courtesy that came from 'yan side of the river.' . . .

"Uncle Ben Bigstaff visited us this year. The old

man is broken in body, having spent himself in his Master's service here in the Kentucky mountains. But he fairly beamed upon it all. 'This is the very thing I have prayed for and waited all my life to see,' he said. 'It is like the leaven that a woman took and hid in three measures of meal until the whole was leavened. Work like this, I tell you, just means salvation to the Kentucky mountains.' But Uncle Ben knows and remembers always what we Blue-grass people seem often to forget — that if the leaven is good, so, also, is the meal."

The Morganton Associate Missions are in North Carolina, in the foothills more than in the mountains. They consist of eight missions, six of them having day schools, which enroll 354 children. As elsewhere, however, the schools are only one feature of the mission work, the house-to-house missionary going into some of the most distant and difficult sections to bring the light of the gospel to those who hear it in no other way.

The Episcopal Church has, besides, inaugurated a work for the cotton mill operatives in North and South Carolina, Georgia, and Alabama, at over thirty different mills. Most of this work consists of Sunday schools and church service, though in several cases a more or less extensive institutional work is done, including night school, men's and women's clubs, industrial classes, libraries, gymnasiums, medical service, and lectures. The cotton mills are mostly in the piedmont, and their operatives come largely from the mountains. The work of the church, especially in its educational and economic features, is generally welcomed and seconded by the mill owners.

In North Carolina is the center of the work conducted by the Northern Presbyterians through their Woman's Board of Home Missions. The Presbyterians were the first to begin special work for the mountaineer, not counting the abortive work of the American Missionary Association before the war. In 1879 they established their first mission school, in Concord, N. C. About the same time Rev. L. M. Pease, a Presbyterian clergyman in ill health, went with his wife to Asheville, even then famous as a health resort. Mr. and Mrs. Pease were soon interested in the children and young people about them, whose school advantages were of the slightest; they opened a free day school, for which they enlisted the support of their church.

This beginning in Asheville was the origin of the Presbyterian mission school work, and of the three great schools now at that place, which make the center of the system: viz., the Home Industrial School (for girls) and the Normal and Collegiate Institute, in the outskirts of the city, and the Farm School (for boys), nine miles up the Swannanoa River.

The Home Industrial School was opened in 1887, to be followed in 1893-94 by the founding of the boys' Farm School and the Normal and Collegiate Institute. The latter is the cap-stone to the Presbyterian school system, being chiefly concerned in preparing teachers to fill the great needs of the mountains. No schools are in greater esteem among the mountain people than these; and while their influence is felt far and wide through the mountains, it is especially evident in that "Land of the Sky" in the midst of which they are situated.

To these higher schools are related more than fifty academies and boarding schools, scattered through West Virginia, Kentucky, Tennessee, and North Carolina. There are, besides, a number of mission stations served by "Bible readers," who establish in their little cottages homes that become models to their communities. They visit the sick, conduct mothers' meetings and sewing-circles, Sunday-schools and prayer-meetings, and do a work that tells for more than that of the school bounded by four walls.

These schools and missions are doing not a little to develop the native handicrafts. A visit to the depot of the Allanstand Industries, in Asheville, where the products of one of their lines of stations are marketed, gives a glimpse into the industries of these mountain people reminiscent of the work of our great-grandfathers. Baskets of cane and hickory splits, whitewood, oak, and willow, in unique and original designs; rugs and coverlets in the colors of the soft wood dyes, and oftentimes in beautiful patterns; and hand-made furniture that defies the assaults of time; these are among the arts that add an important and genuine note to the popular movement in arts and crafts. They are the product of a people who make them from no dilettante interest in art, but to supply their own needs first, and then to reach the general public with the surplus.

"The Presbyterian Church," says Dr. Wilson, "has reached a practical consensus of opinion as to what is its chief mission in the Southern mountains. That mission is to educate, to provide Christian education for the young. This is, of course, recognized as an exceptional case.

"Usually the church looks upon itself as an evangelizing agency. But in the Appalachians it recognizes the fact that here the most successful way to contribute to the coming of the glad day when the mountains will be fully evangelized is to educate the young people of the mountains. What hope of building up good Presbyterianism or good Christianity of any type if the majority of the people cannot read, or search the Scriptures that testify of Christ? What hope of founding a substantial work so long as no educated leaders exist with desire for improvement and progress? It is evident that the Appalachian worker must lay broad and deep the foundation of education and intelligence before he can erect a permanent Christian church that shall largely improve the people for whose good it is consecrated."[1]

A work of great value and interest is that of the America Inland Mission, or Society of Soul Winners,

---

[1] Samuel T. Wilson, *The Southern Mountaineers*, p. 103.

with headquarters at Wilmore, Ky. This society was founded over a quarter century ago by Rev. Edward O. Guerrant, who compresses his forty years' experience in the mountains into these few words:

"When a young man, I went to Virginia, the land of my fathers, to join the army, and rode more than a hundred miles across the Cumberland Mountains. Although not looking for churches or preachers, I do not remember seeing a single one. During the war I crossed those mountains several times, and still found no churches. I was surprised.

"After the war I became a physician, and frequently rode through those mountains, visiting the sick, and still found only a church or two in many miles, though there were thousands of people with souls.

"When I became a minister, I naturally remembered that country where many of my old comrades lived, Christless and churchless, and determined to give them what little help I could."

This "little help" given by the Society of Soul Winners, means this — and more:

"In ten years 362 missionaries have labored exclusively in these wild mountains. They made 51,000 visits, held over 22,000 public services at 10,069 places, had 6,304 conversions, taught 879 Bible Schools with 39,456 pupils, distributed over 250 boxes and barrels of clothing to the poor, over 10,000 Bibles and Testaments, and 125,000 tracts, built 56 churches, schools, and mission houses, including three colleges and an orphan asylum."

Dr. Guerrant, seemingly as active in the saddle as when, fifty years ago, he rode with Morgan's resistless cavalry, now leads his hundred evangelists in tireless journeys over the mountains and through glens and coves from Kentucky to North Carolina. His "Galax Gatherers"[1] is a collection into a book of two

---

[1] *The Galax Gatherers; the Gospel among the Highlanders.* Price $1.00. Published by Edward O. Guerrant, Wilmore, Kentucky.

Redeeming the Time

hundred pages of stirring messages rough-hewn in the field; stories of great heights and solemn gorges; heroic girl teachers in the far interior; highland weddings and cabin prayer-meetings; accounts of Yancey apple caravans and tales of Cataloochee hospitality where "contented poverty lives happily with Jesus;" and preaching services that register audiences of from three little children to mammoth mountain gatherings of three hundred out in the "first church" which God built — a book that carries the reader in a rush of Christian militancy from "Troublesome River in the darkest Cumberlands" to the Estatoa missions under the shadow of mighty Mount Mitchell; fighting the Mormons in Kentucky; conducting a Congregational service with the shouts of Methodist people; closing the saloons with the power of a single sermon; baptizing a score at Puncheon Camp and establishing schools in "Bloody Breathitt" — a book to take the Christian reader by storm, with its vigorous narrative, beautiful descriptions, and flashes of unexpected humor.

When he had made up his mind to devote himself to the mountain people, Dr. Guerrant, a Southern Presbyterian, turned to his church synod in Kentucky, and induced them to send him as an evangelist into the mountains. But soon the church found the work developing too fast, so it thought, for its resources, and asked their missionary not to build so many churches and establish so many schools that they could not keep up with the expenses. Then Dr. Guerrant stood up before his synod and said: "Brethren, if you cannot afford to pay for the schools and the missionaries for the poor highlanders, God can pay for them." And he went out to organize the America Inland Mission, for which he made a general appeal; and "for fourteen years God has supported this mission, which has employed hundreds of workers and cost tens of thousands of dollars, with no dependence but prayer. In every land he has raised up friends whose voluntary gifts have supported the work."

The Southern Presbyterian Church finally took back the developed work under the care of its home mission board, but it is still conducted as a separate department, and "is auxiliary to all denominational work, and seeks only the further extension of Christ's kingdom." It has one hundred three evangelists, for whom are chosen as fields the most destitute mountain regions of Kentucky, Tennessee, North Carolina, and Virginia. It has seventeen day schools, with seven hundred pupils, and four higher schools in Kentucky and North Carolina. Its Orphans' Home in Clay City, Kentucky, is one of its earliest enterprises. This home is ideally situated on a thirty-acre farm, where the children are given an industrial and liberal education. The property of the society — its schools, mission houses, and churches — is valued at $50,000.

But beyond computation is the value of its most precious property, the men and women who are conducting the work at almost less than living wage; as, for instance, the two young men, graduates of a technological school, who left positions at four dollars a day to build with their own hands and to manage the new Beechwood Seminary, at a salary of twenty-five dollars a month. So, too, beyond known value, are the thousands of souls that this dauntless band of missionaries are searching out and teaching and inspiring in the mountains.

Thus have we caught a glimpse of the educational and social work of the churches in the Southern mountains. No adequate presentation is possible or intended in this short review. It has only been hoped to indicate, by a bit of history, a bit of statistics, and a bit of incident, the extent and character of the Christian agencies now engaged in an effort to redeem the lost time of the past century. The field is as yet a virgin field, wide open for workers who are willing to give up some of the luxuries of the age in exchange for the joy of present service and the rewarding glories of an age to come.

First Cabin, and Recitation Hall, Berry School.
"The Berry School makes men unafraid of any task." Page 136.

X

COALS FROM THE ALTAR

ONCE, long ago, a seer saw a vision of the Lord God Almighty, high and lifted up on his living throne. About him were his seraphim, and they sang one to another, "Holy, holy, holy, is the Lord of hosts: the whole earth is full of his glory."

It did not seem to the prophet, cowering there, that the earth was filled with God's glory. Best of earth's blood were his people, the children of a "Prince with God"; yet they little revealed the glory of God. Proud, fierce, ignorant, they darkened the land with their crimes and shamed it with their brutishness. He himself, who should have been a teacher — so ran his self-accusation — had been blind to his people's needs and inexcusably selfish. So he cried, "Woe is me! for I am undone; because I am a man of unclean lips, and I dwell in the midst of a people of unclean lips: for mine eyes have seen the King, the Lord of hosts."

Then flew one of the seraphim to him, with a live coal in his hand, taken from off the altar. He laid it upon his mouth, and said, "Lo, this hath touched thy lips; and thine iniquity is taken away, and thy sin purged."

Immediately came the voice of God, saying, "Whom shall I send? and who will go for us?" Then the seer, fired with zeal and power by that coal from the altar, and seeing as the seraphim a vision of a new earth filled with the glory of God, said: "Here am I; send me." So was born the prophet of the Messiah.

Here, now, is a story of two, a woman and a man, called of God to spread the glory of his presence in the hearts and the homes of another chosen people. Widely separated were these two, in place, in fortune, in station; yet so similar in purpose and resolution that their common mission shows a common origin: the vision of God's glory and the kindling of their zeal by that coal from off his altar. The one was the daughter of a southern aristocrat, with the heritage of culture and wealth; the other was the son of a mountain preacher, with no legacy but an abounding faith. But they were alike, when each had seen his vision, in crying, "Here am I; send me." In what they have seen, and sought, and done for the mountaineer, they may stand as representatives of the forces from within the mountains that are being divinely aroused to teach and lead their people.

Down in the hills of northern Georgia, just where the Blue Ridge and the Cumberlands halt their invasion of the plains, lies the thriving little city of Rome. Two miles north, on a green-swarded, shady hill, is the proud old ancestral home of the Berrys. The big oak grove that surrounds it serves scarcely to hide, down in one corner, a little, low, mud-daubed log cabin, with a stick chimney wide enough to swallow any Saint Nicholas. And many a time it did swallow one of the little Berrys who had forgotten the key to the door of their play-house, where candy-pulls and corn-poppings and chestnut-roastings marked many a holiday.

The children of the Berry household grew up in time; but for one of them the little cabin held all too hallowed memories to permit its being neglected or forgotten. Martha Berry chose it for her "den," and with coon skins and bear skins and plunder of field and wood she made it a lodge to match the legend over the fireplace,

"Kyndle Friendship." The rafters above were hidden behind festoons of peppers and popcorn ears, and outside, by the door, hung the cedar water-pail alongside the gourd dipper. Over in one corner was a little old rosewood melodeon, infirm in its legs, and with its keys yellow from age. Here Martha Berry spent many and many a quiet hour with her books and the wild things of the woods that visited her.

One balmy Sunday afternoon in April three other little wild things crept up to the cabin, and through some unchinked cracks stood peering in at this wondrous palace of beauty and the lady that lived therein. Miss Berry, suddenly conscious of the scrutiny, looked up from her book to encounter the three pairs of gray-blue eyes so wonderingly intent upon her paradise.

"Come in," she called to them. But the three little barefoot, ragged children shrank away in fear. Going to the door, Miss Berry tried to talk with them, but it was only when she held out the temptation of bright-cheeked apples that she could persuade them to cross the threshold. Then, remembering it was Sunday, she began to tell them Bible stories. These were all new to them, as she discovered when she asked them questions.

"Don't know," they said, "don't know. Hain't never been to no Sunday school. We-uns' Hardshells."

Did they have any brothers and sisters? she asked. Yes, indeed. "I got about eight," said one; and another, "I got about ten."

They were the children of tenant farmers near-by, men from the mountains or of kin to them. If Miss Berry like Joseph was seeking to prove these spies as to their families, the proof was forthcoming. She asked them to return next Sunday and bring their brothers and sisters. Then promptly with their departture, her other interests took back her mind, until she had nearly forgotten her promise. The next Sunday she was sitting with some visitors from the city upon the gallery of the "big house," when through the woods she saw a procession that recalled her appointment. Not only children were coming, but men, women, babies, and dogs. Excusing herself from her friends, she hurried down to meet the Sunday school delegation at the little log cabin.

Forming an impromptu program in her mind, she said, "First we'll sing something." The wheezy little melodeon, upheld on all sides by eager children, did its best, a wondrous best, as they sang to Miss Berry's "lining out," "I'm so glad that Jesus loves me." And then she told them Bible stories, stories so new and fresh to these neglected "Hardshells" that not the children only, but the fathers and mothers, sat with rapt faces, while the babies kept silence, and not even a dog moved his tongue. For this Sunday school, mark you, was the laying of the corner-stone of a great temple of service.

Every succeeding Sunday brought more and more and more visitors, some with gifts of shuck mats for seats for the growing audience, which promptly filled the cabin and overflowed into the grove. Miss Berry had become, before she knew it, the head and front of a weekly camp-meeting, an affair that promised an undefined extension. How many a lady, with such a distinction thrust upon her, would not gracefully have withdrawn on about the seventh Sunday? How many would not have found the hot summer good reason to terminate an enterprise that threatened leisure and forbade society? But not so Martha Berry. A Voice had called, "Whom shall I send? and who will go for us?" And out of her leisurely, sheltered life she came to respond, "Here am I; send me." And then a new glory came upon life, the glory of a revealed Christ.

The Sunday school grew. People would come, rain or shine; and soon, impelled by necessity, Miss Berry invested one hundred dollars in lumber, and the men and boys of the Sunday school put up a small schoolhouse, which soon added to itself a little room on the front, then a big room on the back.

Then the Sunday school grew into a circuit. Some of the members moved up to Possum Trot Creek, and they sent word for Miss Berry to come there and open a Sunday school. So she drove the eight miles to Possum Trot, and held Sunday school with them in an old, dilapidated house that had survived the war. One Sunday it rained, and though the superintendent fled from corner to corner, she was soaked before the Sunday school and the shower were over. So she asked the people to put on a new roof before the next Sunday. But that seemed to them a most unreasonable request.

"It mought not rain for a whole month," said one man.

"Yes," replied Miss Berry, "but it mought rain next Sunday."

She pointed to an oak tree near-by which would make good "boards," and told the men that if they would cut it up and shingle the roof she would bring the nails, and treat the workers to lemonade. They came, and she came, and, most indispensable of all, the lemonade came, a most unaccustomed beverage, but one highly appreciated by all, even by the old man who remarked with an amused chuckle that he "never heard of a woman a-bossin' of a house-roofin' before."

From Possum Trot "the Sunday Lady," as the countryside began affectionately to call her, was soon extending her chain of Sunday schools in several directions. Her sister and others were enlisted as helpers. And soon mightily grew the Word of God.

But the Sunday school was not enough to Martha Berry's new-born and abounding interest in these children. Upon the heels of every Sunday school she pushed a day school. Where there was none she made one; and where there was a county school she extended its term, paying teachers from her own purse, and making herself a constant visitor and teacher. A new life suddenly sprang into being at the foot of the mountains.

The immediate and surprising success of Miss Berry's schools invites inquiry as to its cause. Who does not know Sunday schools that are born with the sun and die with its setting? Who is unfamiliar with day schools that would rather send their teachers to Possum Trot than call them from there? What made Miss Berry's work a revivifying power in this dry stubble? It is the secret of the seer: Martha Berry found a life, not a profession. Surprised into a Sunday school, she did not organize an institution; she told Bible stories. When needing a shelter, she did not appoint a committee; she pointed out a "board" tree and ladled lemonade. When she started a day school, she did not write a program on the blackboard; she took her children for long walks in the piney woods, naming the plants and wild flowers and telling stories of the birds, the insects, and the butterflies. Of these things she found her children pathetically ignorant, and pathetically eager to learn. "The Sunday Lady" entered into their lives, making them broader and more beautiful and more purposeful. Who would not follow such a leader, even though she be "a woman a-bossin' of a house-roofin' "?

It was in 1898 that Miss Berry was called from her Sunday reverie in the little log den to become an apostle to the mountaineers. For the next four years she was busy conducting her Sunday schools and day schools. Then she entered another phase. It was as if she had been building board shanties and patching leaky roofs so far: now she would seize pick and spade and dig for solid foundations.

She saw that the day school was not enough. It taught principles of cleanliness, thrift, industry, only to have them overturned when the children went back to their cabin homes. She must have a school home where the right ideas and habits might become fixed by practise, and where pupils from a distance might come and stay while attending school.

Miss Berry tried to interest friends in her project,

but in vain. Then — she did not turn back; for she had committed herself before God to this mission. She went to her iron deposit box and took out an old deed; she went to her bank and took out a thousand dollars. From her father's gift to his little girl she cut off eighty-three acres; she built on it, besides the little schoolhouse already standing there, a two-story home for the school; and all this she deeded to trustees as the nucleus of the Berry School for Boys.

Then the mountain boys came in. They came with mules and ox-teams and on foot, packing their small bundles of clothing and often a week's provisions of hominy and potatoes. Miss Berry and her first assistant, Miss Brewster, went to live in the boys' home. They shared their rough shelter and their coarse food, determined that they would stand with their boys and not above them in their effort to help. They showed them by precept and example how to live and learn by doing. There were no servants; no class but an aristocracy of labor.

This was satisfactory enough to the mountain boy within the bounds of his code. He was ready to plow in the fields, chop in the woods, hammer on the house; he was not wholly off his ground in milking the cows, cooking his food, and making his bed; but there were some things too undisguisedly woman's work. The first Monday Miss Berry summoned her young guard of mountaineers for their first lesson in laundering. The laundry was a wash-tub out under a tree.

"Now, boys," said Miss Berry, "we are going to wash clothes. I will show you how. Then each boy is to wash his own garments."

There was silence, an electric silence, while the mountaineer considered. This was indeed woman's work, nay, more, negro's work. Science was sweet, but was it worth such degradation? The group fidgeted for a minute, and then their spokesman, a tall, strapping young fellow, said, "No ma'am! I ain't never seen no man do no washin', an' what's more *I* ain't goin' to do it."

Calmly Miss Berry played her last card. "If you will not do the washing," she said, "you may watch me while I do it for you." Into the tub went her soft white arms. It was her first washing likewise. Up and down sloshed the clothes over the wash-board, up and down bent the back of the gentle washerwoman. The boys stood sheepishly regarding her. Finally, exhausted, she straightened her aching back and leaned in weariness against the tub. The chivalry of the mountaineer, running in unaccustomed channels, asserted itself at last. "I ain't never seen it done," declared the former speaker, "but I'm a-goin' to wash them clothes." And dashing in, he led his companions in a charge to victory. It was there settled that the Berry School should stand for doing whatever needed to be done, that it should make men unafraid of any task that life might bring them. And perhaps just then was born this motto of the school's, "Be a lifter, not a leaner."

Today there is not only a Berry School for Boys, but, three-quarters of a mile distant, a Martha Berry School for Girls. There are three thousand acres in the school estate, and more than a score of buildings, all erected by the students. Two hundred forty boys and one hundred twenty girls are all that as yet the school can admit, and for lack of room many are turned away.

The buildings are simple and in harmony with the surroundings and the life work of the students. A home life and atmosphere is maintained in the school, the teachers living with their pupils and making themselves in effect the idealized parents of these children. The Bible is a daily text-book in precept and in life. The industries that are most characteristic and most vital in the life of the mountaineer are here taught in developed form: the domestic arts, dairying, weaving, basket-making, carpentry, agriculture, mechanics. And the mountains are feeling deeply the impulse. Scores of Berry graduates are at work in the mountains and the piedmont, in schools, on farms, in shops and offices, molding homes and communities, and helping to develop a manhood and womanhood that will pay to the world their debt a hundred fold.

The Berry estate belongs now to the Berry School; Martha Berry belongs to the age. Most intimately, indeed, is she claimed by her boys and girls, and next by the men and women of the Georgia mountains; but the influence of her faith and devotion has gone, not nation-wide only, but far out into the foreign world. There can be no regret to Martha Berry for the interruption of her reverie by those little wide-eyed children on that long-ago Sunday afternoon.

The spirit born that April evening in the little log cabin has its shrine today in the larger cabin built to commemorate it. This idealized "cabin" stands among its dogwoods and honeysuckle and rose bushes, with its latch-string ever out. Here on Sunday afternoons gather the boys and the girls as their forerunners gathered years ago. They enter and seat themselves upon the skins and rugs and settles about Miss Berry's chair; and again are heard in the gentle tones of "the Sunday Lady" the stories and the lessons of the old, old Book that has been the inspiration of her life and work. And out of hundreds of hearts and minds, strengthened, purified, equipped, ennobled, is flowing forth a stream of answering love to the mountains and the world. Could ever prophet ask for greater reward on earth?

* * * *

It was not long ago that a sympathetic visitor to the Kentucky mountains apologized for there being as yet, he said, "no native leaders in church or educational work among these people." He spoke, doubtless, from his own observation; but only a few miles off the track he took, there stands the monument of the energy, the indomitable leadership, of a son of the mountains.

Shortly after the Revolution, there came wandering

through the wilds of southeastern Kentucky a North Carolina pioneer by the name of Burns. Finding the country well to his liking, he stopped short of his objective, Boonesborough in the Blue-grass, and in this mountain land he reared his family and laid the foundation of his clan. His great-grandson, cast in the mold of his fathers' Calvinism and mantled with the later coming Baptist faith, became a mountain preacher.

The land in which he lived had become, as it has remained to very recent times, the stronghold of the clan spirit, the fighting-ground of the feudist. As in the days of Daniel Boone, so still, it was the frontier, without roads, without commerce, without schools, with law as every man's right arm and straight-seeing eye could make it. Preacher Burns ranged up and down through the mountains, preaching his gospel of election and damnation to a Covenanter breed that made it fit well with their stern law of might and right.

Three or four years before the Civil War, the father, fearing that his sons would become involved in the feuds, moved his family over to Virginia, a land in all respects like his own except for the bloody quarrels of men. Here in the West Virginia mountains was born to the Kentucky preacher his youngest son, James A. Burns.

The boy grew up with the education of the wilderness: rough living, scant learning, hard blows, keen senses alert for danger and advantage. Some of his father's creed and precept was woven into his mental fiber; but as for books, he had obtained, when he was fifteen, the full extent of his youth's schooling — just ten months.

When James Burns was twenty-one years old, his father died, and the young man very soon returned to the home of his clan, in Clay County, Kentucky. Here, as his father had feared, he found the whole community aflame with the spirit of the feud. Many of his relatives had fallen, and the supreme purpose in the lives of those remaining was to avenge their deaths. Burns, big-boned, strong of muscle and hard of fist, quick of eye and unerring with rifle or pistol, was called upon to play a man's part among them, and to the call of the clan he responded.

His party one day made an attack upon a home belonging to the rival faction, but when they tried to rush the place, they found themselves outfought. Young Burns, with empty rifle and at hand-grips with a foe, was hit over the head a mighty blow with a rifle-barrel, and was left for dead upon the field by his retreating party. His genial enemies dragged him by the heels out of the path he obstructed, and threw him over the fence.

The next morning Burns awoke to find himself upon a bed in the very cabin he had so unsuccessfully assaulted. During the night, in his delirium, he had again attempted to force his way in, and had been again knocked down. But his "enemies" then kindly cared for him until he came to himself, and sent him away in peace, explaining, in response to his dazed inquiries, that his injuries had come from his falling and hurting himself!

Arriving at his own home, John Burns betook himself to a densely wooded mountain, where, like another Saul of Tarsus, he remained studying over the revelation that had come with his striking down. For what purpose, he asked himself, had he been brought to life when both friends and enemies had supposed him dead? Had God a purpose in sparing his hitherto unprofitable life? What should he do now?

He determined that he would devote himself to the work of his God-fearing father, but in a new, a broader way, a way that he as yet saw but dimly, but which he believed would clear as he should go forward. The feud, he saw, was the curse of the mountains, but back of the feud was its cause: the shut-in view, the uninstructed pride, the undirected energy of his fellow mountaineers. Their glory they were giving to the beast; their ideal was force, their virtue brutish. But this they did not know. They were not consciously trouble-makers. They desired peace; and in a personal way they held that moral code of the nations, that to enforce a worthy peace they must sometimes make war. As the mother taught her daughter virtue, so she taught her son honor. To maintain the one was no more a moral duty than to maintain the other, by force of arms if necessary. The feudist bedded his code in religion.

But upon young Burns was dawning another vision, the vision of the glory of the Lord of hosts; and in his ears was sounding the challenge, "Whom shall I send? and who will go for us?" And faintly, vaguely, already his lips were forming the reply: "Here am I; send me."

First of all, he saw he must have more education. With almost no money, he made his way to a little Baptist college in Ohio, where he stayed for seven months. He was an Elijah out of the mountains of Bashan. Pondering his vision, he moved among his fellow students moody, silent, responding only to the secret Voice calling him to his work in the mountains. Undiscovered and unremembered in the Ohio school, he passed back into the life of the wilderness, and there began to feel his way toward the fulfilment of his mission.

In 1892 he was back in Clay County, twenty-seven years old, with a schooling that totaled seventeen months, and a fortune no greater than that of the Man who had not where to lay his head. But he had come to help his people to the broader vision. So he taught school on Raider's Creek and Crane Creek and Road Run and Redbird and Sexton and in Manchester, the county-seat. When the scant county funds gave out, Burns organized subscription schools; and with little or nothing of material reward, kept going his campaign of Christian education. As he worked and as he taught, he kept on studying. The walls of a school were to him no exclusive magazine of learning: he raided knowledge and drew his supplies from books and men and God himself. When he could, he went away for a little time to some school where he could be instructed better than he could instruct himself.

Thus in 1898-99 he was in Berea College, and there came to him the climax of his vision: he must start a college in the heart of his own land. To a kindred spirit in Berea, Rev. H. L. MacMurray, he confided his determination, and these two men united to carry it out. Without a dollar, but with a sublime faith that counted the moving of mountains only the matter of germinating a mustard seed, they went up to Clay County.

On the banks of Crane Creek stands an old mill that in those days afforded the largest meeting-room in the valley. To that mill building, in the late days of 1899, J. A. Burns called together the clans, the Burnses and the Allens, the Combs and the Hensleys, men who had never faced one another but warily and with fingers ready to grip the pistol butt. They were called here for a new, a strange purpose, called by one of their own number who had been a feudist, but who was now known and respected for a new sort of power, a forceful preacher and an earnest teacher. Some general knowledge of his purpose they had, but what mixed purposes they themselves had, one and another, they could not tell, and every man of them came armed.

Watchful and alert, the factions ranged themselves on opposite sides of the mill room, and Burns stood up by the old wooden hopper and addressed them. The time, he said, had come for a new era in the mountains. They had been rearing their sons for slaughter; should they not turn them now to salvation? Should men who had heard the gospel of Jesus Christ continue to waylay one another like red Indians? There was a higher call for men made in the image of God. There was a call from God to spread the glory of the knowledge of the Lord through all these mountains. The time was come, and the means must be made. A Christian education was demanded of them to prepare for their mission. Their children should be messengers of heaven instead of agents of hell. A college for Christian training was needed in their midst, and that college he was going to build. He had not a dollar, he told them, but by God's grace he was going to start that college. Did they want to help?

"It was a mighty quiet meeting," says Burns. "I didn't know what they were going to do. But I was right glad when Lee Combs got up, and when Dan Burns got up too, and they met in front of me. They did not draw, but they shook hands. Then I knew that Oneida College was going to be a success." With the handclasp of those two men, the doom of the feud in Clay County was declared.

Then Burns and MacMurray set to work. Henry Hensley gave them fifty dollars. Another gave them a little tract of twelve acres of land. This was at Oneida, where Redbird, Bullskin, and Goose creeks unite to form the south fork of the Kentucky River. With tools fashioned from two old crowbars, Burns quarried the stones for the foundation of his first building. It was at dawn one morning when he set that first stone in place for the wall of Oneida College. Carefully and firmly he set it, in the wish that it might stand long. And then — simple ceremony to his first corner-stone laying — all alone on the hillside he stretched his arms toward heaven and prayed for the souls of the men of his mountains.

As his prayer went up, there came an answering challenge: over the hill beyond a young feudist, drunk with the fury of a fight just closed, came riding against the sun, and its streaming light he greeted with a volley of pistol shots. The new and the old joined battle that morning on the Oneida hills, a battle of principles, not of powder. Three years later that same young feudist stepped into the water to be baptized by Burns, and his surrender was typical of the victory won by this prophet and his divine message to the mountains.

But it was not with ease that the new school grew. MacMurray Hall rose at first under the unaided hands of the teacher, then with the tardy help of some halfhearted friends — a plain, small building of two stories, great only to spiritual eyes that look as God looks upon the heart of things.

Then the pupils came, plenty of them, bringing their provisions in sacks and baskets, with now and then a few dollars meagerly earned but willingly expended in laying the foundation of power in their souls. Food and other needs were knotty problems to the teachers. Night after night, early in the history of the school, Burns and a fellow-teacher sat out by a great flat rock that juts into the river, sat by a fire while they mastered the next day's lessons in studies where some of their students were pushing them hard, sat there poring over their books while their trot-lines led off from the rock to catch the catfish for their breakfast. Catfish and corn — and mostly catfish — helped to lay the early foundations of Oneida College.

The needs pressed. From far away the young men of the mountains came down to this center of new civilization. The first little building was overcrowded at once. At the close of the year their current expenses had put them in debt two hundred dollars. Burns went down into "The Settlements," to try to raise the money. But he found times hard, the churches pressed by the Mission Board to make up the foreign budget, and a general disbelief prevailing on the part of officials in the missionary character of a school in the home land. Not a hearing could he get in a single church, and at last he turned his steps homeward, discouraged but not despairing, for he believed in the God of Elijah.

At Winchester he found a man whose pastor he had been in Clay County, a "feud leader" who had moved away from the troubled zone to save his children. This man called upon his pastor to help, but the pastor said they were sorely pressed to raise money for missions, and the best he could do was to give the pulpit to Mr. Burns and let him state his needs at the close of the sermon. Thus Burns faced his first Blue-grass audience, and taking the text, "The weapons of our warfare are not carnal, but mighty through God to the pulling down of strongholds," preached more for himself than for his congregation. Afterwards he told what they were trying to do at Oneida, and of their needs, whereupon a deacon arose and said, "I believe we ought to help this cause, and I will start the contribution with fifty dollars." At the close of the service, the pastor, rejoicing, brought him a gift from his people of a little more than the amount needed.

Soon after this Dr. and Mrs. J. B. Marvin, of Louisville, heard of his work, and gave him five thousand dollars, which built the ten-thousand-dollar hall that makes the center of Oneida. The mountaineers, converted now and sharing his vision, gave what they could of time and strength and little offerings. They gave, too, their sons and their daughters, but at first only their sons could be received.

One day, down the valley of Bullskin Creek came an old man with two mules and three grown daughters mounted thereon. They forded the river and presented themselves before Burns, an offering of the womanhood of the mountains to his mission, the mission of God. But there was no place for them, and no money to make a place. With tears in his eyes, Burns said to them, "I can't take you. I have got nothing to feed you, and there is no place where you can sleep." Answering tears streamed down the faces of the girls and of the old man, their father. Silently, with the sadness of the mountains' ages upon their faces and forms, they turned back upon their mules, up Bullskin Valley, to the fate from which they had fled.

Said Burns, "That must not be. We must have a home for girls. Our women must not lag behind our men if the mountains are to be reclaimed." Mr. R. Carnahan, of Louisville, who had become their treasurer, encouraged him in his plans to make such a home, promising to help all he could in meeting the bills. Burns started out again to raise money in the churches, but

Oneida Institute.
"Oneida is doing its part in preparing the mountains for their wider destiny." Page 145.

his experience was a repetition of the early part of his former effort. Returning to Oneida, with money nowhere in sight, he had to acquiesce in the decision of his fellows to stop work on the building. Then the president of a building and loan association stepped forward with an offer of a loan which sent the building to completion, and opened a way for the girls of the mountains. Today Oneida College for men and women opens its doors to five hundred students each year.

It feels its mission only begun, and but little developed. Not books only, but applied knowledge, Burns and his coworkers seek to teach their people. A thirteen-hundred-acre farm is the broad foundation upon which the industries have begun to be built, and Burns and his fellows dream — with hands weaving a fabric out of the dream — of industries made from the ancient arts of the mountain home and shop, industries that shall keep the individuality and the beauty of the mountains with their creators, and for the blessing of the nation as well.

The hand of Oneida is reaching out farther into the mountains, up the creeks, through the narrow valleys, upon the mountainsides. One branch school has been established, and others are being planted. Along with the older agencies, Oneida is doing its part in teaching and preparing the mountains for their wider destiny. To it belongs the peculiar power of self-uplift; for the blood of its teachers and its trained workers who are going out into the mountains by the score, is the blood of the clan, the people for whom it is giving its all.

To this dreamer of dreams, this seer of visions, this man of faith and revealer of forces that were hidden in the providences of God, has come the reward of seeing his people put their feet upon the first steps of the ladder on which angels are ascending and descending, and where at the summit is God.

* * * *

No reposeful life are these schools or their founders

spending now. The struggle for maintenance, for greater facilities to meet growing demands, for means to spread their influence in extension work far back into the mountains, press more and more heavily upon the shoulders that are bearing these weights. Time and talents and strength that might seem too precious to spend outside the weaving of the fabric, are spent to exhaustion in the work outside, praying for the warp upon which the school loom is weaving its marvelous patterns from the souls of the mountains. But the Lord that called the messengers, the God that gave the message, he it is that made the quest; and it must be that in the tapestry he has planned, he would have thus revealed the subtle, seamless union of lowland and highland, rich and poor, the thank-offering of them that can give and the more abounding love of them that have received much.

Spinning

A Brotherhood of Service

"The school should be permeated with the religion of Jesus Christ. The mountain people are naturally religious; they love the service of the church. No subject is more attractive to them than the Bible. Nothing will do more for them than the pure gospel. And there is no better way of bringing them under its influence than through a school that is founded and conducted on the eternal principles of God's Word." EDGAR TUFTS.

XI

A SCHOOL OF SIMPLICITY.

TEN miles above Nashville the yellow flood of the Cumberland curves itself into a bottle form known as Neeley's Bend. Across the narrow neck of this bottle, touching the river on either side, lies an ancient estate, a part of the original grant to the Neeley family after whom "the bend" was named. The blue-grass and limestone of its upland furnished pasture for the cattle and intermittent labor for the slaves, as testify the long lines of solid stone fence yet standing. The bottom lands along the river were magazines of fertility that bore long and patiently the drain of a corn and wheat monotony; while, rounding the angles and taking possession of the shaly spots, buckbrush and oak fought with the blue-grass that claimed proprietary interest in the limestone soil.

Far back in the estate, behind its locust avenue and surrounded by a massive limestone wall, stood the old farm house. Its cedar log walls, piled up in early days, had later received the garnish of clapboard and paint, until nothing bespoke its age as well as the massive stone chimneys at either end, whose hewn and squared blocks have darkened under the storms of more than half a century.

To this estate, in the summer of 1904, came a little company of teachers and students to begin a training school for Christian workers among the mountaineers. Whatever the fame of the Nelson Place in ante-bellum days, they found its splendor faded. The rich but shallow soil of the upland had washed until in many places only bare rock greeted the sun. Weeds and briers were overrunning the pastures; the clay of the benchland was baked and hard; and only the river bottoms still upheld the old dynastic pride. Buildings were in disrepair; and the old tip-hatted log barn, sitting among its pig-styes by the wide stone gate, and shaking its leery finger at every passer-by, seemed typical of the state of dissipation at which the place had arrived.

It was not the first choice of the company of educators who had come to establish the school. The previous May, Doctors Sutherland and Magan, who had long been interested in the educational problems of the South, were prospecting for a location. With them were their friends, Elder J. E. White, president of the Southern Missionary Society, and for many years a director of work among the colored people of the South; his brother, Elder W. C. White; and their aged and revered mother, Mrs. Ellen G. White.

Mrs. White had been from early life an earnest worker in the ranks of reformers. As a temperance lecturer she had labored throughout America, and in Europe and Australia, and was widely known as a speaker upon religious and moral topics. Her writings in a score of languages were sown throughout the world. She had been one of the founders of the Seventh-day Adventist Church, and during the sixty years of its existence her teachings had been most influential in the spread of the religious, the medical, and the educational work of that small but active people. The principles of physical, mental, and spiritual health and power which she and her colaborers advocated, had been formulated into a system of education whose aim was the highest perfection of the workers' physical and mental powers for the service of their fellow-men.

A School of Simplicity

Her interest in the problems of the South had been long and deep, and her presence and counsel were highly prized by those who were launching this new enterprise. Their plans, indeed, were much too modest for Mrs. White to endorse. Influenced partly by the smallness of their resources, they intended to go back into the mountains, buy a small place, and give their attention for a while at least to the local needs. But Mrs. White declared that their experience in training teachers and other Christian workers should not thus be buried in a napkin, and that they would do well to locate near to Nashville, in contact with the important educational interests centering there, and in touch not only with the mountains but with other rural sections of the South. She had seen the Nelson Place, and felt it to be favorable in location and character for their work. To their objection that they had not enough money even for the purchase price, to say nothing of development, she replied, "Have faith in God. The Lord has led you through some hard places, and given you deep experiences, and if you will trust him, he will give you more. You will get the money, and I will help you." To the objection that the land was poor and rocky and the fertility of the soil depleted, Mrs. White inquired: "Brethren, whom have you come here to help?" The answer was, "These poor people in the hills."

"And do you think it becoming for you to have the best piece of land in the State to train yourselves to help these people with very *poor* land in the hills?"

The argument closed, and the place was bought. It lies ten miles north of Nashville and two and a half miles east from the little station of Madison.

Four teachers long associated together in school work, were the founders of the Nashville Agricultural and Normal Institute, or, as it is more popularly known, the Madison School. They were Dr. E. A. Sutherland, Dr. P. T. Magan, Miss M. Bessie DeGraw, and Mrs. N. H. Druillard. With them, by twos and threes throughout the summer, came eleven students from Emmanuel Missionary College in Michigan, some of whom were to act as instructors. The first to occupy the place was Mr. E. E. Brink, with two students. Mr. Brink had been an instructor in industries at Emmanuel College; and at the Madison School not only was he the pioneer, but he has remained as a valued teacher and worker in the industries.

Teachers and students alike, they came with no temptation of money or other worldly advantage. They were to have what they could make; and living depended upon their making it. The dean gathered up the reins of the mule team. The lady secretary, in a one-mule cart, drove once a week to town with the butter made by the president in the lean-to creamery. The treasurer, a veteran in finance in institutions home and foreign, laid her hand to the skillet and the broom.

When Mrs. Sutherland came, with Baby Joe and some lady students, the question of lodging became acute. The chief building was the "Old House," but the former owners had not yet given possession, and the next best shelter was the servant quarters in the carriage house, above the horse stables. Into this went the ladies, to be followed in later years by successive relays of new students. The ability of fresh recruits to endure these rough accommodations before receiving better, was something of a test of character; and thus among the students the little old weather-beaten barn came to bear the affectionate title, "Probation Hall."

In October the company took possession of the "Old House." The school was a family; its first classes were morning and evening worship, followed by practical studies of educational conditions in the South, how to make the farm pay, how to bring the stock through the winter, how to get money for furniture, machinery, buildings, etc. The genial, one-sided warmth of the north-room fireplace fell nights on the forum of a young democracy, that mingled discussions of folk-lore and

A School of Simplicity

pedagogy and balanced rations with needlework and knitting and administration of bran poultices to chapped hands.

The Madison School was born under conditions that approximated those of pioneer days. Their tables were of plank, their dressers of dry-goods boxes. Their food was largely restricted to what they had found in their fields and the products of their dairy. This condition of enforced economy, if not exactly the choice, was at least within the plans of the founders. They knew that to train themselves and their students for service to the poor, there was nothing more effective than privation and sacrifice. Not only in the first days of hardship, but throughout its history their school must be a school of simplicity. The body must be accustomed to hard work and simple diet; the reins of the mind must be girded up by self-control and zealous purpose. The closer the living conditions at the school approached those to be met when students should have become teachers, the more adaptable and efficient would those teachers be. No steam-heated, electrically-lighted buildings, no intricate and expensive machinery, no wealth of imported foodstuffs, were appropriate for the men and women in training for service to the mountains.

Vegetarians by principle, they omitted from their diet the most costly food staple. While seeking to provide from the farm and garden and orchard a nourishing and sufficiently varied diet, they denied themselves the world-wide variety in which many families of today indulge. It is the idea of the founders to keep the farm machinery equipment as simple as possible. The student farmer trudges in the furrow behind his mule team. In the laundry, the women rub out the clothes in the hand tub. Few institutional facilities are introduced, and the greatest possible simplicity is maintained in all departments, that the student may not separate himself by too great a chasm from the conditions with which he must deal in his future work.

Buildings there must be; for though the "Old House" and "Probation Hall" were crammed for recitation and dining and lodging requirements, the second comers promptly overflowed into the barns. What should be the form of the new buildings? Should they be large and expensive and equipped with all modern conveniences? If such should be provided here, what would be the wishes and strivings of the graduates who should later go out to establish their own work? The management of the school from the first adopted the principle of making every study, every industry, every improvement, educational not in theory only but in practise, and so suited to the needs of the people to be served as to require little modification when applied to their conditions. The buildings, then, should be small, simple, and inexpensive, yet models of neatness and good workmanship. As the students with their teachers should engage in erecting these, they would receive a practical elementary training in the art of building, a training suited to their afterwork. This educational purpose was the prime consideration, though there were material advantages besides, such as lessened danger from fire and avoidance of large investments.

So the cottage plan of housing students was adopted; and the institution, instead of being comprised in a few large buildings, is composed of a score of small, neat cottages and a few public buildings slightly larger, patterns of simplicity for the smaller schools to be operated in the hills and mountains. The large buildings are Kinne Hall (the boarding department), Gotzian Hall (the main school building), and the Rural Sanitarium. To these is to be added the new hospital, provided through the generosity of Mrs. Josephine Gotzian, a long-time friend of the school, designed, with its treatment rooms and wards, to minister to the needs of sick students and others who may not be able to pay the rates of the sanitarium.

The Madison School has attempted the solution of

a problem which most schools have declared incapable of solution; that is, how a school without endowment may give its students an education without payment of tuition. In other words, can a student pay his way through school by his labor, without the school's having a deficit in consequence? When Hampton Institute, practically the pioneer of the modern industrial school, was challenged on the grounds that "such an education will not pay," General Armstrong conceded, "Of course it cannot pay in a money way, but it will pay in a moral way"; and that "it cannot pay in a money way" has been the concession of most educators ever since, along with the twin conclusion that because of its educational value, the industrial school should be supported by the public, through gifts, bequests, appropriations, and the proceeds of endowments. It is of interest, therefore, to see how the Madison School, without endowment, enables its students and itself to meet current expenses and avoid deficits.

Strictly speaking, the school has an endowment. But it is not an endowment in the usual sense — a capital from the interest of whose extraneous investments there is a steady income of cash. Instead, the "endowment" is a working capital in the form of industries, which by student labor are made profitable enough to meet expenses. Subscriptions were asked from interested friends for the purpose of stocking the farm and equipping it with necessary barns, stables, and machinery. It was believed that these would furnish productive labor by means of which the student could earn the greater part of his livelihood while obtaining his education. It will also be clear that such a system could only live and succeed where there was a spirit of the utmost self-denial and self-sacrifice upon the part of the instructors.

This theory, of course, is neither original nor untried. But as every industrial teacher knows, student labor is, on the average, about the most costly of all labor, and in the matter of profit cannot often be reckoned on the average labor basis. This is one of the facts that has seemingly proved the incapacity of the industrial school to make its expenses.

The other chief factor of this incapacity is that the system of literary education so occupies the time of the student that he is unable to devote enough hours to the earning of his expenses. And so long as he is possessed with the common idea that he must not be expected to pay his way while getting his education, he will not strive very hard to do it. If, however, the student can be inspired with the belief that normal life involves the getting of an education while supporting oneself, if the curriculum can be so adjusted as to give proportionate time and thought to mental, physical, and spiritual matters, and if the student's energies can be so controlled and directed as to make his labor profitable, then by careful management the student and the school (given its equipment) can be self-supporting.

Such a school, obviously, must depart from some cherished ideals of the popular school. It must lay emphasis upon neglected phases of education. It must exchange a scholarly leisure for an intense activity of body as well as mind. Such a school requires the services of self-sacrificing teachers and students. Over all, it requires for its sustenance an incentive so deep and all-embracing that it shuts out all other motives and allurements. Such an incentive is the love of Christ, intensified by the knowledge of his soon coming in power and glory to close the age-long controversy with sin and Satan. To the heralding of that coming are these workers pledged. Not to that alone, but to the sounding of the last notes of the gospel of free salvation through Christ. And not to that alone, but to the revelation of Jesus Christ in his servants today, through ministry to the sick, the needy, the ignorant, and the sorrow-bowed. For the further development of this work was the Madison School established.

Its plan of government is framed to that end. Students and teachers are placed upon the common basis of Christian fellowship. The laws of the school are made and executed by the whole school, in session known as the Union Body. This Union Body relieves the faculty of much of the routine of government. The school family is subject to self-imposed laws, and by a system of checks and reports each member is held to rectitude, first by his own will, and second by pressure of the Union Body. This discipline covers every act of the school life: study, work, physical habits, social life, religious duties, missionary effort, and all the ways in which the individual life is related to the community.

But the Union Body has a far wider field than discipline. Through its committees, it controls all departments of labor, plans for their operation, improvement, and extension, subject only in matters involving expenditure to the executive board.

The daily program is full to the limit, but simple in its operation, rendered so by the adjustment made between study and labor. Labor is dignified by being put on a scientific basis and by being conducted by teachers of mental and spiritual culture. That man was created to work and that work is good for man is more than a slogan in the school; it is an atmosphere that pervades all departments.

In order to maintain this atmosphere it has been necessary to diverge from the program of those schools which give their greatest attention to literary attainments. Here each student carries one major study, spending three hours daily in class work and being allowed an equal time for preparation. During one term the student covers the work for which the entire school year is required when three or more studies are taken at one time. He thus completes his studies in succession instead of in combination.

The following are some of the advantages of this system which have been noted, not only by instructors in the institution but by others of experience in school work who have made a comparative study of the results. The plan enables a teacher to carry one class during one-half of the day and to spend the other half-day in an industrial department. It gives him opportunity to develop the subject in hand, to use the library and the laboratory, to do experimental work, and to correlate with the major subject those fundamental branches so often neglected.

On the part of the student the plan develops concentration of thought, it encourages him to delve beneath the surface and to do original research work, and to pursue to completion one subject before taking another. This advantage is appreciated by the man or woman who can spend but a limited time in school. The student compacts his recitation work into a period of three hours unhampered by the conflicting requirements of his fellows' programs, and the remainder of his day he is free to divide between manual work and study. He obtains both training and practise in his manual subjects, to which he is free to devote five hours a day. His work with the industries is made educational, and for it he receives both credit and remuneration. Thus the business of getting a living is taken from its usual subordinate place in the school and from its usual superior place in ordinary life to occupy its proper place of coordination with intellectual and spiritual activities.

For the institution this program has its advantages also. For while the forenoon is devoted to manual labor by one group of students and to class work by another group, the groups reverse operations in the afternoon, and thus every manual department is provided with a full corps of student workers through the entire day. At the same time the intellectual work is not slighted. This plan makes it possible to keep the equipment of all the departments busy during the working days, and herein lies one reason for the financial success of the industrial departments. The student receives pay for his work at ten cents an hour. His expenses are reduced to the lowest point made possible by large purchases and the production of most of the necessaries of life on the school farm; and the average student is enabled by about six hours' labor a day to meet his school expenses. The student actually produces to the extent of his credit; the school does not merely give him credit and then seek outside aid to cover that credit.

This system of course requires value-producing industries. The various departments of the farm give real productive work. For cash with which to purchase outside supplies, the garden, the dairy, the live stock, and the poultry have been in turn or together depended upon. The later establishment of the Rural Sanitarium (which is discussed in another chapter) has developed an internal market for the farm products, and a source of income which has surpassed most of the others.

Thus the Madison School, by simple living, careful planning, and a rational adjustment of the relations of the mental and the manual work, has for a decade continued to demonstrate the possibility of conducting a school where students earn most of their school expenses, such as board and lodging, and thus learn how to make their after-life a combination of work, study, and service.

XII

LEARNING TO TEACH

THE school at Madison is a normal school in every sense of the term. No part of its life is left unmarked as a factor in the production of teachers. Madison's aim is the training not of mere teachers of abstract sciences, but of teachers of the art of living. The Christian teacher should have a good grasp of scholastic branches; but more than this, he must have ability in the practical things of life, a deep consecration to the highest ideals, and a clear vision of the end toward which he is aiming.

In his daily life he must be systematic, orderly, frugal, industrious, thorough, keen to see, and quick to act. If he misses these qualities in his practise, all his theorizing will go for little. In administrative affairs he must have good judgment developed from experience, broad vision, quick and accurate decision, and energy. Over all things else, he must obtain a sense of the value of lives, of minds, of souls, so that he shall not mistake material advantage for real success, nor displace matters of eternal weight with the light things of time.

At this school the effort is made to give the student, not merely a preparation for life, but an experience in life itself. If by experience in school he learns how to make his living, how to handle difficulties of home

On Madison Campus.
"The Madison School was born under conditions approximating those of pioneer days." Page 153.

and farm and school and church, how to impart his knowledge to others, and how to combine in proper proportion all the elements of life — work, study, teaching, recreation — if he learns all this by experience, he has not merely subscribed to a doctrine and been labeled with a degree; he has had stamped upon him a character, wrought within him a course of life.

The student at Madison works. There is work in the schoolroom, work in the field, work in administration. The students who come there are expected to be of sufficient maturity, and to be able to find diversion and recreation in the varied activities of earnest life. The sports of athletics find no place in the school. The usual rivalry of school life is marked by its absence. No college yells rend the air, no class colors flaunt their silly pride, no strife of teams and clubs and classes distract the life. "Life is real, life is earnest," is the working principle.

But cheer! Good cheer lives in Madison. Everybody is too hopeful to be discontented, too busy to be unhappy. Social life in the school is practically a family life. The students become thoroughly acquainted as they work side by side in the field, nurse at the same bedside, study from the same text, plan together for the conduct of their common interests.

The evening chapel is the pulse-beat of the school. On some evenings teachers lead in studies of principles and purposes for which the school stands. Other evenings are in charge of the students, in the study of current history, the reporting and planning of an active missionary propaganda, and the rendering of programs literary and musical, in which their life interests receive characteristic expression. One evening each week is "Union Meeting," the administrative and legislative session of the school.

Once or twice a year a school outing is planned, usually to one of the hill schools which have been opened by former students. The annual convention of self-supporting workers brings together a company that resembles the old family reunions of a New England Thanksgiving, and in this the school students are as younger members of the family. It is one of the busy holidays that typify the spirit of the work.

The literary side of the school is vigorously conducted. Class work is carried on during practically the entire year. There are four terms of nine weeks each. Between each of these comes a short course of three weeks. These "short courses" are little marvels of concentration. For the most part they are devoted to the consideration of industrial subjects. Carpentry, blacksmithing, cobbling, sewing, box furniture-making, cabinet-making, cooking, and the giving of simple treatments are taught. On account of the nature of the work the student can profitably and without undue fatigue devote the greater part of the day to the one line which he has selected. The results achieved in an educational way have been far beyond anything which the management had dared to hope. It has been demonstrated that by consolidating his time and concentrating his energy on a single branch, the student is able in a remarkably short period of time to attain a practical working knowledge and a creditable degree of efficiency in his subject.

The main departments of the school are the normal and the medical. In either of these are included the industrial studies, which are an essential part of the student's equipment.

A close relation is kept between all the studies and practical life. Madison is fitting the majority of its students to be Christian teachers and health workers in rural communities; its natural science classes all have an agricultural and medical bias, with appropriate textbooks. It is making of its students educational reformers; therefore not only its pedagogical subjects but all of its history and Bible classes are aimed at the study of education's history and philosophy. It is training its students to be ministers to the world's needs; and it maintains in every study and every practise — Bible and physiology, diet and dress — a singleness and intensity of purpose toward that one object. At the close of each short course an exhibit of the work done by each class is displayed in the chapel and the class-rooms. The entire school and frequently a number of visitors come together to see the work which has been accomplished and to hear the students tell their experiences. In brief talks the members of the carpentry class tell of the things they have learned and done; those who have enjoyed the class in simple treatments for the sick, demonstrate a nurse's duties and a patient's patience; those from the bakery class reveal the secrets of their gastronomic successes; and the dressmakers display the simple but neat and tasty garments of their own making.

Two years of work in nursing and health principles are given. A nurses' training class has been a chief feature of the school curriculum from early days. Since the building of the sanitarium in 1907, the medical work of Madison has played a most important part in the institution. It is not the design of this course to prepare the student to stand State Board examinations for nurses' registration. The work is given rather with the desire of fitting those who take it to be teachers of youth in the things pertaining to the care of their own bodies. This line of study and practise combined with the normal courses given in the school equips the student to become a community teacher to a much fuller degree than ordinarily. The idea is inculcated that a rural teacher should be a minister to sick bodies as well as a teacher of mental subjects, that he should be able to instruct those amongst whom he labors in the things which pertain to their material comfort, safety, and welfare.

To those who desire a more thorough training in these lines, a course of another year's study is offered. Personal hygiene and the science of preventive medicine are the strong features of this year's work, together with a thorough knowledge of simple remedies for home use.

If greater stress is laid upon any part of the curriculum, it is upon those things which relate to the daily conduct of life. Finance is made a practical study. Some students pay their expenses partly in cash; none are allowed to do so wholly. The majority earn their entire way by labor. A cash deposit is required upon entrance, both as a safeguard to the school and as an indication of the student's ability to provide for himself. This deposit, or any part remaining above the student's account, is returned to him at the close of his school life.

In planning the student's industrial training, the management have had regard to his future needs. No student is kept continually at one line of work. A young man will spend a while in the general farm department. His ability to handle horses, to care properly for the tools and machinery, is carefully noted by the one in charge; his failures and errors are corrected, and a record is kept of his progress and efficiency. Later this student may be transferred to the dairy or the garden department, where similar methods of training are pursued. Thus in a practical home-spun fashion young men are trained how to do well some of the common things of life.

A shop for the teaching of the rudiments of wood and iron work has been provided. Its equipment is far from being elaborate — the theory being that the interests of the future rural community worker will be best subserved by training him to do his work with tools and appliances of the sort which he is likely to possess and be obliged to use in his own life work. It is held that there is danger of educating men and women in the uses of equipment which they can never afford to own. If this is done the seeds of future discontent and dislike for the humble station in life to which most men and women are called will be engendered and a foundation will be laid for mental, material, and moral failure.

The industries for women embrace nursing, domestic work in all its ordinary branches, and gardening. The young women are instructed in the preparation of simple yet healthful food. The work of the school and sanitarium kitchens is performed by them under the direction of instructors. They are taught how to make out a bill of fare which will give a balanced ration. An attempt is made to apply the lessons of the physiology class to the every-day business of preparing meals for a hungry company of hard-working people. Food values are carefully studied, the various degrees of digestibility of different articles are taken into account. The necessity for due proportions of proteids, carbohydrates and fats are considered in the making up of the daily menu. The caring for dairy products and butter making is also taught and some have become quite proficient in this work.

Every student takes care of his own room. The general work of caring for the sanitarium, for the public buildings, and the laundering of individual and institutional linen, is done by the young women.

What the Madison student learns, he learns that he may teach. He gathers here, puts into practise here, the principles of system, order, industry, frugality; careful planning, perfect execution; breadth of view and decision of character; application of all sciences to practical life, and application of all one's own powers to the problems of life — self-support, study, teaching. The normal work — teaching to teach — goes through every study and every course. As the student learns the laws of language, for example, and has them enforced in class and out of class, the thought is impressed upon him that he must become perfect in order that he may teach others to be perfect. As he nails the studding to the plate, as he turns the furrow in the field, as he mixes the dough in the bakery, as he applies the fomentation in the bathroom, he is taught that these things must be learned perfectly, that they may have their perfect work in the lives of others. Learning to teach, and teaching for the purpose of salvation, this is the principle that animates every phase of the work at Madison.

XIII

THE OUT-SCHOOL MOVEMENT

A STATE senator was speaking at an educational convention: "When I was school superintendent of Sumner County," he said, "we had a district up on the rimlands where there had been no school for seven years. The last teacher we had there was a young lady, but though she drew her salary all right, she quit, and never would go back. She had so much trouble that she thought the best thing for her to do was to get married.

"Well, four years ago a gentleman from that section came down and told me there was a man up there who had actually built a schoolhouse and paid for it himself, and was holding school! We county supervisors were used to sitting on the treasury-lid, and didn't know how any schoolhouse could go up or any school start without our knowing it first. So this report excited my curiosity right away. I wanted to see that man. So I opened communication, and made an appointment with him, and that was my first acquaintance with Professor Alden and his fellow-workers. They are pure gold, twenty-four-carat. I know, and our people know, what they can do and what they are doing. They are in the forefront of the uplift of the rural school. They are helping to develop a love for the country and to bring a solution of its problems that will turn the tide back from the city. If all the schools you people have are like the three in Sumner County, we want more of them. I am glad we have the cooperation of such schools as Goodlettsville and Fountain Head."

The schools thus mentioned are two of the out-schools — the first two — established by workers from Madison. About a year and a half after the founding of the Madison School, two of the charter members, C. F. Alden and B. N. Mulford, were delegated to begin the out-school work. The Madison School itself, in the midst of a prosperous community, was not in direct touch with the most needy classes. It enlisted and trained for the service young men and women from both North and South, who, however, must gain their practical experience through the establishment of homes and small schools in more backward rural districts.

The "Nashville Basin" is a depression in the middle of the State, with a rich calcareous soil, verdant with blue-grass pastures and teeming with bountiful crops. Nearly surrounding it are "the rimlands," a part of the Cumberland piedmont. From the basin below, the land rises steeply for five hundred feet to the rocky, sandy edge of the upland. For ten or fifteen miles back the land is comparatively poor, and in consequence these "rimland" communities have received less development than more favored sections. In conditions both physical and social their people are closely akin to the mountaineers of the Cumberland Plateau.

Fifteen miles from Madison and seven miles from the railroad at Goodlettsville is the community mentioned at the beginning of the chapter. Here in February, 1906, Alden, Mulford, and Charley Ashton went to look for a place.

There was a seven-hundred-acre piece of woods for sale, and out of this they bargained for two hundred and fifty acres, at $2,000, borrowing $700 to make the first payment. The last of February they came up to the place, repaired the chicken house behind the main log cabin for a home, and began clearing land and splitting rails for fencing. There was only a seven-acre plot of ground already in cultivation; and that, a white pipe-clayey land, had been for ninety years devoted to tobacco, until its hard, baked surface looked discouraging.

They had no horse, but carried their provisions on their backs seven miles up the mountain from Goodlettsville. They could bring one sack of cornmeal every trip; and that, with water from their spring, made their corn pone. For the rest, they had been given some prunes, and on prunes and corn bread they lived for some weeks.

But plowing time came. They borrowed a buckskin mule, a turning plow, and a bull-tongue plow, and went after their tobacco field. They went once around with the turning plow, then unhitched, put the mule to the bull-tongue, and made it a subsoiler in the furrow; then they resumed the turning plow, and repeated the process. Thus they prepared their garden, in which that year the tomatoes were the wonder of the land.

In April, Mrs. Ashton, who had now become interested in the work, and had furnished money for it, came with her two other sons, Robert and Ralph, both city young men, nurse and chauffeur, who had never felled a tree nor worked on a farm. But in a short time they had become woodsmen, plowmen, orchardists, goatherders, and bee-keepers.

In June Mr. Alden brought his wife to the place. With gunnysacking, newspapers, and whitewash, they made over the interior of the main log house, until it appeared a mansion to many of their neighbors. In July Mr. John Myers, who had been interested by Mr. Mulford, came from Kansas, with his two mule teams, and a carload of hay, corn, farming implements, and household goods, giving the goods, his own time, and the use of his teams for one year to the new school. His arrival was to these new pilgrims like the coming of the new shiploads of pioneers to aid and hearten the

At Fountain Head School, Tennessee.
"With good cheer, they are looking forward to the building of a new barn and silo." Pages 185 and 173.

Mayflower men who first landed on the rocky, wooded shores of New England. They thanked God and took courage.

Their first source of income was from their timber, in which almost all their land lay. They cut that next winter fifteen hundred feet of timber, had it milled, and hauled it twenty miles to Nashville to sell. They cut the best of their white oak into spoke timber, and were able to boast, for the fifteen days they were at it, the making of six dollars a day. Railway ties brought fifty cents apiece. Thus, living simply and frugally, and working hard, they made their living that first year, and provided lumber for a new story-and-a-half house.

Alden and Mulford went to the community as home-seekers, saying nothing about the possible establishment of a school. They worked with their hands and struggled for a living like the rest of men; and though Alden was a university man, he "was among them as one that labored." But when his wife came, the community quickly discovered that she was a teacher, because she was teaching her young adopted brother. Whereupon they came and asked, "Why can't you teach us a school?" As this was the purpose for which the company had come, they acceded to the request, and in the fall Mrs. Alden began the school, a school which steadily grew until it included seventy-five or eighty children, and required three teachers.

All the workers, whether in the schoolroom or out, are teachers. Thus Mrs. Ashton, who had run a bakery in Pittsburg, soon after her arrival built an out-door oven of rock and lime dust scraped from the roadbed, and in this oven she baked such fine big brown loaves of light bread as were the wonder and delight of housewives for miles about. No one in that community could make light bread, and in a short time Mrs. Ashton was holding a free class in breadmaking, which was attended by dozens; and thereafter corn pone and soda biscuits were not the only breads in the homes thereabouts.

There were calls also for help in accident and disease, and in all the various ways in which neighbors may be of help to neighbors. Charley Ashton became the community blacksmith, and every member of the school family found his services in requisition at one or another duty. And as free as were the neighborly offices, so free was instruction in books or in manual art, to children and grown people alike. The school became, as it was designed, a public institution as free as the tax-fed government schools, but made so through the hard, self-sacrificing labors of the promoters.

This was by no means an easy task, and while the confidence and gratitude of the community was gradually being won, there was more than one episode that threatened disaster to the little company in their unselfish mission. The people are open-hearted, frank, and free, but they are too much isolated from the centers of jurisdiction to have forgotten the prime law that —

"He may take who has the might,
And he may keep who can."

A short time after the establishment of the school, they signalized their power by abolishing a toll-gate which shut them from town, and was often employed in making vexatious and injurious delays, while the toll road was unworked and always in bad condition. Exasperated finally by the refusal of the keeper to let a boy pass who was riding for the doctor, the men armed, and at night, poking their rifles into the face of the sleeping man, disarmed him and set him off for Nashville. Three days later, the owner of the road came back with an armed guard, swearing he would keep his gate against the devil himself. But after a pitched battle, he was glad for the speed of his blooded horse, for he was chased by the angry victors to the very suburbs of the city.

The bullet-marked tollhouse still stands by the roadside, but there is no gate.

Personal freedom, and as little statute law as possible, was the desire and experience of the rimlanders. For one thing, while the county had a stock law, the land in that community was used as free range, and the one who wanted his crops protected must fence against cattle and hogs. To do so unneighborly a thing as to invoke the no-fence law, would be to make undying enemies, as more than one feud testifies.

On the seven-hundred-acre tract out of which Alden bought, one man pastured seventy-five head of swine. Alden had too little fence to protect all his fields, and what he had was rail fence. In his clearing by his new house, the second year, he was raising a good garden, which the hogs were not slow to find out. Those hogs ate his cabbage, rooted out and crunched his potatoes, and devoured his corn and stover. The two boys in the family had their heels twinkling to keep them out, and the dog barked till he was too hoarse to bark any more. Alden was cutting hay on shares away from home, to save an impossible bill for feed the next winter, and he would come home too tired to stand up, only to hear that those hogs had eaten up all his early potatoes. Says he, "I sat down over there in the bushes and pondered what I should do. The potatoes were our main dependence, as they are now, and we were having a hard time to live. I had appealed to the man to keep up his hogs, but he would not; he complained that the country was being spoiled — it was no more a country for a poor man when he could not let his stock run! I would not use the law; it was not wise to do so; and it almost seemed I should have to leave." But Alden is a direct descendant of that John and Priscilla Alden in the Pilgrim company who —"Brave hearts and true! not one went back in the Mayflower." They held on, endured their losses, and now, when the stock laws are observed, they have all but forgotten the episode of the hogs and the early potatoes.

Mr. Mulford remained with the Oak Grove Garden School for over a year, when, it appearing that there was sufficient help to spare him, he married, and with his brother-in-law, Forrest West, set out in search of another needy community. Such a place they found some twenty miles to the east.

In their search they had driven up into the hills from Gallatin, examining a number of places, but nowhere finding what appealed to them. At a little station the storekeeper from whom they bought their lunch of crackers and peaches curiously inquired if they were looking for land. "Yes," they told him, whereupon he directed them to the westward, to a certain farm. They turned in that direction, and after driving a mile or so they came upon a man with his three boys chopping wood. They asked him where his children went to school. Nowhere, he said; never had gone. Could they read? No; none of his six children could read, nor could he and his wife. They drove on, and Mulford said to his companion, "Forrest, we have struck the place. There's a farm for us somewhere in here!"

And they found it; not the farm to which they had been directed, but another of seventy-six acres, on top of a bare clay hill which had been worked and overworked until the neighbors facetiously declared that no one could raise even an umbrella on it. This "school on the hill" has since become famed among the rural-school people for the lessons of faith and courage and persistence its members have written for others to see, and for the leadership it has taken in the development of plans and methods for the out-schools. Some of its experiences are detailed in later chapters.

Mrs. West, the mother and mother-in-law of these two men, later joined the company with her three daughters. Today, embowered by orchards, vineyards, and the old oak grove, and almost overshadowed by the big red barn and silo, three homes stand guarding the neat schoolhouse and the grounds of the Fountain Head School. The building of a small hydropathic home is the latest accomplishment.

The history of these schools is typical of the experience of all those who have entered the out-school work. At the annual convention held at Madison in 1915, thirty-nine groups of self-supporting workers were reported, all but five of which were established by Madison students or those influenced to this work by the Madison people. Thirty of these groups were conducting schools, and all of them engage in some form of Christian work for their neighborhoods. The greater part of these groups are in Tennessee, Alabama, and North Carolina, and in the mountains or piedmont.

These workers are not on salary, except in the case of one school which receives county funds. They have their own living to make from their farms and other industries. Some have received help from relatives or friends, and a few by general solicitation, but money so raised has almost invariably been intended for and devoted to the providing of buildings or equipment, not for living expenses. And with very few exceptions the teachers receive no money tuition from their pupils; for they hold that they are giving the gospel in a concrete way, and that it should be free as preaching. They are not averse to receiving gifts for their support, but they hold that if such gifts are not forthcoming, their commission to teach the gospel leaves them no excuse for neglecting this work. They must do it by some means — by hard work, simple living, self-sacrifice; and where these do not suffice, by simple trust in Elijah's God.

The record they have made, of establishing and maintaining, with industrial and social features, thirty-three schools, with an average school term of eight months a year, and with an approximate enrolment of one thousand pupils, at no cost to the state and none to the church except through a few individual gifts — such a record, it will be admitted, deserves no empty applause merely, but active encouragement. And it gives point to these commendatory words from Mrs. E. G. White:

"The school at Madison not only educates in a knowledge of the Scriptures, but it gives a practical training that fits the student to go forth as a self-supporting missionary to the field to which he is called. In his student days he is taught how to build simply and substantially, how to cultivate the land, and care for the stock. To this is added the knowledge of being able to treat the sick and care for the injured. This training for medical missionary work is one of the grandest objects for which any school can be established. There are many suffering from disease and injury, who, when relieved of pain, will be prepared to listen to the truth. Our Saviour was a mighty healer. In his name there may be many miracles wrought in the South and in other fields through the instrumentality of the trained medical missionary. . . .

"It would have been pleasing to God if, while the Madison School has been doing its work, other such schools had been established in different parts of the Southern field. No soul should be left in darkness if by any possible means he can be enlightened. There is plenty of land lying waste in the South that might have been improved as the land about the Madison School has been improved. . . . The time is soon coming when God's people, because of persecution, will be scattered in many countries. Those who have received an all-round education will have the advantage wherever they are. The Lord reveals divine wisdom in thus leading his people to the training of all their faculties and capabilities for the work of disseminating truth.

"Every possible means should be devised to establish schools on the Madison order in various parts of the South; and those who lend their means and their influence to help this work, are aiding the cause of God."

Pioneering

FOREWORD

In the following sections the identity of persons and places is usually disguised, a course born of the modesty of some of the individuals and communities concerned. The incidents related are true in every particular, and have been selected with the purpose of giving some glimpse into the work-a-day programs of the self-supporting rural mission workers.

"The young man of the mountain, when once educated, is so confident of himself, and so positive of opinion, that he is admirably adapted to be a leader." SAMUEL T. WILSON.

XIV

ON AN OLD FRONTIER

IN THE days of Washington, the frontier of America was the Appalachian Mountains. There the "Long Knives" hunted and trapped, and there the early settlers hewed out their fields from the forest, built their log cabins with the ax alone, and found the necessaries of life within the bounds of their little world. Today, while the border has swept on across the great river and the wide plains, beyond the crest of the Rockies and to the very edge of the western ocean, much of the Alleghanies and the Cumberlands remain in their conditions almost as truly frontier as they were two hundred years ago. And he who would go to minister to the needs of the people there, as teacher, medical missionary, or social helper, may well discover that he is to reproduce the hardy life his great-grandfather lived. Especially is this true to the self-supporting and light-purse worker who makes his post in the far interior.

Let us visit one of these stations far back in the mountains of North Carolina. We alight from the train at a little village huddled in one long street between the gripping hands of the hills, with our journey as yet, in point of time, only half completed. A week before we have sent a letter on its circuitous way through Tennessee and Georgia, asking our friends to meet us with a conveyance. This conveyance proves to consist of two saddled mules, whose first back-woodsy exploit is to take fright at an oncoming freight train and run away with us half through the village.

With suit-cases strapped to the sides of our guide's mule, we take our way out of the town, past a mill site, and across the tumbling Tuckasegee, and set our faces toward the mountains — one of the highest ranges of the Appalachians — which bar our way to the school domain. We are to "hit the trail," our guide informs us, about six miles from town. He might have brought us through by wagon, only that it takes twice as long each way and is much more uncomfortable. The wagon road winds around and in and out over the mountains for twenty miles, with many wash-outs and much steep grade. The trail shortens the distance to twelve miles, but at the cost of taking some of it almost straight up and down. From the county road, at a corner by a country store, we strike into a private road, which gives way in time to a faint wood road, and that in turn to the trail through the Gap.

If you think of a gap as a gateway, you will be greatly mistaken. A gap is merely an aspiring mountain that has failed to make good. It is lowly only in comparison with its towering companions-at-arms. It gives you all the thrills of mountain climbing, all the pulls and wrenches, the puffings and perspirings, all the illusions of early conquest and disappointments of unguessed heights. The trail that lures you on your hazardous way takes you over stony stretches and through oozy wallows where the springs seep out, then upward past deserted tanbark camps into a tangle of fallen logs and briery glades, and last, upon a stairless ascent that makes you certain you are on the roof of the world. Either, like the mountaineer, you dismount and pull your mule up by the reins, or you lie upright along his back and pity him as, with heavings and sobs and grunts, he makes his last successful scramble to the top of the Gap.

And there, under the great chestnut trees, we pause for a breathing spell before attempting the equally terrific descent. In two directions at least, the Gap gives as good a view as the peak. We trace, winding and diving and reappearing, the way we have come, back to the railroad, and beyond, away, away, over seas of ridges and knobs, to the sky-line of the distant Smokies.

But we turn with greater interest to the other side of the Gap; for there, shut in by a great winding circle of high mountains, is the kingdom whose heart, to us, is the little mountain school. Down a certain narrow valley — little and shallow it looks from this height, but sufficiently deep when viewed from within itself — we trace the road that leads to the school, hidden beyond some wooded hills. And down we plunge to the headsprings of the creek that leads us on our way through Eden Valley.

Edenic is this valley, perhaps, in some respects: in its isolation, the primitiveness of its life, and the dainty charm of its springtime, from the early dawn of trailing arbutus to the sunshine of rhododendron and wild rose. But now!— a drizzling rain that set in at the top of the Gap has swathed us in folds of moisture and melancholy, and any memories of Eden that suggest themselves have reference to that last sad day when its gates were shut upon a hapless pair.

Greater, then, the welcome when we draw rein before the home of our friends, and, drenched and cold, stiffly lower ourselves from the saddles. Bareheaded, radiant, Mr. Arthur stands out at the roadside to greet us, and Mis' Margaret's rosy face is framed in the doorway. Behind is a roaring fire in the rough stone fireplace, and the once dark, low room is transformed with paint and pictures to match the glow of love that has come here into the mountains.

It is a rough little shack of a one-room house that the teachers have adopted, but with a triple division and the addition of a two-room lean-to, it serves with distinction not only for their home but for the housing also of three or four students from a distance. Some there are who tramp daily six to eight miles, through sunshine or rain, to and from the school, but others there are, even from neighboring counties, who are begging for a chance to come and live at the school. The triple division of the one-room cabin is a partial answer to the plea.

Two of these students are to arrive this evening, and they come an hour later, trudging through the mud behind their "pappy" with his ox-sled that holds their single box of necessaries and valuables. Shy to the verge of terror they are, especially at having to meet two "furriners" like ourselves; but their father, nothing daunted, preserves an immobile face behind his bushy whiskers, and proves himself in conversation a man of information concerning those things wherein he should be informed.

But soaked through they are, they all make light of this tussle with the elements: "Hain't nothin' to flurry over. We-all's used to gettin' damp here in the mountains." Nevertheless, Mis' Margaret has the girls off for a change to dry clothing — mostly borrowed — before we sit down to the smoking hot meal that has postponed itself several hours for this occasion.

And then comes evening worship and a time of singing around the piano. That piano is the wonder of the valley, and well it deserves its fame, for it came the twenty miles of rough roads over the mountains, with their gullies and ruts and rocks and dips and tippings. It was three weeks on the way, and in expenditure of time and energy and muscle and nerve cost nearly as much for its transportation as its original value. But it makes liquid sunshine now when days are dark, not only for the teacher who insisted on its coming, but for the musical soul of many a boy and girl who aspires to its mastery.

The schoolhouse, up on the hill, asserts its superiority

over the home both in size and finish. It stands out in its pride and paint to challenge the whole valley below, and on such a bright morning as followed our rain the whole valley responds. They come, these children, from up and down the bottoms, and from out the hidden, narrow coves, from off the hill and mountain sides, until there is a muster of mountain forces that remind you of the swift gatherings on Nolichucky and Watauga for the foray against Oconostota or the thrust at Ferguson.

It is a muster, indeed, of forces to threaten a foe; but not that foe. The British long ago ceased to be enemies. The last remnant of the Cherokee nation this side of the Mississippi now live secure upon their reservation but a few miles to the west. Here in the ancient land of the Erati the muster is not for bloody combat, but for warfare against a more insidious and more dreadful foe, ignorance. And is there any one who, beholding these lads and lassies gathered here, in checked shirt and butternut jeans and coarse brogans, in poke bonnet and blue and pink prints, who would deny them as brave spirits, as lofty aims, as deep and willing sacrifice in the cause they have espoused, as any of their fathers in the times of war? They fight a daily battle against poverty and narrowness and a sodden inertia that is more than prejudice; they fight this battle with a cheer and determination that is worthy of its higher use. With their forefathers they share the log home, the hollowed spring, the ox-team, the corn pone and side-meat. They share with them almost equally the homespun and the lack of books, the skill with loom and rifle and ax, and the drab monotony of an isolated life. And when they muster here at the rendezvous of the schoolhouse, there is promise in their courage for a deliverance, not of necessity from all their primitive physical conditions — often of more value than ill — but from the bondage of an ill-instructed and depressing life. Their mud-soaked shoes, for all the service of the door mat, may trace their progress across the white floor of the schoolroom, but their eyes are lifted to the inspiration of the walls, bright with print and map and lithograph and sloyd design, bright, too, with the undying brilliance of the mottoes shining there: "I will lift up mine eyes unto the hills, from whence cometh my help," and "How beautiful upon the mountains are the feet of him that bringeth good tidings, that publisheth peace." And their resolve can be read in their faces, to get that help, to be that messenger.

Out upon the grounds in the afternoon we see another phase of their training. The older boys have gone to the building of the barn and the pruning of the grapes; some of the girls are in the sewing class. But up here in the grove the younger boys are at work with a teacher clearing underbrush. Axes and mattocks are getting out the dead logs, the saplings, and the bushes. But the chief center of attraction is a yearling the boys have been given to break in. We who know nothing about the breaking in of "cattle" must exhibit an innocent faith that these sons of ox-teamsters are doing the proper thing. At any rate, they are going at it with a zest that betokens enjoyment. The stubborn little steer is geed and hawed and whoaed, with pushes and pulls that are meant to teach him these English words; and though he takes it into his little bull head often to cut counter to directions, he and they succeed in time in getting a goodly pile of poles and stumps and brush together for the burning. The boys declare him "breaking fine." Perhaps he will never come to yoke service upon the school farm; for he is an anachronism alongside the mule teams, but he may soon be under the eye of one of these boys or their brothers, drawing sawlogs down to the mill below. He is not out of date in the valley.

Of commerce there is little. An easier route there is to the outside world, through a railroad that runs down into Georgia, but its high rates little encourage exchange, and only the commoner necessities are much indulged in at the country stores. The self-sufficient resourcefulness of the pioneer yet lingers here, from wooden pegs and sunbonnets to grist mills and primitive forges. The school and its teachers must perforce partake of much of the same conditions. It is not their purpose to revamp this society into an imitation of the "foreign" brand. There are, of course, such influences at work, through men who go out and come in; but to the Christian teacher the simplicity, the hospitality, the frugality, even the slower movement of the community life, all these are a precious heritage in this day of pretension, waste, and rush. The learning for mind and hand which they bring is to make helpers, not imitators. They curtail, then, their needs and bind about their wants and wishes, supplying themselves, so far as possible, from the products of the farm, and emulating their people in small expenditures. One of the teachers said that a friend sent her a dollar eight months before, which has been her sole funds for that time, and which still remains intact. In sharing of burdens, alliance of interests, seeing and striving for ideals, they make themselves, not the beckoners, but the leaders, of their people.

*   *   *   *

Not so different in externals, and yet with its own characteristics, is the elevated table-land in Alabama on which some of our schools are established. Its precipitous sides make it a very isolated region. Some of those who live on its rolling top have never been off the mountain. The soil is in some places good, and in others exceedingly poor. The most of the surface is wooded, but the little farms in the several settlements or away out in the clearings have all the characteristics of the properties of our great-grandfathers in this new West. Ox-teams and "jinnys" far outnumber the horses and mules as work-stock.

The second of our schools to be established on this mountain is the one we now will visit. We find ourselves near a famous locality in the valley whence we start to climb. Here along the Tennessee dwelt the Chickamaugas in the days of old, and not a mile from where our feet stand upon the station platform is their most noted stronghold, Nickojack Cave. Into this cave the Indians used to retreat when hard pressed, carrying with them as much as possible of their goods and plunder. As it winds and twists under the mountain to an unknown distance, no pursuing party was ever able to dislodge the fugitive redman once he had made his escape into the cave.

Up the mountainside for two miles to the top, and then on for an equal distance, we make our way to the school and farm of Brother Walter and his wife, Sister Dora. Now you are introduced, in this farm of Brother Walter's, to a reason for the "jinnys." Its land was simply too poor to support a team of horses or mules, and so he bought for eighty-five dollars a team of unusually big "jinnys," with double harness. Mr. Walter's land, a thin, sandy soil, would grow, as he discovered, no more than five bushels of corn per acre. A horse would eat that in half as many months, whether working or idle, but a "jinny" will do with an ear at a feeding, and when not working will subsist quite luxuriously upon the leaves and the scanty grass in the forest range. With his "jinny" team Mr. Walter hauled railway ties, four or five at a load, down the mountain to the railroad. Two loads a day brought him one dollar, and the "jinnys" would not take more than ten cents of that. With his "jinnys," too, he plowed his land, and hauled forest leaves for fertilizer.

Mr. Walter has one hundred sixty acres, twenty-seven of which once were cleared, but having grown up in brush have to be cleared over again. A stiff yellow clay underlies his sandy top soil of two or three inches' depth. Deep plowing the first year would mean no crop, and he had only begun the process of plowing deeper, inch by inch, turning under humus in the form of leaves, for of course he had almost no stable manure, his two cows having also to browse and graze in the forest.

At the moment we come upon them, Mis' Dora and her mother are picking over strawberries for dinner.

"What beautiful wild berries you find here!" is our exclamation.

"Wild!" is the indignant response, "those are our finest garden product." And indeed we find, though they have the best of plant stock, and though they have fertilized with pine needles, the product is little more than equal to the wild berries. And the wild blackberries which are everywhere so abundant can surpass all their garden might attempt. More than that, there are escaped apple trees in abandoned clearings and in the midst of the forest, that furnish no inconsiderable crop, as we learn later at a convention, when Mis' Dora reports that her husband has remained at home to gather such a harvest.

More cheerful, happy, earnest workers could not be found in palaces. Their palace is an ancient, ramshackle house whose leaky roof, though often patched, must in times of rain be supplemented by many pans upon the floor, to keep the soil beneath from being washed away. But they have built a new schoolhouse for the school, which, begun the first year, must be housed in a proper place; and there is a tiny cottage also for Mis' Dora's mother. With good cheer they are looking forward to the building of a new house for themselves next year, when Mr. Walter's father expects to move down from Iowa. And while no tuition is charged they are not unremembered nor wholly unrequited by the people to whom they are giving their lives. A mother brought them a present of her handiwork, a beautiful pattern quilt, and when they expressed their appreciation — "Well," said she, "we think a heap more of the education you are giving our children than you can think of the quilt."

These schools and their teachers are by no means exceptions in the matter of their poverty, self-denial, and courage. They are the rule, and incidents innumerable might be mentioned of workers living on insufficient food for months, of enduring cold in thin clothing and thin walls, of cheerfully facing privations, and anxiously scanning means for meeting obligations; and all this not for a short time only, but as an experience of years. And this they do, not to gain some great end for themselves, but that the poor, the ignorant, and the helpless shall have the blessings of education, health, and salvation.

XV

BEHIND THE BACK OF MAMMON

MAMMON, the god of riches, turns his back upon these self-supporting rural-school workers. If they were seeking his face, they would not enter this kind of work. They have cast their all of time, and strength, and money, at the feet of their Lord Jesus, to be used in carrying the truth and power of an applied gospel to those who sorely need it. Often their time seems insufficient for their many duties and burdens; sometimes their strength, physical and mental, is exhausted; and as for money — always their station is behind the back of Mammon. This is not a complaint, it is a rejoicing: "approving ourselves as the ministers of God . . . alway rejoicing; as poor, yet making many rich; as having nothing, and yet possessing all things." "Therefore I take pleasure in infirmities, in reproaches, in necessities, in persecutions, in distresses for Christ's sake: for when I am weak, then I am strong." This is the Christian's attitude; and the Christian who devotes his all to his Master's use is in the way of being a self-supporting worker, who is always a supporter of others. He finds, too, that the Lord who said, "Seek ye first the kingdom of God, . . . and all these things shall be added unto you," is a better provider than Mammon.

One night in the late nineties, a young man in the

mountains of North Carolina went out to think under the stars. For seven years he and his wife had devoted all their time, strength, and money to a work in the mountains. Now he stared up at the charred remains of a fire-swept building on the hill that had held his all. Their few thousands were gone; they were penniless. Within their temporary shelter lay dying the young woman who had seemed the most precious fruits of their labors in the mountains. In that hour of depression he could see no results of their sacrifice, and an overpowering impulse came upon him to leave the work of the mountains. But then there came to him the experience and the words of Job. His property had been swept away, his sons and daughters slain, his own body tortured with pain. Yet "in all this Job sinned not, nor charged God foolishly"; for he said, "The Lord gave, and the Lord hath taken away; blessed be the name of the Lord."

Not yet, reflected young Marshall, had he given his life nor even his health, and so long as these remained there could be no excuse for desertion. There he registered a vow that with the blessing of health, come what might, he would never desert his post.

Soon after, he had a vivid dream of a place which it seemed he had purchased, with an old log house, gnarled old apple trees, and a tangle of weeds and briers. As he looked off to the right, he saw a man coming through the ruinous place, whose glances seemed to disclose more plainly every unkempt spot. This man began directing him to prune the trees, to clear away the debris, and to lay out a lawn. And the impression came to him that this was to be his future place of work.

Within a few days, while he was pondering this dream, he was made trustee of certain moneys, which he loaned on good security for his wards, while he began carpentry work for a living. But soon one man to whom he had loaned money, came into difficulties, and proposed to turn in his farm for his debt and a further loan. Advised by his bondsmen, Marshall accepted the proposition, and so came into possession, in trust, of just such a farm as he had seen in his dream. Through later developments, this property became devoted to the school work in which Marshall was interested.

With his wife and his two aunts he moved into the log house, planning to make it, as soon as possible, more than a home for themselves. He had long had in mind a work for orphans and aged people, and though having no prospects for such a work, he now planned for it. To provide light farm work for old and young, he set out fruit and began on the old worn-out, sterile land to prepare garden ground.

Another man who had been connected with him, a physician, moved into a near-by log cabin, and joined him in Christian help work among their neighbors. It was a rough and lawless district, where more than one man held his own by right of pistol, and where "woods-colts," as children of unknown paternity were called, were nearly as numerous as the legitimate. There was no school in the community, and when fall came, the question occurred to these two men, "Shall we try to build us better houses now, or build a meeting-house and schoolhouse first?" They decided that the work of the Lord should come first. But they had no money with which to begin. However, said Marshall to Doctor Ed, "We have one thing; that is, a place to build: that nice little wooded knoll on the corner of my land."

Monday morning they went over to the spot with their axes. They knelt down and prayed that God would bless the enterprise they were about to begin. And then they fell to with their axes. Not a ray of light had they as to how they could build a schoolhouse, but at least they were providing the firewood to burn in it.

About ten o'clock a scheme struck Marshall's mind, and he said to his companion: "Doctor, there's a barn up in the woods half a mile away which I believe we can buy cheap." They shouldered their axes and went over to look at it, and they found it a 20 x 29 foot structure, framed up like a house, twelve feet high, and with a lean-to — at least five thousand feet of lumber in it.

That afternoon Marshall went to see the owner, who asked eighteen dollars for the barn. "Is that too much?" he said.

"No," replied the teacher, "it's a bargain at eighteen dollars; but as I'm getting donations, I'm going to ask you for a gift of three dollars. Let us have the barn for fifteen dollars."

"All right," said the man. And Marshall walked away with his bargain in his head and not a dollar in his pocket.

Mrs. Doctor Ed had fifteen dollars which her mother had just sent her for clothing and other needed articles. She gave this to buy the barn. By Tuesday night the barn lumber was all piled up on the school grounds, with every old nail carefully pulled out and saved up for rebuilding. A man in the neighborhood gave fifty dollars, and others gave their labor, while Marshall and the Doctor put in every cent they could get. So the little schoolhouse was built at a cost of one hundred twenty-five dollars, with a valuation twice that. A Sabbath school in Ohio raised twenty-two dollars to pay for the twenty-four seats, made in the shops of another school in the next county. A teacher was obtained, and thus the school began.

In 1914 it had an average attendance of fifty to sixty children, most of whom had previously had little or no school advantages; and a church of devoted men, women, and young people had been raised up to hold a light in that corner of the wilderness.

Two years after the building of the schoolhouse, Marshall felt more strongly impressed to build a home for old people, and he told the Lord that though he had all on his hands it seemed he could do, yet if a thousand dollars should be placed in his hands without his seeking it, he would build that home.

A month or two later, one of his uncles came South, and very soon asked his nephew if a thousand dollars would help him in any way.

"Yes," said Marshall, "that will answer the test I have made as to whether I should build a home for the aged."

Later his uncle added more, and a house of fifteen rooms was erected in which orphan children and a number of old people lived with Mr. Marshall's family. They were supported — food, clothing, and other necessaries — by the farm, on which they raised as money crops, fruit, peanuts, Irish potatoes, a little cotton, and dairy products. By various providences the institution accumulated a property worth five thousand dollars, and did a work incalculable in value. Sometimes the fare was meager, always the work pressed hard, often financial crises came to test the faith of the workers, but repeatedly the providence of God opened the way to success.

A young man who had been under the training of the Madison teachers in the North gave his life to the Southern work. He and his bride spent their honeymoon in driving from Michigan to Tennessee, with an old white horse his father gave them, and with a binder canvass for a tent.

They bought a place of one hundred twenty-five acres, three miles from the railroad, for twelve hundred dollars, partly on time, planning to make of it a stock farm. The larger part was old, worn land. There was an old log house on the place, so leaky that the flour barrel had to have one special corner, and so drafty that a dozen thicknesses of newspapers on the wall could not shut out the cold. At first, however, they had not the benefit of this house, but only of a 6 x 10 shed, for the previous owners stayed some weeks. When in the fall they did get into the log house, they felt it uninhabitable during the winter, and so put up a shack board house which was to serve until they could erect a better home, as they hoped, the following year. With his last hundred dollars young St. John bought another horse. Then came a series of misfortunes.

First one horse died, then the other. Then, while he was away, the shack home caught fire and burned with practically everything in it. He was left without any chance at all to succeed on the farm, but he called on no one for gifts. He gathered together a little lumber, and put up the shell of a new house, and into it they moved. Here he left his wife with a young girl, while he went to the city, fifteen miles away, to work all winter at carpentry; his young wife, a city-bred girl, stayed on the farm to look after the chickens and the cows, and to rescue the young lambs from the sleety weather in the early spring. Every other Sabbath St. John would try to be at home, and once his wife came to stay with him a few days in the city. With this respite, she pluckily held the fort through the winter, until her husband could come back with enough money to add a little more to the unfinished house, and to put up eighty rods of wire fence, and to buy another team on part payment.

Then he alternated days of plowing and sowing with weeks of work on houses and barns in the neighborhood, by which means he earned enough to keep alive, to pay up for his team, and to lay the foundations for a new barn.

Meanwhile these young people mingled with and helped their neighbors. They nursed the sick, taught in the Sunday schools, and scattered much devotional and health literature. They injected energy into the young people with singing and good literature and friendly visits and club work. While not in school work, since there is a good school within half a mile, they are an element of energy and cheer that is leavening the whole lump.

Though the majority of the schools have received little money to aid them, there is one form of help which

Shops, Eufola Agricultural and Mechanical Academy, North Carolina. "Preaching, not by tongue, but by hand." Page 198.

the most of them are glad to have the opportunity of sharing with their neighbors. And that is the barrels of second-hand clothing which some of their friends are so kind as to ship. There is probably not one of the groups of these workers who do not daily see, especially in the winter, opportunity for distributing such charity. And there are few of them whose teachers and children are not often glad to avail themselves of the benefits of these "imported goods," as they have come to be known among the self-supporters. It is seldom that this practise will involve the embarrassment born of the following incident.

The Shamrock School had several young boarding students from the North, members of a wealthy family, who had first come to Madison, and had been sent on as too immature for that school. One week two or three barrels were received from the North, and part of the contents were distributed among the needy neighbors. It happened, however, that none were just then more needy than the teachers, and they were very thankful to get these "imported goods."

Sabbath evening they all appeared in "new" garments, some of which were better than they would ever have been able to buy. After worship, as they gathered around the organ for a song service, one of the boys seemed greatly attracted by the light gray suit worn by Mr. Ore. His attention became so fixed that the rest noticed it, when the youngster explained: "Seems to me I've seen that suit before!" No doubt he had: the barrel had come from his father's house. Mr. Ore naturally felt a little embarrassment, but the incident was passed off with a general laugh and the exhibition of the new clothes of the others.

The experience is not all laughter, however; for one of the above heroes testifies, "I have shed more tears over not being able to get the things for my own family which I felt they should have, than over anything else in our experience," a feeling that will be most fully appreciated by the father who has a developing daughter in her 'teens.

When Brother Josephus' Agricultural and Mechanical Academy was in its beginning, the shop work, on which he was placing his main dependence for support, was at times very light, and again and again his family, including his own children and a number of boarding students, had cause to feel like the widow of Zarephath when she was "gathering two sticks," to go in and dress the handful of meal and the drop of oil, "that we may eat it and die."

In one such experience, when he had used his last dollar and was getting no shop work, his oldest daughter, who had grown into young womanhood wearing "imported goods," and now was destitute even of those, came to him with her maiden's hurt pride at shabbiness.

"Jonnie," he said to her, "we are not here for our own glory, nor to make money. We came here willing to sacrifice. We are having a hard time. I wish you might have these things you need, but what we are doing without we are doing without for Christ's sake. The Lord will send them."

But her patience and faith, spread out over many years, suffered a momentary lapse. "Oh, yes," she responded, "that's what you always say: 'Just trust in the Lord!'" And with tears she went away.

Brother Josephus went by himself and prayed. That night, when the mail came, there was a letter from a man whom he had never seen, had not solicited, and had not even written to for a very long time. In the letter was a check for one hundred dollars, the sender saying that he was impressed Brother Josephus needed it. The father handed the check to his daughter, saying, "I think you can have that dress now." And again she cried, but with a different cause for tears.

One of the two or three schools which have received some little financial aid from the general public is the Chinkapin Ridge School. Its founders were two families from California, Bruce and Lamont. Bruce was a mechanic. Lamont, who had been before his conversion a commercial traveler, and after that an accountant, and whose family in the old days could not live on less than three thousand dollars a year, came here to make a living on a washed and gullied farm, where he scarcely sees one hundred dollars in money through the year. Said he, "We used to be interested, years ago, in sending barrels of clothing into the South through our church; we never thought then that we would some time be the beneficiaries of them."

They moved into a log house one hundred years old, to which they made an addition of two or three rooms. The puncheon floor was full of holes; the attic, where they slept on a straw tick the first three months, was open enough to let three inches of snow drift upon their bed in a February snow storm. But they opened their school in their big cabin living-room, with its puncheon floor, their own children making the nucleus of a group that finally required a schoolhouse.

In the spring of 1912, Mrs. Lamont went back East to get help in building their schoolhouse. With much effort and no little difficulty she secured the interest and help of a number of friends, who gave or pledged nearly five hundred dollars for the purpose. The schoolhouse was going up in excellent form, when one night that winter, as they were away attending a prayer-meeting in the neighborhood, their old log house caught fire and burned, with absolutely everything in it. They had nothing left but the clothes on their back. It seemed a hard blow, for they had not a dish nor so much as a handkerchief left. But it brought forth a showing of sympathy and appreciation from the community at which they were surprised, having been received, when they came three years before, with open and sometimes hostile suspicion. One neighbor woman brought a pair of sheets, with apologies for their poor quality; another furnished two plates, another some steel knives and forks; and every one was ready with expression of sympathy in word and deed. The men came together in a bee and finished up the schoolhouse so that the family could move into it and live. And then from friends farther away came other manifestations of love and interest, until, with a new and beautiful little home and a better equipment than they had dreamed of getting, the Lamonts were bound to declare that, like Job, their latter end was more blessed than their beginning.

The life of self-denying devotion to the good of others is one to be sought, not shunned. In the first place, it disciplines and strengthens the powers of mind and soul to meet the problems which are inseparable from the cause of God. In the second place, while the life must always be one of sacrifice and self-denial, there is an unexcelled satisfaction in the experience of service to others, which finds an echo in the appreciation it gains from the friends of God near by and far away. It pays, from a double standpoint, to stay behind the back of Mammon.

XVI

PREACHING BY HAND

"GO YE into all the world, and preach the gospel to every creature," was the great commission given by Christ to his apostles. And down through the ages has come sounding the message to ourselves. But with it have come the commentations of two millenniums, to the effect that this preaching is to be done by word of mouth. Yet Jesus' own comments and his example signify more. He himself always prefaced his preaching with his practise. He laid hands on the sick and they recovered; he gave bread to the hungry, clothing to the naked, deliverance to the bound. He gave far more time to healing than to talking, and out of his own scanty store of money he relieved the necessities of the poor.

To his disciples, then, when he bade them preach the gospel, he conveyed such an idea of preaching as they had witnessed in himself: not only to speak words of grace, to teach the ignorant, but to minister to the physical needs of men. Especially does he bid them to heal the sick. And when he comes in his kingdom, his test of loyalty is whether those before him have fed the hungry, clothed the naked, visited the sick and in prison; for inasmuch as they have done this unto the least of men, even so, he declares, have they done it unto their King.

Now the feeding of the hungry may mean more than giving a meal to a tramp. If the Christian worker teaches his neighbor how to make a more abundant and nourishing dietary from his own garden and fields, is he not intelligently feeding the hungry? If he is able, through the industrial training of his pupils, to increase their cash income from ten dollars to two or three hundred dollars a year, is he not clothing the naked? If he teaches the community by example and personal help to build better houses for their increased comfort and sanitation, is he not taking the stranger into shelter? always understanding that his motive is not selfish gain, but desire to help his fellow-men. Not that the idea of personal benevolence is taken away from the text, but it is meant to include that and more; it is extended as Christ certainly meant it to extend, to embrace all the processes of life within a Christian motive and to Christian ends. So we may see many men and women who will never thrill audiences with their eloquence in the pulpit, we may see mechanics and farmers and nurses who are by their labors coworkers with evangelists in the fulfilment of the great commission — preaching, not by tongue, but by hand.

Up in the rimlands more than a Sabbath-day's journey from Nashville, lies the happy and somnolent land of Beulah. Here in 1909 came from the Madison School the two brothers Carlson, with their wives. They came without much else, for the expense of getting an education had stripped them of their small savings, and they had neither money nor equipment.

They had been saw-mill men, however, and in this wooded country they believed they might catch a toehold, and be of some use to the community while doing it. They obtained a few acres of wooded ground, a steep ravine that was of no use to any one else, and by some means managed to supply themselves with a small saw-mill. They cleared their own land, sawing up the timber, and also doing custom work for the people about.

Poverty trod hard on their heels in those days, but they had an ideal, and they held to it. Their earliest home was a shack built of slabs, in no way better, in many ways worse, than the homes of the people about them; but it furnished them shelter, and more than that, an inspiration. They would yet produce from this scant beginning a worthy temple of Christian living.

They sold the best of their lumber, and with the third grade they built first a schoolhouse, and after that a cottage for themselves, which, neat and handsome in style and finish, quickly became models that were copied up and down the ridge. Then the Carlson brothers turned over the property to a family of teachers and moved fifty miles away to another community where a school was just being established. Here they set up their mill in a country in which are extensive forests of hardwood, and developed a large business. They prospered until they had a plant worth two thousand dollars, with a twenty-five horsepower engine, saws, planing and siding machines, and a dry kiln.

Upstairs at one end of their mill is a pretty complete little repair shop. Ingenious and capable workmen, they do all their own repairing, making their own planer bits and other parts of the machinery. In consequence they have almost no loss in wear and tear of machinery.

In the winter of 1913 their plant was burned with almost total loss, but they rebuilt and stayed at their post. The results of their work are seen all through the country about them. Very neat houses were built at the school by themselves and their coworkers, which proved patterns in architecture and finish to the whole community. Having a grist mill as well as saw-mill, they were visited by scores of customers from the vicinity, who took away not merely their grist less its toll, but a thousand good ideas without toll except the satisfaction these workers have in seeing the blessing and improvement of their neighbors.

Shortly after the establishment of one of the early schools, three of its workers were one day going along the road near their home when they found an old man lying unconscious by the roadside. At first they thought him drunk, but upon examination found he was not. They carried him to their cabin and revived him. He was an old man whose mind had become enfeebled. He lived in the neighborhood with his married daughter, but it was almost beyond any one's power to care properly for him, as he was incompetent to attend to or even to make known his most common wants. That day he had started out, unknown to any one, to go to another house in the vicinity, but had fallen with a stroke of paralysis.

The young men cared for him in their own home for several days, until he died. This, almost their first experience in the neighborhood, gave them the reputation of good Samaritans, and they were at once looked to as persons to whom to turn in time of need.

Not long after, as one of these young men, Winthrop, was logging in the woods near the road, a man came running to him, crying that his child was choking to death. When he described the symptoms, Winthrop pronounced it a case of worms.

"If there's anything you can do," pleaded the father, "please come down at once."

"I'll go," said Winthrop, and ran to the house to get some worm medicine and castor oil. With one of the ladies of his household he went to the home of the child, and soon gave her relief. When he returned to the place where he had left the father helplessly crying, he found that the man had taken up his work, and, says Winthrop, "He had hauled more logs than a company ordinarily would have hauled in that time. He had been a little bit off with us, too, but he never was after that."

Somewhat later still, as Winthrop was hoeing in his new strawberry bed, a little girl came running up the road, crying to him, "Father is bleeding to death." He had cut his foot, she said, with the ax. Mr. Winthrop got some antiseptic cotton, disinfectant, and bandages, and started on the run down to the man's house. He found him standing up helplessly in the middle of the floor, the blood running out into a great pool. Winthrop had him sit down and put his foot up on a chair, cut off his shoe, stopped the flow of blood, and washed and disinfected the wound. Then he covered it with carbolized vaseline and cotton, which he bound on with adhesive plaster, and bandaged the foot. But, fearing that the bone might have been cut, he urged the man to send to town for the doctor. When the physician came, he took the bandages off, looked at the wound, and pronounced it all right. Then he said, "That fellow has done it up in better shape than I have the appliances to do it with. I wish you would go down and get some more cotton and plaster from him."

Another man in the neighborhood broke his leg one spring, and Winthrop and Emmet and the boys went down and offered to put in his crop for him. The old man was a little offish. He was evidently afraid he would be running a big bill. But he had no one who could do it for him, and as they pleasantly insisted, he let them go ahead. It was well into the summer before he was able to do much, and they not only put in his crop, but regularly tended it until that time. Then, when he thought he could manage it himself, he asked for their bill. They told him they were not doing it for money, but because he was their neighbor and needed help, and that their bill was just nothing.

He gave them his thanks; but he more plainly showed his gratitude later, in a characteristic way. He was one of the most influential men in the community, a type of the old clan leader of Scotland transplanted into America. Some weeks after he had gotten around with his mended leg, there came up into the community a deputy sheriff who was hungering for some ready cash. The Sunday law in Tennessee provides that a reward be given to the informer against any one convicted of Sunday labor. This deputy had heard that the school men were not Sunday-keepers, and might very likely be found working on Sunday. Now Sundays are largely employed by the workers at this school, as at most of the others, in Sunday school work, visiting the sick, distributing literature, etc. But it is true that they sometimes attended on Sunday to farm work which was pressing, though avoiding it as much as possible, and always working out of sight and hearing. The deputy, not being well acquainted with the neighborhood, thought he might employ this old man in his search, and so he came to him and proposed to divide the reward with him if he would pilot him where he could see the school men at work on Sunday.

The old man eyed him until he had finished his proposal, and then, saying not a word, he stepped back within his door and took down his rifle from the pegs above. Then, as he expressed it, he "looked into the eyes of him and spake into the teeth of him," saying, "Them boys are true men. They've worked for us here. And all I've got to say to you is, Git!" The fellow *got*, and has never been back.

This incident is of value not as showing how Christian service may be repaid by protection, for that is the last thing of which the Christian worker thinks; but it shows what bonds of sympathy are created by Christian service, which may be used for the conversion and blessing of those who are thus drawn. This same old man is now superintendent of the Sunday school which meets in Winthrop's schoolhouse, and leader also of the mid-week prayer-meeting. The last time the Visitor was at the Pine Knot School, he met the old man on the road going to Winthrop's house. He gave a hearty greeting, and asked him to speak to the neighbors at the next meeting; but the Visitor afterwards learned that his errand just then was not at all a religious or peaceable one. At a recent "wake," or carousal at the house of a dead man, he had been threatened by his drunken son-in-law with a pistol, and he was now going to request the loan of Winthrop's buggy to go down and swear out a warrant for the miscreant. Mr. Winthrop told him he might have the horse and buggy, but talked with him a little about the Christian's duty and privilege of forgiving. The old man went home to think it over. He studied over it for twenty-four hours, but the next day he came back and told Winthrop he would not need the buggy now; he had gained the victory over himself; and though his son-in-law had drawn a gun on him — that almost unforgivable offense in the hills — he would forgive him. That night was prayer-meeting night, and the clan leader, big, bony, white-haired, leonine, had a glowing face as he led his fellows in prayer and testimony. The leaven was working.

The "ministry of the word" of most value is that ministry of the Word which was made flesh and dwelt among us, going about doing good, and healing all that were possessed of the devil. Preaching that is unaccompanied by works of faith and helpfulness is not the kind of preaching that Christ did. The proclamation of the truth by oral preaching is indeed of value, but it is of value only when it has the power of the Word within it; and that power is the power to minister to men.

"Our Lord Jesus Christ came to this world as the unwearied servant of man's necessity"; and when his followers take the same position, there will be power in the word they have to speak; they will be able to speak as those having authority, and not as the scribes and Pharisees.

"Nothing will so arouse a self-sacrificing zeal and broaden and strengthen the character as to engage in work for others. Many professed Christians, in seeking church relationship, think only of themselves. They wish to enjoy church fellowship and pastoral care. They become members of large and prosperous churches, and are content to do little for others. In this way they are robbing themselves of the most precious blessings. Many would be greatly benefitted by sacrificing their pleasant, ease-conducing associations. They need to go where their energies will be called out in Christian work, and they can learn to bear responsibilities.

"Trees that are crowded closely together do not grow healthfully and sturdily. The gardener transplants them that they may have room to develop. A similar work would benefit many of the members of large churches. They need to be placed where their energies will be called forth in active Christian effort. They are losing their spiritual life, becoming dwarfed and inefficient, for want of self-sacrificing labor for others. Transplanted to some missionary field, they would grow strong and vigorous.

"But none need wait until called to some distant field before beginning to help others. Doors of service are open everywhere. All around us are those who need our help. The widow, the orphan, the sick and the dying, the heart-sick, the discouraged, the ignorant, and the outcast, are on every hand.

"We should feel it our special duty to work for those living in our neighborhood. Study how you can best help those who take no interest in religious things. As you visit your friends and neighbors, show an interest in their spiritual as well as in their temporal welfare. Speak to them of Christ as a sin-pardoning Saviour. Invite your neighbors to your home, and read with them from the precious Bible and from books that explain its truths. Invite them to unite with you in song and prayer. In these little gatherings, Christ himself will be present, as he has promised, and hearts will be touched by his grace.

"Church-members should educate themselves to do this work. This is just as essential as to save the benighted souls in foreign countries. While some feel the burden for souls afar off, let the many who are at home feel the burden of precious souls who are around them, and work just as diligently for their salvation.

"Many regret that they are living a narrow life. They themselves can make their lives broad and influential if they will. Those who love Jesus with heart and mind and soul, and their neighbor as themselves, have a wide field in which to use their ability and influence.

"Let none pass by little opportunities, to look for larger work. You might do successfully the small work, but fail utterly in attempting the larger work and fall into discouragement. It is by doing with your might what you find to do that you will develop aptitude for larger work. It is by slighting the daily opportunities, by neglecting the little things right at hand, that so many become fruitless and withered.

"Do not depend upon human aid. Look beyond human beings, to the One appointed by God to bear our griefs, to carry our sorrows, and to supply our necessities. Taking God at his word, make a beginning wherever you find work to do, and move forward with unfaltering faith. It is faith in Christ's presence that gives strength and steadfastness. Work with unselfish interest, with painstaking effort, with persevering energy.

"In fields where the conditions are so objectionable and disheartening that many are unwilling to go to them, remarkable changes have been wrought by the efforts of self-sacrificing workers. Patiently and perseveringly they labored, not relying upon human power, but upon God, and his grace sustained them. The amount of good thus accomplished will never be known in this world, but blessed results will be seen in the great hereafter."[1]

---

[1] Mrs. E. G. White, *Ministry of Healing*, pp. 1, 151-154.

XVII

SERMONS IN SOIL

THE greater number of these rural-school workers in the South look to the soil for a livelihood, and this will be the case with the large majority who come in the future. This is as it should be. Families with children should not go to the cities. The natural conditions of life are in the country, and there the children should grow up into Christian life in the midst of the handiwork of God.

Moreover, the farm is the surest means of support. The whole structure of the economic world rests upon the farm. The world is fed and clothed, and in great part provided with shelter and warmth, by the farmer. As a forceful writer puts it: "We realize (we farmers) that we are the foundation: we connect human life with earth. We dig and plant and produce, and having eaten at the first table ourselves, we pass what is left to the bankers and millionaires. Did you ever think, stranger, that the most of the wars of the world have been fought for the control of the farmer's second table? Have you thought that the surplus of wheat and corn and cotton is what the railroads are struggling to carry? Upon our surplus run all the factories and mills; a little of it gathered in cash makes a millionaire. But we farmers, we sit back comfortably after dinner, and joke with our wives and play with our babies, and let all the rest of you fight for the crumbs that fall from our abundant tables. If once we really cared and got up and shook ourselves, and said to the maid: 'Here, child, don't waste the crusts: gather 'em up and tomorrow we'll have a cottage pudding,' where in the world would all the millionaires be? . . . Moreover, think of the position of the millionaire. He spends his time playing not with life, but with the symbols of life, whether cash or houses. Any day the symbols may change: a little war may happen along, there may be a defective flue or a western breeze, or even a panic because the farmers aren't scattering as many crumbs as usual (they call it crop failure, but I've noticed that the farmers still continue to have plenty to eat), and then what happens to your millionaire? Not knowing how to produce anything himself, he would starve to death if there were not always, somewhere, a farmer to take him up to the table." [1]

If there is any place where the Christian worker may be able to weather a storm, either financial or religious, it is on the soil. There he may, indeed, suffer privation, but so long as God's bounty continues, he cannot be utterly crushed out. Panics, bank failures, strikes, riots, boycotts, may refuse him cooperation in exchange of products, may deprive him of ready cash with which he might buy silk dresses and oranges, but he can raise his own wool and corn and potatoes, and if necessity demands, can convert his cotton or wool or skins into serviceable garments. The last stronghold of independence that will remain to be taken is the farm. The last troubles in this earth's history may, indeed will, drive God's people to the caves and deserts and swamps, but for long before that culmination comes, they will find refuge from the common woes of a distracted, chaotic world, on the ground where God placed the feet of their first parents.

But far more than the mere making of a living,

---
[1] David Grayson, *Adventures in Contentment*, pp. 115, 116.

the soil, with its products, is to be the medium of an important education. "There are lessons that our children need to learn. To the little child, not yet capable of learning from the printed page or of being introduced to the routine of the schoolroom, nature presents an unfailing source of instruction and delight. The heart not yet hardened by contact with evil is quick to recognize the Presence that pervades all created things. The ear as yet undulled by the world's clamor is attentive to the Voice that speaks through nature's utterances. And for those of older years, needing continually its silent reminders of the spiritual and eternal, nature's teaching will be no less a source of pleasure and of instruction. As the dwellers in Eden learned from nature's pages, as Moses discerned God's handwriting on the Arabian plains and mountains, and the child Jesus on the hillsides of Nazareth, so the children of today may learn of him. The unseen is illustrated by the seen. On everything upon the earth from the loftiest tree of the forest to the lichen that clings to the rock, from the boundless ocean to the tiniest shell on the shore, they may behold the image and superscription of God."

"Patient, painstaking effort needs to be made for the encouragement and uplifting of the surrounding communities, and for their education in industrial and sanitary lines. The school and all its surroundings should be object-lessons, teaching the ways of improvement, and appealing to the people for reform, so that taste, industry, and refinement may take the place of coarseness, uncleanliness, disorder, ignorance, and sin. Even the poorest can improve their surroundings by rising early and working diligently. By our lives and example we can help others to discern that which is repulsive in their character or about their premises, and with Christian courtesy we may encourage improvement." [1]

---

[1] Mrs. E. G. White, *Education*, p. 100; *Testimonies for the Church*, Vol. VI, p. 188.

A New Industry.

"The substitution of the strawberry crop for tobacco was begun." Page 212.

It is not only the farmer's neighbors, but the farmer himself, who is to be taught. Indeed, it is most necessary for any farmer entering a new country to learn all he can of local conditions from his neighbors. The less time it takes him to make his living, the more time can he find for Christian work among them. And not only his financial success, not only his missionary activities, but his own spiritual growth, is dependent in a degree upon his successful farming. If, because of poor crops, he is overworked and worried, he is in no proper frame of mind to listen to God or to speak for God. The spiritual lessons which the Saviour taught us to find in seed-sowing and harvest, are belied by poor farming. A thin, sickly, straggling field of grain or vegetables is a poor figure for the kingdom of God, as is also a batch of sour bread. A sound, scientific, intelligent understanding of the laws of God in nature, and how to control and use their operation, is an excellent basis for sound theology.

One whose experience is typical of many thus acknowledges it: "I made an astounding series of mistakes when I first tried to teach my neighbors how to farm. In the first place, I could not bring myself to the idea that I had to plow around the hills. I would not do it; I ran my rows the way I wanted to, and that was, straight. The result was that the most of my soil washed off the hillsides into the hollows.

"My second mistake was to plant my crops too thick. I expected two or three stalks of corn to mature in a hill, just as they used to in my native State. I thought it was just a notion that only one stalk could grow in a hill. So I planted my corn just as I wanted to, with the result that I got plenty of leaves, but little or no grain.

"My farm is in a country that practises 'terracing.' I did not believe in terracing, and at first plowed right through the ridges. I spent much money for fertilizer, only to see it washed away. Then I tried to ditch and terrace for myself, but not understanding how, I only made bad matters worse. Finally, the fourth year, I employed a neighbor who knew what he was about, and we laid the hills off on a proper system of terraces. It took me about four years to learn that although I had been considered a successful farmer in the North, I was not yet fitted to be a teacher of farming under Southern conditions. Now, my neighbors and I consult freely together over plans and methods. I am able to teach as well as to learn, and we all recognize that there is much for us yet to learn together."

Another, who is foremost as an authority on agriculture among the self-supporting workers, and who has been employed by the State to teach the subject in some of its teachers' institutes, says:

"Every successful farmer recognizes that he must modify his methods of soil cultivation to suit climatic conditions. Many of the methods that make for successful farming in one section cannot be followed in another. For instance, in the North the soil is left to weather during the winter, locked up with frost and snow. In the South, if that method is followed, it results, because of open weather, in the leaching and evaporating of a large portion of the most valuable plant foods during the winter. An uncultivated soil in the South during the winter may mean the loss of twenty-one per cent of the whole year's heat units, and of a large amount of available nitrogen, the most costly of plant foods. Southern farming needs to be studied from the standpoint of the South, and not subjected empirically to Northern methods."

Not every one, of course, can have the advantage of even a short course in scientific agriculture, but reliable scientific instruction is now so common in books, in bulletins, and through the personal help of representatives of State and federal agricultural bureaus, that no man has the excuse that he cannot learn. Sanctified common sense, as well as practical experience and wide-awake interest in the new, will do wonders for the missionary farmer.

Take the farm at the Shamrock School. The main part of this farm lies up on a tongue of land that is bounded below by brooks or "branches." When the workers went there, that old gray hill lay up bare to the sun, like the scraped dry head of a tonsured monk. Around the house was a fringe of weeds and sassafras shoots, but the fields resisted even the sassafras. They went there with almost nothing, having put what little money they had into buying the place. They grubbed the brush, and they plowed and harrowed the fields, but they found them too poor to grow even legumes. They tried cow peas, and then they tried soy beans. They put them into the ground, and on some of their land they got back not even as much as the seed. Some of the beans sprouted, grew an inch or two high, and then died. They decided that it was cheaper to work out and earn money to live on, and turn their crops under for fertilizer. They succeeded in growing some rye, and turned it under; then soy beans gave a little more promise, and they turned that crop under; rye again in the winter, followed with corn, which made some forage, but was also partly turned under. Not all their land was so poor as this, however; so that they did get some returns, but the most of it was poor enough. Today, by feeding their soil, they have raised the productivity of some of their land to forty bushels of corn to the acre, and they get very fair crops of legumes and vegetables. They have used very little commercial fertilizer, but realize that their land needs liming. They have a splendid little vineyard and a good peach orchard. Their milch cows, though few in number, have played an important part in increasing the fertility of the land, for the manure has been carefully conserved and used where it would have the most telling effect. The transformation of that old gray hill in the last six years has been a marvel not only to the neighborhood, but to the friends who have visited these brethren. But it has meant hard, grinding toil, as well as careful thought and planning. Many a time they have come to close places for both food and clothing, but cow peas and wild blackberries have never entirely failed, and "imported goods" have been the mainstay in clothing.

A very important side industry at this school is the cannery, which was opened four years after the school began. It was not merely an economic reason, it was chiefly an educational idea, that started the cannery. Tobacco is the chief money crop in that part of Tennessee, and all the mission schools in that section have struck at the base of the tobacco habit by teaching against the culture of tobacco. Two of them, studying how to strike a practical blow at the business, determined to introduce other crops. At one, the substitution of the strawberry and potato crops for tobacco was begun, and the workers demonstrated to their friends both in the school and in the field, that there was more money actually to be made by these crops than by tobacco. At the other school, the raising of garden produce — tomatoes, beans, sugar corn, etc.— was advocated, and, first for themselves and then for their neighbors, the school-men began canning such products. They established a town market for their own produce, and then offered to can such things for their neighbors, if they would raise them, and to find a market for all they desired to sell.

The cannery at the Shamrock School became a very considerable industry, employing not only the children and several of the older people in the school, but a number of hands from the neighborhood. A small but neat building, with canning apparatus on the ground floor and storeroom overhead, was erected. The utmost neatness and cleanliness was required in the small establishment. No tobacco-chewing or snuff-dipping was allowed, the workers must scrub their hands and faces, their hair must be combed, and then they were arrayed in enveloping white caps and aprons, with pocket for handkerchief to wipe away perspiration. They were made to feel that the cannery stood for something besides money-making: it exemplified the virtues of order and cleanliness, inside and out. At first the customers were indifferent to the condition in which they brought their produce, but they soon learned to sort it carefully and to bring only sound and properly prepared material. The hands were paid by the piece, and custom work was done on the same basis. New customers appeared every season. A neighbor who had ventured to plant a surplus of Kentucky Wonder beans came bringing them, thinking to try the canner.

"You're sure they'll keep?" he inquired dubiously.

"O yes; we have tested them three seasons now."

"How many beans will it take for a mess for two of us?" was his next question.

"You will have enough for dinner and some to warm over for supper, out of one of these cans," was the very exact information given him.

"Well, then," he concluded, "I want some. It'll be mighty fine to have something besides hog and hominy this winter."

The little cannery had a capacity, when running full, of 500 cans a day. In 1912, 2,900 quarts were canned for the neighbors, and the patronage grew. But it was the endeavor of the Shamrock teachers to induce them to can for themselves, with small outfits. And some began to do it. Thus they created a business each for himself, which displaced the tobacco business, and still with no danger of overstocking the market with canned goods.

In the neighborhood of both the schools mentioned, the lure has worked well. Tobacco-raising is a laborious and disagreeable task. No plant is so selfish as tobacco. It makes great demands upon the soil, and not a weed must be suffered to grow in the tobacco field except itself. Then comes its enemy, the tobacco worm, which is followed assiduously from end to end of the field, searched out on the plants, and usually smashed between the thumb and forefinger. This work falls to the lot of the children, and the children hate it. Oftentimes a child will appear in the school with swollen face and inflamed eyes from bending over the poisonous plant.

"What's the matter?"

"Oh, been working in that old tobacco patch. Wish tobacco had never been born," is the reply. Where the cultivation of tobacco depends chiefly upon white labor, which means the farmer and his children, the crop is heartily detested; but still the farmer continues to raise it, because he knows of nothing else which will have the ready and profitable sale that tobacco has. When it is demonstrated to him that there are other crops which cost less in soil fertility and less in labor, and bring equal or greater money returns, he begins, slowly perhaps, but surely, to turn away from tobacco. Listen to a report of how the matter was taken up in one of the rimland schools:

"Now with our children in the school," said the teacher, "I take up the first elements that are in the soil, those elements that are especially short in this country, which are nitrogen, lime, phosphorus, and, in a less degree, potash. We put it up on a chart right back here on the wall. We compare two crops: one, Irish potatoes, perhaps; the other tobacco. We show what elements each of these plants takes from the soil, and they see that tobacco is taking most liberally just those elements of which we have the least, while potatoes take but little of those elements. It takes more potash to build up a thousand pounds of tobacco than it does for three thousand pounds of wheat. It takes more potash to build up a thousand pounds of tobacco than it takes to build up five or ten thousand pounds of Irish potatoes. So the continual raising of tobacco on these hill lands has not only depleted them of humus, but has so lowered them in their supply of these elements that the farmers find it necessary, in order to get a crop of anything, to supply these elements at the rate of two to four hundred pounds of fertilizer per acre. At the high price of commercial fertilizers, the cost of labor, and the expense of marketing, tobacco is the most expensive crop that can be grown. To get the farmer and the farmer's boy and the farmer's girl to see this, we take these different crops and put them on the board and show what they cost in these elements, figuring each at the market price; we figure in the time of the grower and the cost of the marketing. We have these boys and girls do this themselves, from the statistics which we give them. And you never saw boys and girls more interested. They will stay in at recess figuring on these things, and come around to us to get a bit more information on this and on that. And the conclusion they reach — you can see what it is. They discover that from an economic standpoint they cannot afford to raise tobacco, and they see the desirability of raising a crop that will furnish food for them.

"Now this has its effect especially on the younger people. The old farmers are dubious, when they hear these things through their children or direct from us; they shake their heads and go on the same old way. But among the younger men there comes evidence of a break. One young man of our neighborhood just came to me this week, and said, 'I believe we have got to stop raising this tobacco, though it has been our only money crop. It would be the best thing for this country that could happen if we would stop raising tobacco. And,' he said, 'I am going to try a good big piece in Irish potatoes this year, and see what I do.'

"Then in the physiology class we have our next chance. This study of statistics which they have worked out themselves, as to the economic value of tobacco as compared with other crops, has impressed them, and they are ready for something more. We show the effects of tobacco on the lungs, the throat, the heart, the membrane of the mouth, the blood, and the brain, showing how it stops the energy of the child, making him indolent and lazy, making him careless, making him rude. Do you know it makes them rude? I made a point on that. To my class over in the county normal, I put this thing: 'Have you noticed and compared those of your acquaintance who use tobacco, and those who do not? Who is stunted, and who is well developed? Is the color of the skin rosy or sallow? How are the teeth? Is the eye bright or not? What are the manners, slouchy and sloven, or well-poised and civil? How does the boy do in his studies?' I had them give the names of boys. Every one of them using tobacco fell down on the desirable attributes. It astonished the class to have their own knowledge thus brought before them.

"So there is a lever to help pry with in the physiology class. Tea and coffee are taken up in this connection, and their effects as well as the effects of alcohol are taken up. I have done this in the normal school. I have said to them, 'You have a great campaign on against alcohol, yet you are poisoning yourselves with tea and coffee and tobacco, which are as deadly as arsenic or opium or alcohol.'

"This combination of the study of agriculture and physiology on the tobacco question has affected in a very strong way many of the serious-minded students. Many of them have ceased drinking coffee and tea, boys have quit the tobacco habit, and some grown men and women who have attended these lectures have also put it away, and in their fight on this habit have come to me repeatedly, asking me for help and advice.

"A few days ago a young woman, a teacher, came to me and asked, 'What can a person do who has used tobacco for thirty years, to make it easier to quit the habit?' She and her husband had been attending the lectures. I had not noticed any apparent effect of the studies on the class; that is, no break in habit or ap-

At Cowee Mountain School, North Carolina.
"Through the study of the work his hands performed, he was to learn higher and higher truth." Page 217.

pearance. And I said to her, 'Why, I don't know of any such case. Where is there any such person?'

"And she said, 'Well, here is one. That is my case. And my husband is another.'

"I said, 'When did you begin to leave it off?'

"She said, 'After your first lecture. We see what it means, and we made up our minds not to be slaves any longer. And we are still determined. But if you know of anything which will help my husband, I wish you would tell me — something that will stop the terrible pain in the head, and the nervousness. Isn't there anything you can tell me that will make it easier for him?'

"Now that was a heart-touching thing. They had heard the truth, and without any ado, any talk, any announcement of it, they started out to obey the truth, and they struggled on with it for three weeks without saying anything. She had stopped using tea and coffee, and he had stopped using tobacco. And now all they wanted to know was if there was any help for them. There was no question of turning back, but there was a cry from overtaxed nerves and will, a cry for help from some one who had the truth. And that, my brethren, was an opening for more truth."

But is there any teaching of vital truth in all this work? There is, indeed! It has become the habit of modern Christianity to regard truth too much in the abstract. The next natural step is to regard truth, the abstract, as unimportant. It was not so with the Christianity of Christ and the apostles. The healing of the sick went on with the telling of principles of truth; the life was reformed as the mind was instructed. The salvation of Christ meant higher living, better methods, greater life and power.

God makes truth concrete. He set man in a garden home at the first, to dress and to keep it. And through the study of the work his hands performed, and the objects with which all his senses dealt, he was to learn higher and higher truth. "The system of education instituted at the beginning of the world, was to be a model for man throughout all after-time," and even "under changed conditions, true education is still conformed to the Creator's plan, the plan of the Eden school."[1]

It is of no value to a man that he be induced to subscribe to a dogma of faith, if it have no concrete meaning in his life. The best method of instruction is to reveal the doctrine by a practical application in life. It is upon this basis that the rural mission schools are endeavoring to proclaim the truth, and there is this commendation for them: "In the work being done at the training school for home and foreign missionary teachers in Madison, Tennessee, and in the small schools established by the teachers who have gone forth from Madison, we have an illustration of a way in which the message should be carried. . . . Let us strengthen this company to continue the good work in which they are engaged, and labor to encourage others to do a similar work. Then the light of truth will be carried in a simple and effective way, and a great work will be accomplished for the Master in a short time."[2]

---
[1] Mrs. E. G. White, *Education*, pp. 20, 30.
[2] Mrs. E. G. White, MS., January 6, 1908.

The Medical Missionary

"How best to accomplish the work in this field is the problem before us. Great progress might have been made in medical missionary work. Sanitariums might have been established. The principles of health reform might have been proclaimed. This work is now to be taken up, and into it not a vestige of selfishness is to be brought. It is to be done with an earnestness, perseverance, and devotion that will open doors through which the truth can enter, and that to stay." ELLEN G. WHITE.

XVIII

FOLLOWING THE GREAT PHYSICIAN

CHRIST is no longer in this world in person, to go through our cities and towns and villages, healing the sick; but he has commissioned us to carry forward the medical missionary work that he began." [1]

There is no class who have greater influence than physicians. Whoever relieves distress of body (and thereby often distress of mind) possesses a hold upon the affections and confidence of people which can be gained by few others. The farther the medical profession has advanced out of quackery and empiricism, out of drug medication and speculative prescription, the more completely has it gained influence with men. That influence, when devoted to rescuing men not only from disease but from sin, is a precious possession; but too often it is turned into another direction. Yet when the missionary records of the world take from among physicians such glorious names as Livingstone in Africa, Grant in Persia, Mackenzie in China, and Grenfell in Laborador, there is surely inspiration to their fellows to devote their splendid talents to more than the getting of money and reputation.

In the mountains there is need of physicians who will be at once philanthropists and educators. It cannot be said that there is any greater lack of physicians

---

[1] Mrs. E. G. White, *Testimonies for the Church*, Vol. IX, pp. 168, 169.

here than elsewhere, at least in the more populous and wealthy sections; yet there is the greatest room for physicians who use simple means of cure, and who will teach the people how to preserve as well as to regain health. And there are many isolated sections where the services of competent physicians are sorely needed. The difficulty in inducing Christian physicians to settle in such places is the same difficulty that has debarred other physicians: the isolation of the location, and the poverty of the people. The one shuts the physician largely from that contact with the rapidly advancing science of his profession which he desires, and the other prevents the remuneration which he counts his due. Yet the rewards of such service have been found by some as precious as the equally laborious and self-sacrificing work of medical missionaries in foreign lands.

In the spring of 1907 a Christian physician who had had an important part in medical work in the South, found his health so impaired that, leaving the large city where he was practising, he retired for rest to a place his father had bought on a part of the Cumberland Plateau. It was a quiet enough place, almost out of the world, it seemed, and Dr. and Mrs. Cornwall settled down with a sigh of relief in their little log cabin, to rest and study. But, like the great Physician who retired in his weariness to a desert place in Galilee, the doctor found that there was to be little rest for him. Only three or four days after their arrival, he was called out at midnight by a boy on muleback, who had come to guide him four or five miles through the woods to attend a dying woman. She was a poor outcast, who had been left alone in a log hut, where she had a few days before given birth to twins. Some of the neighbors attended her at that time, but afterwards left her alone; and, neglected and uncared for, she had sunk into a fever in which she was thought to be dying.

Out there in the black wilderness that night, there came to the doctor the vision of a needy people such as he had never seen in his years of official life and institutionalism. In that lowly cabin he ministered to the needs of this young woman, passed the crisis successfully, and afterwards brought her to health. From that time on he was besieged by people from increasingly greater distances, until he began to have calls from as far as twenty miles away. There was not another physician on the breadth and length of that mountain plateau, twenty by one hundred miles.

The sympathies of Dr. Cornwall and his wife were drawn out in many directions for this people, and soon they were busy in more than one phase of work — school, social, and industrial, as well as medical. The doctor's attention and energies were called twenty ways at once. Was a tray of cans just ready, in the canning shed, to go into the tank, was a wall being laid by unskilled hands, was the garden crying for cultivation, there would surely come riding up a messenger, crying: "My neighbor's daughter is took powerful sick. She et too big a bate of fresh meat, and her misery's raging terrible. They're skeered she won't live, and want you to come over quick. They live on the fur brow of the mountain, on a cross-road 'tother side of the big ravine. I'll show you the way." What could he do but go, perhaps not to get home until early the next morning, and then tired, hungry, and cold? The familiar, "Hello! Where's the doctor at?" was one of their greatest hindrances, and still one of their most precious opportunities. Physical suffering was a goad that drove the people with decreasing reluctance to those who could help, strangers though they might at first be.

Miss Rexall, a trained nurse who had accompanied them, was a mainstay in the doctor's work, and she developed surprisingly a resourcefulness not only in meeting emergencies, but in finding her way through almost trackless stretches of country, to carry out the doctor's directions for treatment in some needy home. His directions might be: "Go down this road till you come to a fork. Take the left-hand one and go till you come to a blazed tree on your right. Then you'll see a little trail going to your left again. Follow that until you come to an old field that's nearly grown up. Go around the corner of it and along by that fence, and you come to a branch that you have to ford. You may have a little trouble in getting Fanny across, but if you insist she'll make it all right. Well, go straight ahead and you come out on the big road in about eighty rods. Turn to your right now and go two miles. You'll come to a road going to your left; don't take that; and then a turn in the road to your right; follow that, because the dim road straight ahead only leads down where they've been getting out cross ties. It is only a little turn. You can tell when you've gone about two miles; then you will see a clump of big pine trees and a fork in the road. And down to the left, at the end of a lane, is the house. You'll find a sick woman there. Give her alternate hot and cold to the spine, a tepid sponge bath, and a cold mitten friction. Don't forget the ice-cap; the spring water is cold enough to answer for that. She needs a hot pack, but there is no chance to give her that. Get her quiet before you leave her, and leave this sedative for emergencies."

And on old Fanny, the mule, Miss Rexall would make her way, guided by the signs and doubtless by the angels, coming back again with an interesting tale of need and ministry and hospitality, and usually with a message or two from other cases found en route. And always her story would end with, "Oh, if we only had some place where we could put that poor thing, where we could feed her and give her better care."

And the doctor would return from a piece of critical surgical work done in a little cabin where surgical cleanliness was almost impossible, to declare: "Oh, how clean our own dirt seems! It was terrible to do surgical work in such a place, but I feel that he'll get along all right. He couldn't live without it, and I believe the Lord will make up for what we couldn't do. But we've got to have a place near by that we can keep clean."

To meet the needs of hospital and school, they planned, and, through many difficulties, at last succeeded, in putting up a small two-story building, with basement. Measured by their importunate needs, the work of excavation, masonry, and carpentry seemed to crawl, but it was at last energized and finished by the coming of one of that company of missionary mechanics whose work has meant so much in the building up of some of these schools.

The financial resources of Dr. Cornwall were at this time slight. He carried no fortune into the wilderness with him, and his medical work was largely charitable. All that he could earn, what little came to him from other sources, was speedily eaten up by the needs of home and farm and school and building, until the work grew so heavy that he decided he must seek an opportunity for greater earnings.

Just at this time, in the spring of 1908, several nurses who had previously been with him seemed to have no prospects for employment, and, planning with them, he decided to open a small sanitarium work in the nearest large city, thirty miles from his railway station in the valley. It was the doctor's hope that it might prove a means of financial assistance to his work on the mountain. And so it might, if it had not been, for him, three men's work. During the day he attended to his practise in the city, while his wife, with two or three helpers, held the fort on the mountain; at night he would travel to and from his home, sometimes carrying provisions in his arms three miles up the mountain road, returning early in the morning to the city. Often his rest at night was broken by a call from some sick highlander, and sometimes he was prevented by his work there from reaching the city. His faithful nurses in both places made up all they could for his absence. But such a life could not last forever. Sickness in his family brought additional anxieties and burdens, resulting in a nervous breakdown, which necessitated his retiring from the field for several months. With deep regret the work was surrendered to others; but the influence of that unselfish and devoted effort remains today in the hearts and lives and minds of that elevated community.

XIX

THE RURAL SANITARIUM

SEVENTH-DAY ADVENTISTS from their earliest history have earnestly advocated simple, right living and rational methods of healing. These principles have made a deep impression upon the denominational character, and have given a distinct trend to their work. They believe that the divine plan of country life is based upon right laws for the development of the entire man and for maintaining health of body, mind, and soul. It is reasonable, therefore, to hold that an institution whose object is the restoration of health has great advantages if located in the country.

The tendency of the world is toward centralization and extreme specialization, as seen in the rapid creation and development of cities, monopolies, and tyrannies, but there are men who, grasping the plan of God, are moving their homes and their institutions away from these centers of artificial activity to the more normal environments found in rural communities. Here the tenor of men's minds is changed by dwelling upon the objects of nature.

For the healing of diseased bodies and minds, there is no environment so favorable as the country, and no agencies so powerful as those gifts of God, pure food, fresh air, sleep, sunshine, work, and unselfish service for others. The sick need to be brought into close touch with nature. An outdoor life amid natural surroundings has worked wonders for many a helpless and almost hopeless invalid.

This truth has been well expressed in the following words: "The noise and excitement and confusion of the cities, their constrained and artificial life, are most wearisome and exhausting to the sick. The air, laden with smoke and dust, with poisonous gases, and with germs of disease, is a peril to life. The sick, for the most part shut within four walls, come almost to feel as if they were prisoners in their rooms. They look out on houses and pavements and hurrying crowds, with perhaps not even a glimpse of blue sky or sunshine, of grass or flower or tree. Shut up in this way, they brood over their suffering and sorrow, and become a prey to their own sad thoughts.

"And for those who are weak in moral power, the cities abound in dangers. In them, patients who have unnatural appetites to overcome are continually exposed to temptation. They need to be placed amid new surroundings, where the current of their thoughts will be changed, they need to be placed under influences wholly different from those that have wrecked their lives. Let them for a season be removed from those influences that lead away from God, into a purer atmosphere.

"Institutions for the care of the sick would be far more successful if they could be established away from the cities. And so far as possible, all who are seeking to recover health should place themselves amid country surroundings, where they can have the benefit of outdoor life. Nature is God's physician. The pure air, the glad sunshine, the flowers and trees, the orchards and vineyards, and outdoor exercise amid these surroundings, are health-giving, life-giving.

"Physicians and nurses should encourage their patients to be much in the open air. Outdoor life is the only remedy that many invalids need. It has a wonderful power to heal diseases caused by the excitements and excesses of fashionable life, a life that weakens and destroys the powers of body, mind, and soul.

"How grateful to the invalids weary of city life, the glare of many lights, and the noise of the streets, are the quiet and freedom of the country! How eagerly do they turn to the scenes of nature! How glad would they be to sit in the open air, rejoice in the sunshine, and breathe the fragrance of tree and flower! There are life-giving properties in the balsam of the pine, in the fragrance of the cedar and the fir, and other trees also have properties that are health-restoring.

"To the chronic invalid, nothing so tends to restore health and happiness as living amid attractive country surroundings. Here the most helpless ones can sit or lie in the sunshine or in the shade of the trees. They have only to lift their eyes to see above them the beautiful foliage. A sweet sense of restfulness and refreshing comes over them as they listen to the murmuring of the breezes. The drooping spirits revive. The waning strength is recruited. Unconsciously the mind becomes peaceful, the fevered pulse more calm and regular."[1]

The Rural Sanitarium in connection with the Madison School stands in close adherence to this ideal. At the time the school farm was being bought, Mrs. E. G. White pointed out a site in a grove, some three hundred yards from the old farm house, saying, "This would be a good place to put your sanitarium." Nearly on that spot today stand the simple buildings of the Rural Sanitarium.

It did not seem within the possibilities, during the first few years of struggle, to take any steps toward establishing a sanitarium. But the foundations were early laid, in the training of nurses. While yet the old farm house, with its low, dark rooms and drafty doors, was the only home of the school, Mrs. Druillard took in hand the education of the first nurses' class of five girls.

Their class was held in an upper room that also

---

[1] Mrs. E. G. White, *Ministry of Healing*, pp. 262–264.

served as a sleeping room. Here they heated their water for fomentations in an iron pot in the fireplace; they demonstrated massage upon a pallet of two planks laid from one bed to another. They studied dietetics and hydrotherapeutics and psychotherapy under conditions such as they would find little exceeded out in the mountains. That class has since proved its superior efficiency in a number of trying positions of responsibility and authority.

But it was not until the managers felt that their hands were forced by circumstances, under great disadvantages, to take up the healing work as an institution, that the first steps were taken toward making a sanitarium. One day in the summer of 1905, there came to the Madison School a man whose home was in the city of Nashville. He was suffering from disease, and wanted a quiet place in which to recuperate. He stated that he had heard something of the Battle Creek Sanitarium, and he thought he could get those treatments there at Madison. But they told him that, while they expected some time to provide facilities for helping sick people, they were not yet in any condition to receive patients. They had but two or three cottages erected, and several of the teachers and most of the students were still crowded into the old farm house.

But he begged that he might stay. He said he would sleep on the front porch; he would eat at the family table; he would not ask for special treatments. Such importunity could not be denied, and he was told he might remain. A blanket partitioned off one end of the veranda, and there he slept. Plain and simple vegetarian food was served him on a tray. There was as yet no bathroom, and the only hydropathic facilities were a common wash-tub and a boiler in which to heat the water on the kitchen stove. But sunshine was free, pure fresh air was abundant, and cheerful determination was the key-note of the school.

Under such conditions the man's strength gradually

returned to him, and he went back to the city and resumed his business. To his friends he gave the credit for his recovery to the healthful diet, the quiet surroundings, and the cheerful atmosphere of the school.

To the school management it seemed that God was pressing them by this and similar circumstances, even before they had sufficient facilities for their school work, to establish a sanitarium in connection with it; and therefore they planned to do it. It was their purpose to build the sanitarium, not as a distinct institution, but as an integral part of the school. It must partake of the simplicity of the school, it must make the same appeal to country environment and life, and it must have its part in educating the students for service.

To many people the name "sanitarium" conveys the idea of an immense building, with elevators, steam heat, expensive apparatus, gymnasium equipped with many artificial appliances for exercise, and an atmosphere of artificial life. When one comes upon the Madison Rural Sanitarium, the contrast is so strong that it frequently calls forth an exclamation of wonder. Arranged on three sides of a hollow square, with every room fronting on the veranda and open to light and air on two sides, the little one-story sanitarium seems not an institution, but the quiet retreat of a country home. The building is surrounded by trees and blue-grass sward. The sweeping view is beautiful, the quiet is impressive and restful. Patients accustomed to the noise and smoke-laden air of the city, at once appreciate the quiet of the Rural Sanitarium.

The equipment is simple, consisting mostly of the hydropathic appliances in the two small treatment departments. For the healing of the sick, reliance is placed upon the natural remedies of fresh air, sunshine, water, proper diet, exercise, peace, and joy. Quietly and gradually the patronage has been built up. Influential people in Nashville and neighboring towns have found that within easy reach of their own homes there is a quiet little retreat where rational treatments are given, and where patients are well cared for.

The sanitarium patients are much interested in the development of the school. They become acquainted with the system of self-government, the industrial work, and other features of the school. Frequently they attend the Union Meetings, the legislative sessions of the school family. They can be found wandering over the farm where the young men are at work; and they visit and sometimes work in the garden from which the sanitarium table is supplied with vegetables, and the dairy, with whose products they have already become acquainted at the sanitarium. Their attention is called to the fact that the buildings are the work of the carpentry class, and this in itself appeals strongly to men and women who are interested in practical education. And last, their close association with the students makes them thoroughly acquainted with the chief product of the school. More than once patients have remarked that they have never met another class of young people having so definite, determined, and high a purpose in life.

Each day at the sanitarium, worship is held in the parlor. From time to time lectures are delivered on health topics, and the minds of the patients are directed to the importance of diet reform, correct habits of living and thinking, the value of the simple life, the reasons for establishing a sanitarium in the country, etc. The home life of many of these patients has been changed as the result of their stay at the sanitarium. They become acquainted with the principles here held through conversation with nurses and physicians, by attending Sabbath services with the school family, and through meetings which are held in the sanitarium itself, as well as by the literature at their hand on health and other topics. Often in warm weather the Sabbath vesper service for the entire school family is held on the sanitarium lawn. It is the custom of physicians, nurses, and workers to hold a daily prayer service in behalf of the patients and the work in general.

The Rural Sanitarium is a very small institution, but its very simplicity is in its favor. Each patient is dealt with individually. He comes daily in contact with physicians and helpers in a way impossible for patients in a larger sanitarium. The institution maintains the closest cooperation between school and sanitarium workers. In the case of the Madison School and the Rural Sanitarium, there are not two institutions. The sanitarium is simply a department of the school. The members of the school faculty are physicians, matrons, and helpers in the sanitarium. The nurses trained to carry the work at the sanitarium receive their training under these same physicians and other instructors in the school. They give a part of their time to the sanitarium and a part to the other work of the school, according to the varying needs of the several departments, thus avoiding a wastage of labor. There is absolutely no division between the sanitarium workers and the rest of the student body.

It is not designed to increase greatly the capacity of the institution. The policy of the management is rather to encourage the providing of treatment facilities in the out-schools, and to direct patients there whenever their cases seem favorable to the conditions provided.

The prospects for health homes or treatment-rooms in connection with the rural schools have developed as the result of neighborhood work among the sick. Some among their workers are trained nurses, and practically all of them have acquired some experience through answering the calls of the suffering about them. In this work they have often come in contact with the physicians of the community, who on acquaintance have become their staunch friends. "Whatever Mr. Emmet does," one of them sent word to his anxious patient, "let him alone. He will do everything all right."

One day there was a surgical operation to be performed in a little house near Mr. Emmet's school. A boy had an abscess, and the doctor finally decided it would be necessary to remove a rib in order to drain the cavity. "When I do that," he told Emmet, "I want you to be there." Mr. Emmet was visiting the boy twice a week, treating him under the physician's directions, and trying to teach his parents how to care for him — for instance, to feed him fruit and toast instead of side-meat and biscuit.

When Mr. Emmet arrived on the day of the operation, the two surgeons were already there. The boy was lifted upon a rickety kitchen table, the father with a leafy branch kept the flies off, one doctor gave the anaesthetic, Emmet handed the instruments and held open the wound, while the surgeon did the cutting. When they had gotten the boy back to bed, they stepped out into the yard, and the nurse asked, "Doctor, what do you think about it?"

He said, "Emmet, the odds are against him, but it is surprising what these people can go through. If I just had some good clean place where I could take some patients, there would be some sort of hope in treating them."

"Would you," the other asked, "cooperate with us if we could build a little place on the hill where we could take care of your patients?"

And the surgeon replied with emphasis, "Yes, sir! You will have all the cooperation I can give."

And today there stands "on the hill" the response to this appeal, in the form of a neat two-story health home, with treatment appliances and room for a dozen patients. Several other schools have provided similar facilities, and practically all are planning to do so as soon as circumstances permit. The gospel of health is an integral part of the mission of these rural school workers, as it was of their Master.

XX

THE NURSE AND THE MEDICAL MISSIONARY

CHRIST, the great Medical Missionary, is our example. Of him it is written that he 'went about all Galilee, teaching in their synagogues, and preaching the gospel of the kingdom, and healing all manner of sickness and all manner of disease among the people.' Matt. 4: 23. He healed the sick and preached the gospel. In his service, healing and teaching were linked closely together. Today they are not to be separated.

"The nurses who are trained in our institutions are to be fitted up to go out as medical missionary evangelists, uniting the ministry of the Word with that of physical healing. . . .

"All around us are doors open for service. We should become acquainted with our neighbors, and seek to draw them to Christ. As we do this, he will approve and cooperate with us. . . .

"There should be companies organized, and educated most thoroughly to work as nurses, as evangelists, as ministers, as canvassers, as gospel students, to perfect a character after the divine similitude. . . . There should be workers who make medical evangelistic tours among the towns and villages. Those who do this work will gather a rich harvest of souls, from both the higher and lower classes."[1]

---

[1] Mrs. E. G. White, *Testimonies for the Church*, Vol. IX, pp. 170-172.

Such a work as is portrayed above is distinctively that of the self-supporting workers. There is doubtless not a single group of these workers who do not have constant practise in Christian help work — relieving distress and healing the sick. From every one of the rural mission groups, experiences could be related like that of Rachel Black at the Meadowdale School.

Typhoid is a plague in that section, and when the word came that a neighbor woman and her four children (the father of the family having but recently died) were all down with typhoid fever, not a person in the neighborhood, not even their relatives, would go and stay with them. Rachel, an eighteen-year-old girl, packed her valise with a few clothes, and went down to the stricken household. There she stayed for four weeks, doing the cooking and housekeeping, and attending to all five of the cases, night and day.

When she went there, they had a doctor, an old man, who was dosing them all heavily with drugs; but Miss Rachel induced them to let her try water treatments, whereupon the old doctor refused longer to attend the cases. They sent farther away, to a railroad town, for a younger physician, who, when he came, was delighted as well as astonished to find in those backwoods a nurse who understood hydropathic methods of treatment, and he readily gave her permission to go on with her work. It was a strenuous life for the nurse, who perhaps presumed too much upon her abundant health and vigor. In one day she gave eleven mitten frictions and oil rubs, besides her other work. She nursed the mother and three of the children back to health, though before they were through with the fever the children were attacked with whooping cough — which the disgruntled old doctor ascribed to the water treatments! While the fourth child was still convalescent, Miss Rachel herself was stricken down with the fever. The news of her sickness electrified the community, and persons who had refused to care for the sick were heard to say that they would rather give their own lives than to have Rachel Black die now.

Her mother brought her home, with a temperature of 105°. The doctor called to see her and was welcomed, but no medicines were given. It was January, and Mrs. Black placed her sick daughter on a couch by the open window, where the cool winds could pass over her. She packed her in ice, fed her nothing but blackberry juice — the only fruit obtainable — and in ten days she had the fever broken. Rachel Black was back to visit her last patient before that patient — again attended by the old doctor — was out of bed. This exhibit of the efficacy of the treatment and the Christian love of the nurse gained the high favor of the community, which has, besides, had more than one similar experience with this school group.

Something of the medical missionary work of certain schools has already been mentioned in other connection, and other schools have had similar experiences. Of a wider nature is the work of Mr. Thomas Patrick, who with his wife and two little girls, after a stay of some months at the Madison School, removed to the neighborhood of Mr. Walter's school in the Cumberlands. Patrick was a pharmacist, and had had some experience as a nurse in a hospital. On the broad and long expanse of the plateau he found himself nearer being a physician than any other man there. Physicians, when needed for any case, had to come up from the valley, and it was with difficulty that one could be persuaded to climb the steep sides of the mountain, even if he could be gotten in time.

On Mr. Patrick's arrival he found Walter with a wounded hand, which he dressed. This act was quickly known thereabouts, and he was surprised when he went abroad to be saluted as "Doctor." There came to him soon after, a man who had in his spine eight open sores, which had troubled him for many years, constantly discharging pus, and causing him great pain. He had been to many doctors, and had had much treatment, but without being cured. He now asked Mr. Patrick to try to heal him. Patrick said that he was not a physician. Still the man begged him to try. He replied that he did not know whether he could help him, but he did know that the Great Physician could, if he would conform to his laws. So he took him in hand, cleansing the sores and disinfecting them. Then he knelt down and prayed for the man.

When he had risen and was about to dismiss his patient, he asked him, "Do you use pork?"

"Yes," answered the man.

"You must stop eating pork, or I can't do anything for you, because it pollutes your body, and is no doubt partly the cause of your bad condition."

The man promised and went away and told everywhere about the man who made him stop eating hog meat. As he continued to get better under further treatments, and finally was completely cured, the people gave no little heed to the idea that pork-eating should be stopped.

Mr. Patrick soon found himself in demand for miles about, wherever there were sick people. He had bought a small place on the mountain, intending to support his family from the soil, and he now had his garden planted, but he could get no time to tend it. Calls came from one direction and another, and soon a familiar sight on the lonely mountain roads came to be this nurse, going on foot from place to place to attend the sick.

The matter of a living seemed just then a serious matter to Mr. and Mrs. Patrick. They had come out from an affluent life, and were quite unused to the wilderness and its hardships and privations; and now how they should get their daily bread was an immediate problem. Mr. Patrick never charged fees for his work: he gave as freely as did the Great Physician in the days of his ministry; and seldom, at first, were gifts made to him. His garden grew up in weeds, despite the best endeavors of his wife; for every time he would set himself to garden making, a call would be sure to come from some one in distress, and he could not refuse to go. Nevertheless, that garden, under its weedy blanket, yielded wonderfully, as well as most cultivated gardens, a blessing which they took as a direct favor from the Lord. And now and again, at some critical time, when no dinner was in sight, some unexpected providence would furnish them with bread.

Meanwhile Mr. Patrick continued his itinerant mission to the people of the mountain. He would first treat his patients for their immediate pains, then he would pray for them, and afterwards he would instruct them in habits of right living. Always he would tell them that they must stop using tobacco and liquor, and he would not treat them unless they did this, because, he said, these are the laws of God, and it is God who is doing the healing. Far more than his treatments, the faith and the earnest prayer of the man impressed those who came under his charge, and a great reformation was begun.

One day, early in his experience, Mr. Patrick passed by a schoolhouse out in the woods. He stopped to rest and watch, and thus became acquainted with the teacher and the boys and girls. Their conversation soon turned to topics of health, and Mr. Patrick began to introduce some thoughts of hygiene badly needed there. The teacher finally invited him to come to the school and teach the boys and girls, and also to teach him, so that he might help his pupils. The children took great delight in the physical exercises and marches, and listened with eagerness to the health principles taught. A very considerable change was made in the surroundings; outhouses were built where there were none before, personal cleanliness became a gospel to the school, and appreciation of the value of God's remedial agencies — fresh air, sunshine, pure water and food — was brought into many homes. The teacher himself became an enthusiastic supporter and exemplar of these physical truths which bear so close a relation to mental and spiritual purity and health.

It was chiefly through the interest aroused in the children that Mr. Patrick succeeded in founding a health club composed largely of adults, a club which early reached a membership of seventy-five. The members of this club pledged themselves to maintain purity of thought and life, and to follow a program of exercise, pure food, and cleanliness. The influence of this voluntary health association, not only against the grosser evils of liquor and tobacco, but upon the inner life of thought and will, is an incalculable ally of truth and purity.

Meanwhile, this itinerant medical evangelist goes his way over the roads and trails of the mountain wilderness, seeking no gain but the blessing and happiness of his fellow-men, and following far in the steps of that Master who "went about doing good, and healing all that were oppressed of the devil." It is a work that is yet to be imitated far and wide by those who see value in the Saviour's methods, who are willing to sacrifice themselves to the heavy work and the meager living that invariably accompany the peace and joy and power of the close followers of Jesus of Nazareth.

Madison Rural Sanitarium.
"The Rural Sanitarium at Madison stands in close adherence to this ideal." Page 229.

School Work

"THE old education fails to reach the mountain problem because it is not adapted to mountain conditions. The kind of education needed is education which shall have a larger bearing upon the life which the people are to lead. The school by which this education is to be provided must establish a practical connection between education and work. Its course of study must have to do with the industries of the environment." ANDREW J. RITCHIE.

XXI

THE SCHOOLS OF GOD

GOD made the first school upon earth, which he intended to be a model for all after schools. The teachers were himself and his angels, and the pupils were the first man and woman, the schoolroom was a garden, and the text-books were the created things of land and sea and sky. In this school, work was study, and achievement was the companion of study. The service which man received from all creation, he repaid in service; yet so evenly ran the course of nature that service was not toil, and life was joyous because the powers of mind and body were ever fresh and eager for use.

Sin spoiled the perfection of man's life, deranged its course, and made infinitely hard its conditions; yet even under the changed conditions, true education still seeks to conform itself to the original plan. The inability of parents may force the partial substitution of other teachers, the niggardliness of nature may require more work for the support of life, and dulled minds and depraved natures may thwart much of the Creator's design in study; yet the schools of God today will seek the conditions and the methods of that school of Eden.

At the present day, the popular system of education is a child of medievalism. It has freed itself from many of the shackles bound upon it by the Dark Ages, and every day is struggling still clearer; yet in many of its forms and its ideals it shows its parentage and its servitude. In this the public mind lags behind the scholastic mind, and it is difficult to get rid of many ideas and practises which lie embedded deep in popular prejudice. Most parents of school children yet make booklearning a synonym of education, and the modern reforms of educational handicrafts, from sloyd to machine shops, are begrudged by almost a majority of parents, who grumble that they can teach these things to their children at home.

If they could and if they had, the burden would not be upon the school; but the history of the home in the past century has been a history of progressive abdication. It has successively resigned to institutional hands, to governmental hands, to ecclesiastical hands, or to no hands at all, its ancient privileges of instruction in arts and handicrafts, in the principles of obedience and control, and in the tenets and practises of Christianity. When Horace Mann began his agitation for government control of child education, it was yet at a time when the parent was capable, and not altogether neglectful, of giving his children an education in everything but literature. America was a land of farms, whereon the boys and girls were taught how to live practical lives, where only for book knowledge was there a famine. And America, despite its free thought, was a land of religion in home and church. And it was a land of homes, where the day saw the united efforts of family workers, and the evening saw their gatherings around the fireside, the work-table, or the festive board. But with the growth of commercialism, of irreligion, and of urban life, the family group has been dissolving. The average home today is little more than a lodging house and a restaurant. Rarely does it hear the voice of family prayer or of parental instruction, seldom is it the center of communal industry and association. It has thrown the burden of the one upon the church, and of the other upon the institution. And thus to thoughtful educators the state's training of the child, neglected by the home and in all practical senses by the church, has become a problem not merely of literature and science, but of a fitting for complete life. And for sufficient cause they have instituted reforms.

To the degree to which these reforms approach the ideal of the home, God's original school pattern, they are in the right direction. But that the state can ever make a satisfactory substitute for the home in the complete education of its children was refuted long ago by the experience of old Sparta, which took the child almost from the cradle, making the state his father and mother, and succeeded in creating patriots but not nation-builders, and by usurping the home destroyed the state.

The public teacher, with all the ability he may possess and all the facilities he may create, cannot take the place of the parent in the home, unless he fully puts himself in the place of that parent, and makes his school a home. It is not possible as it is not desirable, that the teacher become the parent of the community. But it is possible, as it is altogether desirable, that he help the parents and the homes to be all they should be to the child. This is the teacher's greatest work, and success in the effort will become his greatest triumph. For in the restoration of the home to its prime place as a school, lies the hope of the nation and of the church. That nation which has no proper homes will cease to be a nation, and that church which is not composed of Christian homes is no church of Christ.

To do this work, the teacher must rely not so much upon lecture as upon demonstration. He must make his school a home, that it may show the home how to be a school. In attempting this, he may not be able to succeed wholly. Untoward circumstances or his own disabilities may make his effort but partially successful; yet by the degree to which he succeeds, so near is he to the kingdom of heaven, so much is his school a school of God. If he shows the beauty and the value of a country environment, if he establishes the dignity and the joy of labor and achievement, if he inculcates the virtues of obedience and good cheer, if he inspires the spirit of service, he has with his students entered the school where God put the first pupils of earth, and where he will establish the last and everlasting university of the universe.

The school, then, that seeks to do God's work will be a school not merely of books, but of work and of religion. This is the ideal toward which the schools of the rural mission system aim. As an illustration of their methods, let us take the program of the Shamrock School.

It is in the early spring, and the neat white schoolhouse in the oaks up on the clay hill is making an urgent call to the boys and girls of the neighborhood for a term's work before they must get down to solid toil in the corn fields, the tobacco patches, and the experimental gardens. They come, from the youngster of six to the youth of twenty, and fill the two rooms of the little schoolhouse to overflowing. No tuition is required. Thus even the children of the poorest are welcomed to the school. Three teachers there are belonging to the schoolhouse, and as many more outside, for every man and woman engaged in making the living, in house, in sawmill, or on the farm, must hold himself ready to teach the younger ones the things he is doing.

The morning session is literary in the main, though mingled with many sounds and echoes of the industrial work. Mr. Emmet, the principal, opens the day by leading the school in religious exercises of song and Scripture reading — or sometimes of Scripture recitation — and prayer. The Bible classes (Bible history) taught by himself and his wife, are open to all, though not obligatory, and are entered by practically all the pupils. The quieting, steadying, character-developing influence of Bible study is evident in the daily lives of the students, and the leaven is observable through all the community.

The Word of God is the foundation of any stable school and community, as also of the home. And not alone in the Bible classes is the Scripture unfolded. Its precepts are interwoven in all the instruction, and embodied in the practises of the school and the lives of the teachers. There, indeed, it exerts more influence even than in the spoken word.

Mrs. Emmet carries the main burden of the upper classes, while her sister, Mabel Ore, is engaged with the primary pupils. The literary work of the school is not especially peculiar from that of other progressive schools, though distinguished from many by the plentiful employment of illustration through charts, maps, and drawings, and by the use of special text-books in reading and science, which shun, on the one hand, the myths, fairy-tales, and legends of paganism, and on the other the untruths of popular science. These teachers are Christians guided in their teaching by a firm and simple faith in the Word of God.

But the morning hour passes, lunch time arrives and is passed; then come the industrial classes. While the little children, below the age of twelve, are given drawing and practical, homely sloyd — sewing and mending, making button holes and matching the buttons to them — besides the more artistic basket weaving and the nerve-relaxing, muscle-stretching work of caring for the yard and the garden, the older students are being trained in the higher duties of home and field. The boys and young men are taken into the field and the carpenter shop. They all know how to hold the plow, and they may need only instruction as to the benefits of deeper plowing and fertilizers and cover crops, but practical work they must have in propagating, planting, and pruning fruit. The plants they set are watched by the class, and so far as their attendance permits are cared for by them through the season; and the bearing fruit trees and vines which they prune in the spring give them employment in the fall in the gathering of fruit, a science in itself. They must also study live stock, and the school furnishes objects for study in its sheep, goats, cattle, horses, and mules. While the agriculture study given them is of course elementary, it is nevertheless intensely practical. It is the same education that the farm home used to give, with the addition of some of the science which modern study has added to the subject; and, primary though the study is, it is the basis for a thorough work to be concluded later in the agricultural college or at least conducted in the agricultural books and papers that come to the farmer.

The carpentry work has been partly in the shop, much more fully on the buildings — the cottages and the barns which the school has been erecting from time to time. This, too, is of the most practical nature, such as the home would naturally furnish. Some fathers in some homes do give this instruction, but the majority do not, and in all cases the usually superior advantages of the teacher make the school instruction valuable.

The first half hour of all this work is given to class study, usually out of doors, under the trees, or in the fields and orchards, or out in the pasture, or at the bench, or before the building. And then immediately comes the practical application of the instruction. Six to eight boys are usually handled by each of the men teachers, and strict attention to the work in hand is enforced, the same as in the schoolroom. The boys are taught that this work means as much in the development of mind and character, as the studies conducted in the schoolroom, or possibly more. Their conversation is kept upon the work they are doing, for where their words are, there their minds will be.

The girls, meanwhile, are taken by Mrs. Emmet and Mrs. Ore into the teachers' homes, and taught the science of home-making. While the greater part of the girls' industrial work comes in the afternoon, the necessities of housekeeping and cooking require some work in the forenoon. As with the boys, so with the girls, the first half hour is given to the study of the work they are going to do. Cooking is a daily practise, for certain ones of the girls are detailed each day to get the dinner for the school family under the leadership of their teachers. And practically every day there is a study in the science of cooking. Charts giving food values, composition, combinations, etc., are in daily consultation, as well as the cook-book; and schoolroom classes, such as physiology and hygiene, drawing, and arithmetic, are closely related to this cooking class. Besides, the days devoted to certain industries have studies in those arts. For instance, on Monday the girls study how to wash before they bend over the tubs. (And incidentally, they are taught that it belongs to the men to furnish sufficient water, either by piping it to the house, or pumping it up, or carrying it from the spring.) On Tuesday there comes a study in ironing while the irons are reaching the exact temperature. Another study of great importance is housekeeping: sweeping, scrubbing, dusting, and the making of beds.

The work is divided among the girls in each home. One girl may have to sweep and dust, another to help with the dishes, another with the washing; but during the term every girl gets her experience in doing the things they have had together in class study. The girl who bakes bread one week has an all-day job which she must attend to at intervals. The making of light bread is an art highly prized, and none too common, in the hills and mountains, and the girl who can carry to her home the perfect art of breadmaking has brought a boon into that home more prized, perhaps, by the household than any other practical art.

On all these subjects, domestic, agricultural, and mechanical, examinations are held periodically, the same as for other studies, and the industrial branches are in every way put on a par with the literary studies.

While not a few highly appreciate this kind of education, there have sometimes been parents, naturally, who objected to it. They held the ancient doctrine that children go to school to "learn books," and they felt that time spent in living practical life was wasted or unjustly given to teachers instead of to parents. Though the parent may himself be extremely impatient about teaching his child these things, because he thinks the child is slow and dull, or careless and indifferent, yet it is hard to convince him that the teacher is giving more than he gets out of the labor of the student. What every industrial teacher knows as an axiom, that student labor is unprofitable commercially, is a truth unknown to some parents. But as the Shamrock School charges no tuition, and attendance there is not compulsory, the teachers are in a position to say that if objection is made by the parent, he has the privilege of taking the child out, a privilege that none so far have accepted.

A means of better reaching the parent, however, with the value of this system, is found in the monthly parents' meetings held at this school. Some schools hold them more frequently. There the problems of the home are studied, the parents' perplexities may be brought forth, and instruction from the Word of God, from other good books, or from the teachers' experience, is applied. The betterment of the home, in material as well as in social and spiritual matters, is also studied, and this interchange of thought and this social contact are powerful factors in uniting parents and teachers. In regard to the industrial features, parents are taught to see that while school and work have been popularly divorced, it is in God's plan that they be closely united, and that the teachers, while professing no greater ability than the parents to teach the child, must nevertheless unite the three features of education, piety, literature, and useful labor so as to give the child a rational philosophy of the life he is being educated to live. The home, they are taught, is to be a school, and the school a home. They are urged to bring into the home every element of the school which they can, and thus make themselves the teachers in greater and greater degree of their children. This view appeals to the parent, the most intelligent and the most ignorant, and the influence of this teaching and practise has become very evident in the community, in better and more attractive homes, and in some cases in a closer union between parent and teacher. It is the ideal of the school, not to separate parent and child by a gulf between learning and ignorance, but to make each the helper and supporter of the other; for service to the lowly as well as to the great is the maxim of the kingdom of Christ.

XXII

THE MOUNTAIN CHILD AND THE WORLD

NARROW and broad are relative terms; and, according to standard, the views of every man may be either narrow or broad. In God's view we are all narrow, for our knowledge is confined mostly to this round ball on which we live. My nearest neighbors, indeed, differ from me in not believing that we live on any ball whatever. They maintain, with much show of scriptural authority, that the earth is flat and stationary, while the sun moves around it; for does not the Bible declare that the sun stood still when so commanded by Joshua? Likewise, they scout much of the information I have laboriously gathered from books and hearsay. They refuse to believe that there is such a thing as a cannibal. Did I ever see a man eat another man? Then how do I know! Who says there is no water on the moon? Has any one ever journeyed there to see? Also, they believe in "ha'nts," and I despair of convincing them of their unreality, for they would receive no testimony as final save that of disembodied spirits.

Yet what right have I to call my views broad and theirs narrow? If measured by the standard of the universe, the comparative difference in width would be infinitesimal, and whether my views or my mountaineer neighbors' would be ahead, I cannot say. The most I can say is that there is a difference in direction. I may consider myself capable of teaching them geography, but they, on the other hand, rightly regard themselves as able to instruct me in a horse deal. If I (supposedly) overtop them in height of knowledge, they outdo me in wealth of heart. And I believe that my only hope of enriching them with knowledge is first to share, till I can exceed, in the riches of love. They will listen to one they love.

The mountains have all classes, rich and poor, cultured, learned, and ignorant. When, therefore, we speak of the mountain child and his relation to the world, we must consider several classes. First, there are the children of the wealthy, who have all the advantages, not only of common education, but of travel and broad social life. Their knowledge and measure of the world are in no sense peculiar. Second, there are the children of the cities and other communities where the schools and other public utilities are the best. Whether for good or ill, their advantages differ little from those of the children of other sections with the same advantages.

But traveling down through a succession of less favored classes, we reach the child of the isolated mountain community, either far away in some valley or cove, or up on some plateau, where the world is bounded by a horizon but few miles away. To such children even the blessing of literacy gives only a limited field; for the figures and allusions of literature are often but dimly if at all comprehensible to them. The mental life of their community furnishes no stimulus to imagination, and the stories of the Bible, of secular history, or of chance travelers, are localized within the narrow rim of the child's experience, or left altogether outside, uncomprehended. As illustrating the character of the teacher's work under such conditions, we are privileged to quote from a report by one of them at a convention of rural school workers:

"We first met our new neighbors in a Sunday school

about a mile away, and, owing to a previous introduction, my husband was invited to take the Bible class, and the younger members were turned over to me, and I was supposed to do something with them till they were through asking questions over in the Bible class. But had I stopped half an hour before, the children would have waited quietly without pinching or pricking or doing one of the many impolite things any other children I ever taught would have done.

"I can hardly describe to you the difficulty I met in trying to really present to them the lesson, to really bring before them a mental picture of it. We were studying the book of Matthew. Take, for instance, the 'Stilling of the Tempest.' Saying, 'Jesus went into a boat,' meant little to them. They never had seen a boat or hardly heard of one. A picture would help somewhat, to be sure. 'And started across the lake, when a mighty storm came up.' But they have no mental picture of the lake. I might say, 'Well, you've all seen a "branch," and have been wading in it. Suppose it were deep enough to cover these tallest pine trees and as wide as from here to that far brow of the mountain. And if the water were standing still, as you've seen it in big puddles after a rain, it would be a lake. When the storm raged upon the lake, the water looked rough and white like the "Big Falls," or like a "swillin bullin,"'—a name the children gave to water backed up in the spring during a heavy rain, derived, I suppose, from "swelling billows."

"And so I had to invent and contrive to make for them anything of a mental picture of the lesson story. But by the answers and looks of animation that crept into some of the faces, I knew, in time, that I was at least partly succeeding.

"Other work pressing upon us made it impossible to attend this school very long, but the short connection with it confirmed our belief that schoolroom work should be one of our first efforts.

"It was easy to find the 'work,' but where was the

'room'? After a deal of careful study of the problem, we went down to the little 16 x 24 canner building by the spring, nailed some boards over the most open places, put in four small half-window sashes, packed the canning outfit up in one corner, took down the shelf used by the solderer, and put up a smaller one to be used by the teacher, borrowed some wobbly benches from the public school building a mile away, brought in plenty of cedar and golden rod, and opened school.

"My husband had expressed some serious misgivings as to the wisdom of requiring the children to use their eyes in such a poorly lighted place, but we were somewhat encouraged to try when a young man who was assisting in the preparation remarked, 'Well, one thing's sure, you-all will have plenty of light in your school.' Four little streams of light coming through glass into one room was more than he had ever seen in that region before.

"There were just six pupils enrolled that first morning, besides the three little natives we then claimed as our own, two of whom were too young to enter as regular students. But we sang, and I believe with something of the spirit and understanding, 'I'm so glad that Jesus said, Let the children come to me.' And it seemed as though the birds and the breezes took up the song. So the children came, until in two weeks there were twenty-one enrolled, and that was the limit of accommodation. But the spirit in which they came was the notable feature. One burly little fellow who expected one or two whippings a day every one of the few days of public school, came there as docile as a little lamb, and seemed childishly happy and contented every moment. Boys and girls who squirted tobacco juice right and left when at home, did not soil the rough boards in the canner schoolhouse, as we called it, with one little drop.

"I chose for the central thought of the school work — or I might say for *my* motto —'Importance of obedience to law.' For I was in a community where too many knew no higher law than their own caprice or the tradition of their fathers. I never gave the words of my text to the children, but sought to bring them frequent illustrations, as, for instance, the many examples nature was affording us at that time of year. We found, by marking on the floor at noon, the point the sun reached, that he was gradually traveling south, and that this was his obedience to the law given him to 'be for signs, for seasons, for days, and for years.'

"The teacher's shelf was filled often to overflowing with things brought in by the children, as nuts, beans, corn, etc., as illustrations of herbs 'bearing seed after their kind, whose seed was in itself.' And in harmony with a great universal law, not written in books, nor dictated by man, every one of these, along with many animals and birds, were preparing for the decreed winter. Disobedience to this law meant hardship, if not death.

"Because we were handling so many good things to eat in our nature work, we began physiology (largely oral work) with the digestive system, and discovered a few simple, inexorable laws of digestion and chemistry; and as we were studying the Bible by course, we came in time to the giving of the law in Sinai, and a few of the older ones learned the Ten Commandments, and all came to enjoy that sweet hymn, 'How Gentle God's Commands.'

"Thrown in parenthetically at Thanksgiving time, we had an illustration of the bondage of cruel human law in the story of the Pilgrims. The story was all so new to them, but evidently very interesting. But it was no stranger to them than facts about their own State and county. We had a simple little Thanksgiving program, and the older members of our family came down to help with the music. We had learned to sing 'America,' so after helping us with that, they gave us 'Dixie,' but even it was as new and strange to those little mountaineers as the Pilgrim story.

"In place of dictated physical culture work, they sometimes played the animating game of 'dare base,' which I had taught them. (They seemed to know no games,— had not even felt the ball craze.) We held ten-minute parliamentary sessions three times a week, and made our own code or rules for the game, elected a secretary, and did things in a *lawful* manner. They cleared a little place, and made careful measurements for the bases. It was very interesting to note how much they *enjoyed* being law-abiding.

"At Christmas time we prepared a little more elaborate program, though still very simple and crude. Our little room could hold no more, and so we took our organ and stove, and went over to the public school building, and with mistletoe and cedar, mottoes and decorations, Miss W. transformed the place into a thing of beauty. There were two Christmas trees, hung with candles, apples, bright bags of popcorn and nuts and a few inexpensive little gifts we were able to prepare, and some others were brought in by the people, besides a sample of canned stuff for every family in the neighborhood.

"It was really a bitter cold night, but the house was full. We sent what extra clothes we could spare to some of the poorer neighbors to enable them to come. One flock of children came to ride over with us — the girls of four and six wearing old worsted basques for cloaks, and with bare knees. And so they came in all kinds of apparel, and listened to every word of the program with deepest interest. The faces of the parents whose children took part, fairly beamed with delight. It was the first experience of the kind to the children, and they certainly did themselves credit.

"It seemed to me I should freeze stiff before it was out, but at the close one woman said, 'I didn't think about the cold. I wish it had been longer. I could sit and listen to such as that all night.'

"The wonders of that evening were talked about for miles around. The strangest of all was, no one had gotten drunk, there was no whiskey passed around or pistols shot off, and the simple little songs and poems and stories of the Babe in the manger and the guiding star, had touched a chord in their souls that they enjoyed having played upon.

"The home life of a large majority of these people is almost a blank in the sense in which we think of the word "home." In so many instances it is to them merely a place where they warm themselves (one side at a time), 'lay down' at night, and get something to eat.

"We are instructed, when entering a field like this, to 'begin by correcting the physical habits of the people.' 'Physical habits' must mean their manner of eating, sleeping, dressing, treating their sick, and general habits of home life. And we asked ourselves, 'How can we hope to correct their habits along these lines? Simply to tell them they are doing all these things in almost the worst way, will do no good unless we provide for a better way and teach it to them.

"The calls already coming opened the way for a physician and a visiting nurse to deal with one phase of this work, and it could be self-supporting, though but little more than that. In the physiology, cooking, and sewing classes, the *how* of the other phases could be taught, but what use to teach the value of fruit as an article of diet, and the best manner of preparing vegetables, grains, etc., when the home larder provided nothing but pork and corn meal and tea? And that was often the actual condition.

"No, the school work must go farther, and teach them how to make the land (and nearly every man owns a good-sized farm of woodland) yield them a proper dietary.

"Take, for instance, the tomato. Let it be studied in the nature class from a botanical standpoint, its value as a food and conditions of growth considered, hot-beds made and seeds planted by the students, and

The Mountain Child and the World 259

a piece of ground properly prepared and some plants set on the school farm; but also let each student have a piece of ground at home which he prepares just as the class do the one at school, and then give or sell him at a low price, plants enough to set his land. The teacher ought to be free to visit these gardens often. When the crop matures let the school canner can his fruit on shares. He then has one healthful thing put away for winter. If he grows more than he can use, the canner may sell the surplus for him, and the teacher in nearly every instance can control the use of the money, especially if he requires the pupil to keep a 'Garden Book,' and is teaching, as may be done even in the lowest grades, the keeping of simple accounts. The money will be spent for books, clothes, etc., rather than for tobacco. Other fruits and vegetables could be dealt with in a similar manner. The school farm and canner must help in 'correcting the physical habits.'

"In spite of all the difficulties, the work there has steadily won the interest and confidence of those dear superstitious, tradition-ridden, hospitable people. I have never worked among a class more needy, but at the same time one which yielded better results for a given expenditure of energy and material. They have a latent love of the beautiful and appreciation of what counts for the highest and best in life; and in spite of their poor English, their tobacco-stained faces, and their uncouth garb, they possess a true refinement which might silence any boasting of superiority from the average well-dressed city boy and girl, or man and woman. These mountain brothers and sisters of ours are true Americans, independent and highly sensitive to any suggestions of non-equality."

Many, though not all, of the rural mission schools are operating under somewhat similar conditions. The work of a teacher in such a case is the most delicate given to men. His must be a nice touch, a sensitive perception. To enlighten and broaden without wounding, to inspire and lead to higher things while still keeping in contact with the conditions and the needs about him, is an accomplishment for which only the wisdom of the Master Teacher is sufficient. But the teachers' hearts are cheered with a sight of the results. Some of the North Carolina schools can point with satisfaction to graduates in various occupations, from farmers and mechanics to ministers and physicians. One is a missionary in Africa. The first of the Madison out-schools, the Oak Grove School, though but a few years old, numbers among its graduates several teachers. One of them — a fine, manly young fellow — has been for several years principal of a graded school in the valley. He came at the first session of Mr. Alden's school, knowing nothing of grammar and not so much as common fractions in arithmetic. His mental progress was rapid, but his advance in moral and religious matters was most interesting. Early in his school life he was introduced, as are all the older pupils, to the custom of occasionally leading the school in its devotional exercises. The natural reverence of the hill child deepened in him, and though he was undemonstrative, and therefore not specially a leader in the church, his sturdiness of character was recognized throughout the community, and he was a silent power for good.

But one habit, which seemed ineradicable, troubled his conscience. He had used tobacco from his early childhood, and though thoroughly convinced from the studies in the school that it was doing him harm bodily and mentally, and though he tried various plans to rid himself of it — tapering off, and using anti-tobacco remedies — he could not cure himself. He finally began teaching in the valley, and, determined to make himself an example to his pupils, he began a rigid limiting of his allowance, till at Christmas time he was down to "three chews a week." But he could get no further, and came in great distress to Mr. Alden, who had now been laboring with him especially for two years to give up his tobacco. Mr. Alden told him he could not do it by degrees, nor by his own strength; he must settle the matter by prayer, and then take the plug he was chewing and throw it away forever. The young man followed the advice to the letter. He was plowing in the field at home the next day, and suddenly coming to the resolution, he threw himself on his knees by his plow, and prayed for deliverance. Then he rose, took his plug from his pocket, and threw it as far as he could. His taste for tobacco left him that moment, and he has been free ever since. His activity in religious matters has greatly increased. He is now not only a leader in the Sunday school, but in the prayer-meeting, while pushing on in his profession and winning golden opinions from his educational superiors.

The teachers who take such boys from the pit wherein they have been mired, see in such victories an evidence of spiritual as well as of physical progress. The one who begins a "spiritual" life with the handicap of evil physical habits will have a hard time to maintain spirituality. The farther, the faster he overcomes physical evil, the more rapidly do his conception of truth and his living of truth progress. Every victory gained, every step forward, is so much more received of the character of Christ, and if that course is unfalteringly pursued, it will end in the imprint of the seal of God upon a perfect character.

XXIII

VICE AND VICTORY

THE main purpose of the Christian school, in its work both for the children and for the grown people of the community, is to lift to a higher life in body and mind. It seeks by teaching and inspiration to rid the people of vices great and small, that they may become true Christians and earnest workers for Christ. In the mountain and hill schools the great and almost universal vice is the use of tobacco, especially in its two most loathsome forms, chewing and snuff-dipping. The extent to which this habit dwarfs and stupefies the mind is responsible for not a little of the backwardness and the blunted moral sense with which the teacher has to deal. Little boys six and eight years old not infrequently are found with the quid puffing out their lean cheeks, and little girls of as tender age are proud to hold the snuffstick between their stained lips.

The standard is, indeed, rising, and in many communities women who are desirous of social respect are ashamed of the habit of snuff-dipping, while men are making the dubious advance of substituting the cigarette for the plug; but as yet in the outskirts of the mountain country this is not so, and the teaching that tobacco is bad comes as a curious doctrine to many a mountaineer who, even when a willing disciple, often needs continual instruction and correction. To the Eden Valley School, hidden behind the high mountains of a North Carolina district, came a man with his family from an adjoining county, who from reading had begun to keep the Sabbath. There had been many things to teach him, and little time for instruction, but he was watching for every point of faith and practise that he could find. On Sabbath, when Mr. Nelson with his wife went down to this man's house on the lower part of the school farm, the new convert offered him a pipe. Mr. Nelson quietly refused, with thanks, and the man, wondering within himself, concluded that it was not right to smoke on Sabbath. He himself therefore refrained during the day, but as soon as the sun went down, he got out his pipe and began to smoke. Again he offered the visitor tobacco, but this time was informed that Adventists never used it. In a few words answers were given to his questions, and, convinced that tobacco was harmful, he immediately threw his into the fire, as his wife did her snuff, and thereafter they did not touch the weed.

It has been a question with the teachers in the hill schools exactly what position they ought to take in regard to the use of tobacco by their pupils. On the one hand, the injury to mind and body, and the nauseous character of the habit, incline the teacher absolutely to prohibit it; on the other hand, too early and abrupt a prohibition might result in turning away unreformed many a pupil who by more gradual means could be reclaimed. It has therefore been the more general practise to prohibit the use of tobacco within the schoolhouse, appealing therein to the students' sense of cleanliness and desire to progress, while leaving its use on the school grounds and elsewhere to be affected by the studies of the school in physiology, hygiene, and moral laws.

At the Eden Valley School, which shares with few others the distinction of ministering to the most isolated and unprivileged classes, the beautiful new schoolhouse, clean and attractive, with its white walls artistically relieved by pictures, maps, and the drawing and sloyd work of the school, there is a resistless esthetic appeal to the children who come — many of them — from dingy, crowded, and unlovely homes. Though on the school grounds at recess, or in the afternoon industrial classes, there may here and there be detected on children's breaths the unspeakable stench of the molasses-filled "store plug," or the less offensive smell of the home "dry twist," in the schoolroom there is never spot nor stain from the unhallowed thing.

At the infrequent times when the school entertains a visitor from the outside world, and he is announced to speak publicly, the news, carried far and wide by the children, fills the big main room of the schoolhouse to its fullest capacity, with eager, open-eyed children, with parents slower of motion and duller of eye, along with the groups of swaggering youth and shy-faced maidens inevitable in every rural community. But though in their own church and social gatherings the older ones are used to the free exercise of the right of expectoration, and sometimes to regular journeyings of the whiskey-bottle, the firing of guns outside, and a few private or free-for-all fights, up here at the "school on the hill" they are as well behaved, attentive, and courteous, as at the best-ordered Episcopal service in the city, and not a sight and scarcely a smell of tobacco is to be found. The influence of the school, its principles and its practise, is telling.

Mr. and Mrs. Arthur, the teachers, tell of this one and that one and the other, five or six in all, who during the year have quietly forsaken the habit of tobacco-using, constantly swelling the numbers of the band of defenders around the school principles. These principles, given in precept in the schoolroom, and reinforced and exemplified in the students' life with the teachers in home, field, and woods — for all the local as well as boarding students take the industrial classes in the afternoon — are setting before them ideals of life that lift them above the sordid pleasures symbolized by the birch twig and the tin tag.

While the Visitor was there, one evening there came in the mail from a Chicago friend a postal order for two dollars, with the explanation that it was "bribe money." This suggestion of Chicago graft at work so far from home interested the Visitor, who straightway made inquiry as to the nature of the bribes. Nurse Bryan explained that the term was coined in Chicago to fit her description of Mis' Margaret's operations on the tobacco problem.

One little eight-year-old boy, a "woods-colt," who had found refuge in the "school on the hill" from the taunts of his child companions, was beggarly furnished with shoes and hat. The mud and water oozed in through his broken soles, while his old felt hat served less to cover his red thatched head than to hide his blue eyes. Mis' Margaret found means to supply the needed articles from the stock of "imported goods" and from her own meager purse, and the little fellow thereafter, with dog-like devotion, trod in her foot-prints, with an eye for every little personal service he could discover. His grateful devotion was touching; and it sprung an idea into Mis' Margaret's head. From his mother no less than from his companions he had learned to chew, and the quid was seldom absent from his mouth outside school hours.

"Henry," said Mis' Margaret one day, "do you want to do something that would please me very much?"

"Sure I will, Mis' Margaret," was his ready response.

"Then promise me never to use tobacco any more."

It was a request for half his kingdom; but he had given the word of a king. The struggle was short. He knew the principle of the thing; the school had taught him the harm of tobacco; but he had grown up with it, and never yet had found his boyish stock of courage great enough to throw it away. Now his blue eyes shifted from Mis' Margaret's face, wandered down the hill, across the valley, and away to the far-off heights. Before his eyes, perhaps, stood out the motto on the schoolroom wall, "I will lift up mine eyes to the hills, whence cometh my help." From those far hills, at least, his gaze came back to the eyes of his teacher. It was only a minute before he said, simply, "I will, Mis' Margaret." Slowly he drew the "dry twist" from his pocket, and with a quick fling sent it spinning down the steep hill. He did not touch tobacco after that.

When he went home and told his mother what he had promised, there was another convert; for, as she afterwards told the teacher, "I thought that if Henry was a-goin' to fight that fight, he couldn't see me around dippin' an' chewin'. His mother ain't a-goin' to be a millstone hangin' round his neck." Girl victim of man's passion and cowardice though she had been, and slave besides to the most nauseous of vices, she had played a mother's part to this boy of hers as best she knew how, and now she answered the next appeal to her motherhood, and stepped one step higher with her son.

Another little chap there was in the school whom ordinary bribes would not affect. His mother, though she herself used snuff, had offered to get him a new pair of shoes if he would quit chewing; and his uncle promised him a flour-sack full of candy. But he shook his head; he loved his plug.

But he also loved music. He had a rare talent, indeed, for it; and voice or organ, but especially piano, would charm him almost into heaven. He knew by heart half a hundred songs, and his voice rang out the cheeriest in the morning exercises of the school. One day, after school, he was telling his teacher of the bribes his relatives had offered him, and of their failure.

"I'll tell you what I'll give you, Charley, if you'll quit tobacco," said Mis' Margaret.

"What?" And the shrewd speculation of the mountaineer showed in his eyes.

"I'll teach you to play the piano," she said.

"Will you?" His voice rang with pleasure; but immediately it changed to a note of doubt, "I don't reckon I could stick," he said.

"You think it over, Charley, and whenever you get ready, let me know. Whenever you have let tobacco alone for a day, come and tell me, and I will give you a lesson that very night," she promised.

But he did not come that evening. He slipped away without being seen. The next day he kept out of the way of any conversation or inquiry, and the teacher wondered if he had taken up the gage of battle at all. But that evening he came to her with shining eyes.

"I get my lesson tonight, Mis' Margaret," he said. "I would of last night; I pretty near did it. But you know when I go out to the well for a drink, I always take a chew, and yesterday evening, when I let down the bucket, it kind of slipped into my mouth before I thought. I hit him a lick today, though. Hain't touched it, and it's right there,"— hitting his hip pocket with an emphatic hand. "It'll stay there till I've forgotten it, too.".

His mother said to him afterwards, "Charlie, why didn't you give up tobacco when your uncle offered you a sack full of candy?"

He replied, "I reckoned it wouldn't last very long."

"Why did you do it, then," she pursued, "for the music lessons?"

And the young philosopher answered, "I reckoned they'd last as long as I would."

Four months had passed when the Visitor heard this tale; and parents and friends all testified to the fact that Charley had never taken a chew since. And probably he had "forgotten it," as his hip pocket no longer bulged, and he was becoming an accomplished pianist.

But the tobacco habit is only one of the vices against which the schools are striving, and from which they are endeavoring to uplift their children with the parents. The lax moral conditions prevailing in some places are responsible for a degree of misery and degradation that goes beyond any other trouble.

Let it not be understood, here, that the South is peculiar in having these conditions. Indeed, after careful and somewhat extensive observation and inquiry, the belief has grown that the sins of impurity are less prevalent in the mountains than in more sophisticated communities. But they show more in open than in secret vice, and in the general society rather than in a segregated class. And further, this peculiarity will be noticed in the rural white South: that a highly moral community may be located only a few miles from a notoriously immoral community, a peculiarity due sometimes to the boundaries fixed by mountains and hills, and always to the smaller degree of travel and mingling of communities with one another. Thus, a community which has the benefit of a good ancestry of high principles, is likely to keep that high moral tone, and vice versa; whereas in the North the greater amount of travel and commingling of peoples tends to make nearly a dead level.

Take, then, from the shady side of the mountain, two stories of needs and ministry, stories exceptional and extreme in their showing of hard conditions, but no wise extreme nor exceptional in their bright promise of reward.

In the neighborhood of Mr. and Mrs. Short, at the Long Trail School in the Cumberlands, lived three little children, the illegitimate offspring of a man who had held a high place in the mountain community. He had been assassinated a year or two before, and now the children's mother, dying, left them to the care of an older half-brother. He, however, was as unwilling to care for them as he was incapable. He took them, however, into a cabin with him. The two older children were girls, eleven and nine years of age; the youngest, a boy of seven.

One day the Shorts heard from a neighbor that the

little boy, David, was dead — had died a day or two before. They went over to the place to see if they could be of help. The cabin was closed, with no sign of life, and all their pounding and calling brought no response. But looking in at a hole near the chimney, Mr. Short spied two shod feet protruding from the bed, and with this advantage he succeeded in arousing the owner (the half-brother) and in bringing him to the door. They asked if it was true that David was dead.

"Dead!" he echoed, "yes, he was dead — dead drunk!"

Then they had the story. The boy had gotten his brother's whiskey bottle, and drunk a whole quart of the poison; and when his sisters found him he was unconcious, scarcely breathing, his head lolling, helplessly drunk, and in danger of death. The girls dragged the little fellow out to the road, in a frightened effort to revive him. They dashed cold water over him, and tried to waken him, but not until ten hours had passed did he regain consciousness. He was now, however, nearly recovered from his debauch.

To save the children, Mr. and Mrs. Short considered taking them into their own home, but they found the relatives ill-disposed to permit this. The clan was large, and some of them in good circumstances and of fair culture; but none of them wished to take the children so illy bred and nurtured into their own homes, yet their pride revolted at the thought of strangers' giving them charity.

Christmas time came. At the Shorts', there was discussed between the parents and the children how the Jones children's lives might be brightened a little. Should they have a Christmas tree? Oh, yes! and Katherine and Charlotte would give them their own dolls and ribbons and other presents. Christmas day they loaded a wagon with a tree and presents, covered them with a canvass, and drove over to the home of the waifs. It was a new, two-room house the older brother had just erected out of green lumber, and there were now wide cracks between the upright boards. The children were alone within, trying to keep warm around a coverless stove. They were inveigled outside and away by some of their visitors, while the older people took the tree in, set it up, decorated it with strings of popcorn and bright paper, and hung the presents upon it. Then the children were brought in again, and their eyes opened wide with astonishment.

"We tried to keep awake all last night," they said, "to see if 'They' would bring us a doll, but 'They' didn't bring anything." And they fingered with some misgiving mingling with their delight, the first dolls and Teddy-bear they had ever owned. With the wagon they all went out and brought up a load of dry wood to warm them as well as might be. And then they were left alone with the tree.

A week later they began to come to school, the first they had ever attended. They were delighted with it, especially the dinner part, a part which they found by persistent venturing into the teachers' home at the proper hour, and which they took to be a legitimate feature of the free school.

In the midst of winter as it was, the girls were wearing only a single garment, a thin dress, the boy a waist and a pair of knee pants, both in tatters, so that his skin showed through in strips. All were barefooted. Some new clothes—"imported goods"—were provided for them, but it was ordained that they must first be bathed. They were brought over from the school, one by one. The girls willingly took their baths before they donned their new clothes; but the boy, no! After a while they succeeded in getting his rags off, but he persistently refused to be wet with water. Even a celluloid duck plunged into the tub gave him no reassurance. Then his sisters, who, bathed and clothed, were in the schoolroom, were successively sent for, but they could not succeed with him.

They showed him his nice new clothes. "Oh, I want those clothes *so much*," he would say, but he would not get into the bath. At last they did induce him to put one foot in, but he immediately jerked it out; and that was all the bath he got the first time. He got the clothes.

Soon after, the clan became more generally disposed to turn the children over to the school people, and they were taken into the Short's home. Again the battle with the bath was on with David, "I ain't goin' to take no bath!" he announced with decision. Mr. Short said nothing, but to clean the boy's head he doused it with creoline, and then —"Oh, David, your shoulders are wet with this creoline. You'll have to have it washed off."

"Yes," he said, with interest, "it's rainin' down," and with no protest he was set into the tub. There, after the first gasp, he sat splashing, and shortly began to say, "Oh, I do like a bath! I do like a bath so!"— an expression iterated for the next half hour over new clothes, new apron, and so on. And soon the bath hour came to be one of his chief delights.

The head cleaning was no small affair. The hair of all the children was matted with nits and alive with lice. There were great sores and patches of loose skin which served as hiding places for the vermin. The two younger ones had to have their hair clipped close, but the older girl begged so hard of Mrs. Short to have "nice hair like yours," that an effort was made to save it. Mrs. Short and a friend worked for hours on it. It was greased, soaked with creoline, and carefully, very carefully combed, the vermin being destroyed as fast as they fell. But her raw, sore head caused her great pain, careful as they might be.

"Susie," said Mrs. Short, "you will have to let me cut it."

But she said, "Oh no, no; I can stand it. Do go on! I'll stand anything if I can only *be somebody!*" And so they worked for five solid hours, till midnight, and saved the hair that was to her the badge of being somebody!

Those children came into that home having no real knowledge of God or of prayer, having no clear conception of correct behavior at table or elsewhere, their young minds besmirched and besotted with bestial ideas. They remained nearly a year, fathered and mothered equally with the own children of that home; they learned to love their Jesus and to pray to him in a quaint, original way that was the soul of sincerity, and which time and again brought tears to the eyes of their benefactors. They became well behaved and well mannered, their minds were purified, brightened; and the time finally came when some of their relatives, in one of the largest cities of the South, were glad to open their doors to this trio, rescued and prepared for a higher life.

The teaching of the schools is to the end that those who are helped shall themselves become helpers. Nothing can so rejoice the heart of the teacher as the sight of those whom he has helped turning with the true spirit of Christ to the rescue and uplifting of others. When his young men and women, saved from debasing habits and trained in truth and purity, become the instructors of other boys and girls; when families in his community freed from the filth and stupor of tobacco and the craze of liquor, freed from the pains of dyspepsia and rheumatism and boils and eczema by radical changes in diet and manner of living — when these become messengers of light and blessing to others in the community and outside; when children and youth, standing on higher planes of living, reach down helping hands to those who have not yet responded, and whom none but themselves can help so well; that, all that, becomes a reward in comparison with which the highest salary and the most honored position in the world are as nothing. This experience is one in which every member in the self-supporting workers has had a part.

There was in the neighborhood of the Pine Knot

School a family composed of a decrepit father, four grown boys, and a fourteen-year-old girl, the youngest of them all. The mother was dead; and the girl, Anna, had never had any instruction in housekeeping, and scarcely in cooking. The family never sat down to meals together; they took their food from the pot and the bake-kettle on the hearth, and ate as time and fortune favored them, by the fireplace or on their way to the field. The house was unkempt and dirty. Outside, the farm was in keeping with the house. The rail fences were down and weeds and briers covered the field. The girl seemed to her brothers not as a sister, but as one of themselves, and she, as well as they, was called upon for field work.

This girl, along with others, came to the school, but for two years she seemed incapable of making progress. Her dress — gotten however she might get it — was ill-fitting, torn, and buttonless. Her hair was uncombed, and she had often to be sent out to wash her face and hands. Mrs. Winthrop and others of the ladies went time and again to her home to clean it and teach her how to make and mend her clothes and those of her brothers. But very soon things would be almost as bad as before. For two years this went on, and the school workers almost despaired of making her better.

But at the end of the two years, suddenly there seemed to come an awakening. She came to school neat and tidy, her dresses she kept in repair, and visits to her home revealed the fact that the lessons taught her had at last borne fruit. The home began to be transformed, and the girl herself blossomed into womanhood like a flower from a dull weed. Her brothers opened their eyes at her in astonishment. For the first time they seemed to realize that they had a sister, and what a sister meant to them. They began to take pride in her, to give her little presents, and to help her make the home a home. The reform began outside as well, and the farm began to look up. The change in the family, begun in the girl, was marvelous and complete.

Some time after this transformation began to take place, a younger girl, a neighbor, came up to Anna's house one morning. She was much such a girl as Anna had been, dirty, ragged, and untidy. Anna looked upon her with the eyes of a new apostle.

"Dolly," she said, "I'm going over to Aunt Belle's this afternoon. Wouldn't you like to go with me?"

"Yes," said Dolly.

"Then let me help you slick up, and I'll take you."

She took off Dolly's dirty and torn dress, putting one of her own new ones upon her while she washed the other. She gave Dolly a bath, scrubbed her face and hands, and combed her hair. Then she ironed Dolly's dress. But it was torn in several places. Where she could, she caught the edges together, but there was one rent too big to be spanned without a patch. And though she searched her small house over, she could find nothing to make a proper patch. All she had was a clean flour sack she had dusted and washed. And since she had nothing better she took the white flour sack and made a patch on the little pink dress. Then they went together over to Aunt Belle's.

Anna saw her aunt looking with curiosity at the transformation in the neighbor girl, and supposing she was taking special note of the flour-sack patch, she said, "It was all I had. I did the best I could."

But there were other thoughts in her aunt's mind. "Anna," said she, "how did you come to do all that for Dolly?"

"Why," answered the girl, "I was helped: why shouldn't I help others?" It was a hill girl's simple expression of Christianity's deepest principle: salvation for service.

Her home became neat and tidy; on the farm the fences were built up and the fields were cleaner. Prosperity attended the work of this girl and her brothers.

Her father died. She developed into a good woman. From this poor hill cabin, from a flour-sack patch, she came to be a young woman who would not become conspicuous because of dress on the boulevards of Nashville. And holding still that idea, "I was helped: why shouldn't I help others?" she developed into a true womanhood, a helper indeed among others.

Well is it said that this work "will have a far stronger influence for good than the preaching of sermons." Let the Christian worker show the life that is within him by his practical ministry, and the ranks of the Lord's army will continually be swelled by the new recruits he thus creates.

Going to Market

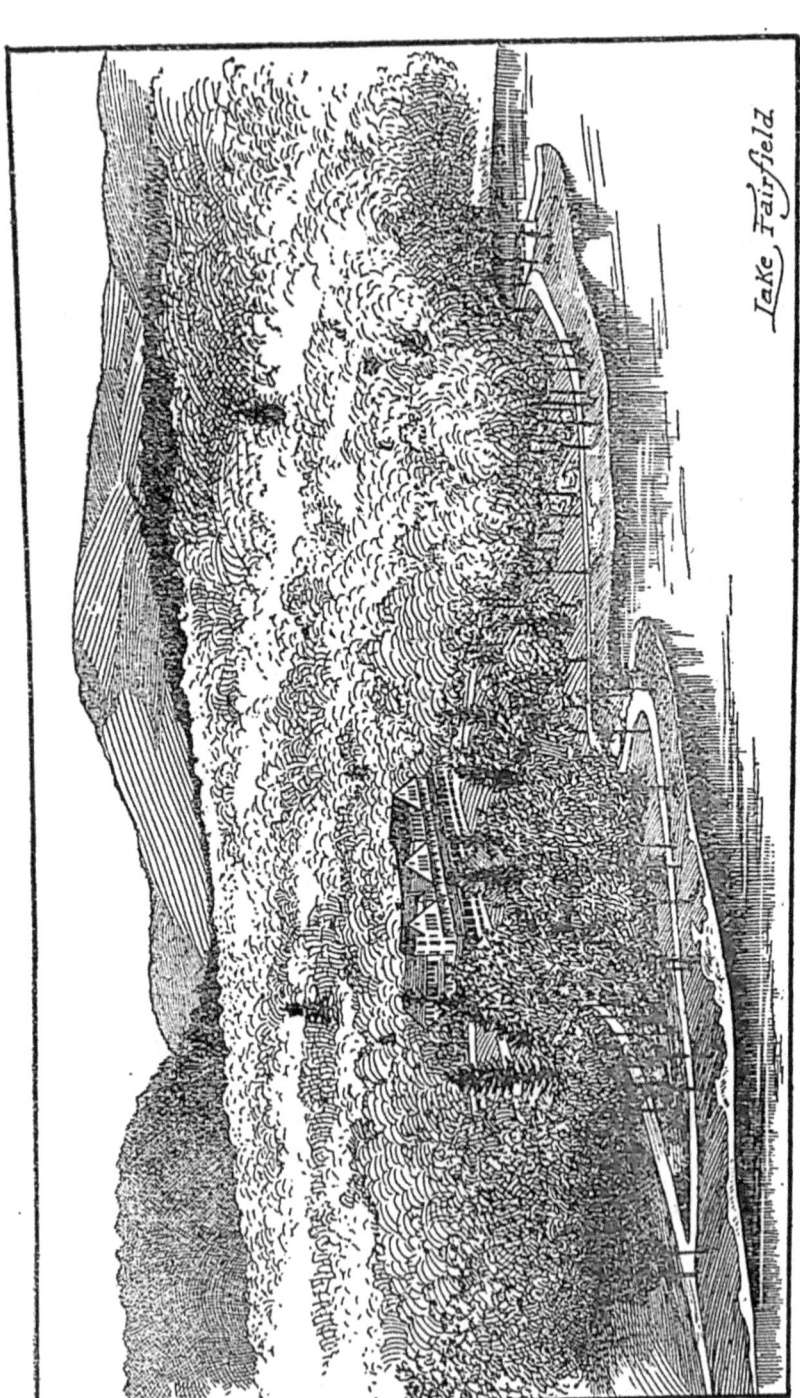

In the Sapphire Country

Cooperation

"The temple of knowledge is not to be found by searching through far lands; it stands here at our hand. Nor are the great men and the leaders to come mysteriously from some distant place; they are here at our doors, pleading for a chance."
Martha Berry.

XXIV

WHOSOEVER IS NOT AGAINST US

JOHN, the "Son of Thunder," one day with some of his fellow disciples came upon a scene such as they were accustomed to associate with only their Master and themselves. They saw a man casting out demons. Whether they knew anything of the case, how much and how long the man had suffered, how worthy or unworthy was the healer, we are not told. But their spirit is manifest in John's report to Jesus. "We saw one casting out demons in thy name," he said, "and we forbade him, because he followeth not us." They did not think of the relief and joy of the healed demoniac, they did not think that Jesus' fame and power were being spread through others; they felt only jealousy that one not named or associated with themselves should presume to do the work they were doing. These others, they assumed, could not accomplish their mission, could not rightly represent their Master. They were specially privileged, they believed themselves therefore specially capable, and they did not intend to sanction usurpation of their place and work by any other.

But Jesus rebuked their action and their policy. "Forbid him not," he said, "for he that is not against us is for us." The disciple who gets Christ's attitude will be a ready worker with all forces for good. In the world, and in other churches than his own, he will find men and women giving their lives to the betterment of their fellow-men, some in one way, some in another. Some he will find have grasped Christ's conception of the kingdom, working to persuade men to enter therein; others have dimmer views, and while zealous to procure good works in men, and church, and state, try largely the force of law and legal combinations. With all, the true disciple of Christ can and will show an open-minded helpfulness, giving to each the full measure of his strength and cheer so far as he can go with them. He will be no narrow sectary, requiring the brand of a particular sect or society on any work in which he is to engage, and withholding his sanction and cooperation because he fears he may be swept from his moorings. He can cheer on the prohibition movement, though he does not believe that law will conquer the liquor habit; and meanwhile he can put forth his strongest efforts to educate for temperance. He can aline himself with those who are fighting the social evil, though he may not believe that prostitution is completely curable by either law or economic improvement; and he can at the same time be devoting himself to the inculcation of personal purity and the upbuilding of the home. He can add his efforts to the efforts of those who are struggling to banish illiteracy, though he may differ with them as to some of the agencies used. And he can join the Christian worker who is seeking to bring righteousness into churches and communities, by preaching, and praying, and personal work, though he may not sanction all the doctrines advanced nor the methods used. And in all this work he can and must retain his personal connection with God, and receive wisdom from on high that he may neither betray his sacred trust of truth nor offend his fellows by a parade of his peculiarities. He can be made, as Paul declared himself to be, "all things to all men," and a coworker with all the good.

It is the peculiar temptation of a people who have radical differences from other peoples, and who especially are fearful of losing their children and perhaps themselves out of their communion, to isolate themselves and associate only with one another. Thus did the Jews in their late national history, in order to avoid the backslidings and apostasies of their early experience. And by this means they built up a middle wall of partition between them and the Gentiles to whom they were meant to be lightbearers. Some of them were indeed active enough in proselyting among the Gentiles, but so narrow and distorted had become their religion, largely because of their exclusiveness, that Jesus declared they made every proselyte "twofold more the child of hell" than themselves. They lacked the inner power which comes from communion with God, and which is the protection of the Christian against the influences which he meets in his intercourse with men. Lacking this, they sought to supply a defense by those walls of partition, first between Jews and Gentiles, then between the rich and the poor, and last — the highest step of holiness — between their strictest sects, like the Pharisees, and the masses of the people. The result was an ecclesiastical haughtiness, a formal religion, a spiritual death, a failure in their mission to the world, and finally, a rejection of their God and Saviour.

Thus will it be today with any people who repeat their course. So long as the battle rages between God and the devil, so long must the soldiers of Christ encounter the world. Failure to do so is cowardice and desertion. The only safety is not in shirking the battle, but in being armed with the armor of God. Christians trained in the truth of God and having a personal connection with him, will retain their faith and love, though assailed by all the temptations to which their mingling with the world subjects them. "I pray not," cried Jesus to his Father, "that thou shouldest take them out of the world, but that thou shouldest keep them from the evil." Following their Master, Christians today will give themselves whole-heartedly to the service of mankind, and will with gladness cooperate with all whom they touch and whom they prove worthy of Christian fellowship, be they of whatever name or Christian cause. The only ones who think all the good is in their own church are those who have never worked outside.

None have greater opportunity for this cooperative service than the rural mission school workers. Situated, for the most part, far from other churches or members of their own denomination, they are the more keenly alive to the influences for good manifested in other churches and individuals. Holding with the utmost earnestness the belief that the second coming of Christ is very near, and that preparation for his coming involves a very definite reform on many points not recognized by some of the churches, they nevertheless welcome the cooperation of all agencies which, though failing to stand on their own platform, yet aim at the betterment of society and the salvation of men. They recognize the splendid service given in the field they are entering, by individuals and organizations which have preceded them, a service far more extended and better developed than their own now is or may ever be; and they esteem the earnest efforts of members of the communities of which they have become a part to lift higher the standard of morality, education, and efficiency.

Thus it is their aim to cooperate with all who will receive their aid in any of their manifold channels of service. Nearly all the groups of these workers are members and workers in Sunday schools, several of which they have organized where there were none before. Free ministry to the sick is always one of their chief cares, and out of their poverty they have created the means of helping the poor, in clothing and sometimes in food and shelter, in this uniting with those of the community who are able and willing to dispense charity. To the upbuilding of the agricultural work they have contributed their help. One school led the neighbors in the purchase of a community-owned rock-crusher, to furnish crushed limestone for the soil. Several have been leaders in the development of new and valuable money crops, to take the place of tobacco or less profitable products. All have taken an interest in local agricultural movements whether organized or unorganized.

One school in middle Tennessee has for some time held an annual agricultural rally, that calls together farmers and farmers' wives from a considerable section of their country, and to these rallies they have brought not only help from their own schools, but from the State and national departments of agriculture. Deep appreciation has been shown of this feature of the school work by representatives of the government farm demonstration bureau, the boys' corn clubs, and the girls' tomato clubs.

In hygiene especially the influence of these workers receives appreciation from the guardians of health and those who have lost their health. The health principles of this people are more radical than the majority of men wish to accept, but they are recognized by all as being an advance in the direction of rational science; and many who are brought through their schools or their sanitariums to an adoption of the curative regimen of a simple dietary, healthful dress, water treatments, active labor, cheerful religion, and prayer, testify to its blessing and pleasure in their lives. In no more practical way is shown the ability of the workers to cooperate with their communities and with other workers for the world's good, than in the matter of health and disease. The Rural Sanitarium at Madison, as well as various humbler enterprises among the out-schools, has received the grateful testimony of many prominent in professional and government service, and their cooperation is assured in the work which these interests are endeavoring to forward.

In the library extension work of the state, several of the schools have cooperated, helping their communities in the selection and understanding of the best books, adding in most cases a number of their own not included in the library's lists.

So also in the efforts of the state to reduce the illiteracy among the adult population, some of the schools have added to the burdens of their gratuitous work of daily teaching, the additional work of night schools and a campaign to include in these evening exercises every one of the unlearned in their communities.

In all this cooperative service, it is the ambition of these workers, emulating their Master, to merit the testimony given by one who, returning from a stay at the Rural Sanitarium, was questioned as to how much of religious indoctrination she had received, to which she replied: "They do not need to talk their religion; they live it."

XXV

THE TIMES OF CHEER

ONCE a year the self-supporting workers come up to look one another in the face, to exchange experiences, to encourage one another, and to lay plans for more aggressive and extended work. That is, all who can, come. It is a difficult thing for the most of them to make the journey; for to solve the problem of shelter, the gathering must be in a warm season — summer or early fall — and at that time the crops are requiring attention, while few of the workers can easily find expense money. Those who are near enough, drive through in their wagons; and many a tale is told by the more distant, of providential incomes to pay their way to the meeting.

One brother and his wife, teaching in Alabama, wished very much to attend a convention, but they were practically without money, while they had two or three small debts in the neighborhood, and no means appeared to offer a way out. But they were in a peculiar situation just then, which they felt required the council of their brethren in order to decide their future, and whether they should stay with the work at all, and they believed it was God's will for them to go to the convention.

So they began to pray for the way to open, and prepared their clothing and arranged their affairs for the journey. In praying, they took their little daughter,

Dorothy, ten years old, into their confidence. She had been trained to have perfect faith in whatever she asked for and in what she did; and as soon as they had all prayed for God to send money, she climbed up into her father's lap and said, "Papa, how long will it take God to answer? Will it be five minutes? Or will it be an hour?" Her Father told her that God could answer in a minute, but that he often tested our faith by having us wait for a longer time, and he reminded her of the experience of the prophet Daniel, who prayed for three weeks before he had an answer to his prayer.

"Oh, but," she said, "it will not be three weeks this time, because we have to go in two days. And I believe we will get the money tomorrow."

Her father had a year-old colt which he decided to try to sell to pay his debts and furnish money for the trip, but he thought he could not expect a sale on the mountain, as valuable horses were rare in that locality, twenty- to thirty-dollar "jinnies" being much more common, and long time usually being given on the sale of a horse. So he planned to take the colt down to Lock-and-Dam, on the Tennessee River, a camp at the place where the government was making improvements, and which offered a better market than any other place near by.

He started out in the morning to walk the twenty-four miles there and back, leading the colt. But he had gone no more than three or four miles from home, and was still on the mountain when a woman came out of a house, calling, "Do you want to sell that colt?"

"Yes."

"How much do you want for him?"

"Seventy-five dollars."

"Well, I'll take him," she said, and going into the house produced the money.

It was a transaction unheard of for rapidity on the mountain; and in two hours from the time of his leaving, he had returned to his home, where Dorothy ran out to meet him, crying, "I knew it would come today. I knew it would when I prayed." The next day they were en route for the convention, where they received courage and inspiration to continue their work in the midst of unusual difficulties.

The first of these annual gatherings was held in late August, 1908, at the Madison School, where each succeeding convention has been held. The different meetings have varied more or less in character of constituency and program, but they have been alike in their main purpose of helping and cheering those already in the field and in giving inspiration to others to enter it. The schools nearest Madison have naturally been most fully represented — Oak Grove, Fountain Head, Chestnut Hill, Spring Farm, Hawk Ridge — though scarcely more so than schools from fifty to one hundred miles distant, like Bon Aqua to the west, Lawrenceburg to the south, and Daylight and Sequatchie Valley to the east. Alabama has seen members from its four schools nearly always marked present. Farthest away within the States, Georgia, Florida, and Virginia, and the Carolina group of schools, have seldom failed to have representatives present at the convention. Occasionally there have come from the Cuban and Honduran schools teachers who were in the States on business or furlough, and also missionaries from South America, Central Africa, China, India, and other foreign fields, some of whom have had more or less experience in this kind of school work.

Six miles north of Nashville is the Hillcrest School, which, though younger and as yet not so well developed, aims at the same position in relation to the negro work as the Madison School holds in relation to the white. It was established in 1908, and has made good progress in its mission of training negro workers as self-supporting teachers and farmers among their own people. So far, however, being conveniently near to Madison, its white teachers have joined the workers assembled there, and their assistance has been of marked value in making the convention successful. Their students also have the privileges of the convention for at least one day, the Sabbath.

The students of the Madison School usually constitute nearly half of the congregation at the convention, and their presence is far from being a formal matter; for they are almost without exception planning and studying to do the same work, to meet the same problems, which are discussed in the convention by those who are now actually meeting them. The eager attention shown by these students, the questions and the suggestions that come from them, make no small part of the value of the gathering.

We would invite you to attend with us a typical convention. Let us arrive the night before its opening, for promptness is a virtue highly prized, and there are material reasons besides why it is better to be early than late. If you go with us, you will walk the two and a half miles from the station to the school, but the road is macadam, and so, stowing our grips in the vehicle where the most delicate ride, we cheerfully follow this road through the garden spot of Tennessee until, at the rise of the fourth or fifth long hill, we reach the sign that says, "Rural Sanitarium," and turn to the left on the new stone road of the school.

Shortly, topping the crest of the ridge, which the water tank marks as the highest point on the farm, we pause to behold the panorama spread out before us. Just beyond us, scarcely below, stretches the long campus, from the old farm house up to the Rural Sanitarium, a road bordered on each side by cottages little and big — the little for homes, the big for public uses. Cool and inviting it lies in the luxuriance of its blue-grass sward, under the shade of the mighty old oaks and the locusts.

Sleep is sweet in the dewy nights of blue-grass Tennessee, and unless you are a light sleeper, it is not likely that you hear, late at night or early in the morning, the rumbling of the wagons that come in from Goodletts-

Third Annual Convention, Madison, 1910.
"Once a year the self-supporting workers come up." Page 285.

ville and Fountain Head and Portland, or even, perhaps, from Bon Aqua and Lawrenceburg, bringing the teachers and farmers who spent their last moments of light in the corn field or in the canning factory or the mill, and took the dark hours for their *de luxe* traveling to the scene of the convention.

But in the morning we greet them. There is the jovial Alden and the lean-jawed Irish Mulford, first of the out-school pioneers; there is Martin from Bon Aqua and Johnston from Eufola, who help us to remember, come Sabbath, what old-time preaching is like; there is little Leitzman from Alabama, and the bluff, hearty Artress from west Tennessee, to talk to us about building and blessing. And Clifford Howell from the Cumberlands and Marshall Johnston from the foothills of the Blue Ridge, are among those who represent a work antedating Madison, yet welcoming its magnificent aid. Tolman and his family and the Scotts from Sand Mountain, and Groesbeck from Sequatchie Valley to the north of them, Waller and Steinman and Graves from the French Broad plateau, and Watson from his celery lands and orange groves by Tampa, and Pflugradt from the Tidewater of Virginia, Diehl and Jacobs from Kentucky, and Kendall and Rudisaile from Arkansas — all these bring news from near and far of the progress of the self-supporting school work.

And not alone from the school work are we to hear. Down from Chicago comes the virile, rapid-fire Dr. Paulson, with the gospel on his tongue and the *Life Boat* in his hand, fresh from experiences in prison ministering and platform lecturing, from rescue work in the slums and the care of his great sanitarium — comes to offer a union of city work with the work of the wilderness. And with him is Dr. Kress, world-wide medical evangelist, a leader alike in temperance crusades and personal evangelism. Dr. Hayward, veteran among the medical missionary forces in the South, comes up from Georgia, with his wife, a sharer in his work of ministry to the mountaineers. And closer by, in Nashville, so that he can alternate attendance with practise, is Dr. Harris, earnest advocate and practitioner of medical philanthropy. Then there are nurses like Glatter of Alabama, Kate Macey and her corps in North Carolina, and Elma Jeffries in the Palmetto State, and last of all, Oswald, with his report of needs and service and miracles. By all of these the note of medical evangelism is sounded, and emphasis given to the place the healing art is to occupy in the work of the gospel. It is a note fitly sounded at Madison; for a third of its students are nurses, its president and its dean as well as other teachers are physicians in charge of the sanitarium, and ministry to the bodily ills of men is interwoven with all the work and the teaching of the school.

The convention opens with a praise and experience service. Dr. Sutherland, who is invariably elected chairman year by year, strikes, as is his habit, the note of cheer and courage, and the testimonies that roll in in response are no ordinary recitals of hopes and fears and desires, but rather live, specific reports of deeds accomplished, needs inspiring to service, difficulties financial and spiritual overcome, and joy in the realization of fellowship with other laborers and of oneness with Christ. Sometimes a minor note is sounded by some struggling soul new to the work and almost overwhelmed with the obstacles in the way, but invariably the chord of triumph is also struck, feebly perhaps at first, but full and strong before the close of the convention.

On Sabbath, the time of the Sabbath school is occupied by a general study of the day's lesson, and then by a discussion of Sabbath school and Sunday school work. Experiences from many quarters in methods and results are ready for relation by practically every one, but the Sabbath school superintendent (a student) keeps the discussion brisk, short, crisp, and to the point.

Listen, thereafter, to a sermon that is neither the ancient exposition of a text nor the modern vogue of a harangue upon some sensational theme, but rather a sermon based upon the model of the Sermon on the Mount. Says the speaker: "The words of Christ in reference to the Good Samaritan are addressed to the church for all time: 'Go thou and do likewise'— not merely to preach the gospel, but to minister to men. To our sick people in our sanitariums we do not give all the same treatment — a cold plunge. We study the needs of each individual, and treat each one accordingly. Just so it must be in the science of salvation. The manifestation of the love of Christ is the last message to the world. As we go out as workers, we are not only to study Christ's methods of work, but we are to carry with us Christ's spirit of work."

Saturday night begins the discussion of the subject of agriculture, so important to the rural worker, a subject which is continued on Monday, a special agriculture day, on which many speakers from the State and national departments of agriculture and education are present. The presiding officer of the day is the county superintendent of schools, and an enthusiastic audience responds to the speakers' instruction, their appeals, and their words of appreciation for service being rendered by the teachers and workers before them.

Sunday has been a red letter day, when large numbers from the Nashville publishing, educational, and medical interests were present, and often from greater distances. The discussion of experiences in the hill and mountain schools begins on this day, and principles and plans are thoroughly studied and illustrated by the varied experiences of those who present and discuss the topics under consideration. On this day, too, first appear on exhibition the displays of the workmanship of the schools. It must be said, however, that though these exhibits bear fair comparison with similar exhibits in sloyd of paper and woodwork and weaving and drawing and sewing to be seen elsewhere, the real exhibits, which best tell what these schools are doing, are to be seen only by visits to their various neighborhoods, where the more permanent and valuable evidences of their energy, care, and patience are shown in the homes and farms of the communities.

The teachers enter heartily into a discussion of one another's circumstances and peculiar needs. Oftentimes these can be and are discussed in public meeting with the greatest profit; at other times private conferences are arranged between those in peculiar circumstances and those who have experience and wisdom to help them. The assembly room of Gotzian Hall, where the sessions are usually held, is a forum of world-wide subjects. Now it is the struggling farmer, but lately detached from the accountant's desk, who is anxiously inquiring about the use of fertilizers, and the answers come from the radical's utter condemnation to the expert's succinct advice and recommendation of bulletins for study. Again, it is a request for information as to the best text and auxiliary books, and a physician responds with the recommendation of the newest physiology, or a litterateur (rare bird in this practical, next-the-ground collection) tells of a list of helpful juvenile books which appeals for book donations may possibly bring in. Again, there are tangles of government and cooperation whose general principles may be dwelt upon in public, but which for specific discussion require private conferences. And yet again, a brother brings a report of threatened opposition and obstruction of his medical evangelistic work, a thoughtful discussion of which results in the division of the convention into groups for prayer and study, that there may be unanimity in the final course adopted.

And all this while the two or three committees which the simple organization requires, are busily at work collating and condensing and relating the ideas and suggestions of the body for a report at the last meeting. It is a notable thing with what speed and unanimity these final recommendations are put through, because the discussions consist almost wholly of commendation and exhortation, and are brief at that. The members of the convention are for the most part better accustomed to deeds than to debates.

Five days is the utmost time that such a meeting can be held. With difficulty have the workers left their farms and shops and homes to be present on these days of cheer. Always in the midst of the joy of this association the call of the needs at home is sounding in their ears; and they are at once loath to leave and impatient to be back at work. But of their faith and joy there is no better testimony than that of a young teacher in the last morning meeting. One cannot give the conviction that lies in his tones, in his eyes suffused with tears, as speaking of a worker, he says, "If I had no other result for all my struggles there, single-handed, overwhelmed with tasks, perplexed about money matters, knowing myself inadequate to the needs — if I had no other result than the salvation of this young man, I should thank God eternally that he has permitted me to undertake this work."

The evening sees some of the wagons depart; the morning says farewell to the scores who go by rail. They bid one another good-by with affection, with clasped hands and embraces, with smiling lips but oftentimes tearful eyes. Their words and their looks declare that the brotherhood of these times of cheer shall be maintained out on the frontier, as, few or single-handed, they continue the work they have so bravely begun. It is a little band, this, training in the wilderness for great things; and many there must be to join them, like Zebulun of old, "such as went forth to battle, expert in war, . . . fifty thousand, which could keep rank" and "were not of double heart,"

A Kentucky Homestead

The Help of the Hills

"Here is our Jerusalem, the children of the hills; our neighbors; our kith and kin. Begin with them and save them and let them help us save the world." Edward O. Guerrant.

XXVI

THE TORCH-BEARER

THE limestone bed of the Cumberlands is honeycombed with caves. Memory runs back to a day when a school outing promised the unexampled joy of exploring one of these caves. A lazy, hazy Indian summer day, bronze-leafed and stubble-paved, opened its right of way to the dark mysteries it might never look upon. At the hole in the mountain's face, the varied crowd of youth and children, with one or two elders, stopped to get ready their lights, for which perhaps half the company had provision. The great majority bore "lighter wood" torches — fat pine knots, with adhering splinters for handles. There were two or three lanterns, one of them a huge, old-fashioned black japanned affair carried by a little girl named Emmy. But the chief interest centered in the newfangled light of the teacher, who, deploring the ravages of the smoky pine knots upon the alabaster treasures of the cave, had brought with him a powerful electric torch, the object now of envious and half-scornful raillery from the dozen youngsters who bore the time-honored "lighter."

Within the cave the pungent censers of the pine knots threw their gleams on the walls, or darted glints of smoky fire upon the path as we stumbled along. But so dim was their light, and so erratic their restless carriers, that only fleeting glimpses were to be caught of the great high domes with their clusters of glittering stalactites. Or, when they were held near to the crystal-tipped daggers lower down, their oily smoke so quickly killed the beauty that we thrust them away.

Then little Emmy, lifting her lantern, sent its shaft of light along the rows of "The Dragon's Teeth" or round the circle of "The Queen's Necklace," and made all their jeweled points glow with passion or with pride.

But it was to the teacher's torch that we owed our vision of the grandeur and glory of this hidden world. Down the winding, rough-floored corridors we passed from chamber to chamber, piloted through the darkness by that clear, streaming light, ever steady, ever playing just right to show the pitfalls or to reveal the beauties of the way. Here we lay flat to gaze over a precipice into a Stygian gulf that even the flashing eye of the electric torch could but vaguely explore; there we saw, rough-cast by nature and shaped by imagination, a trio of squat stone gods that might claim rule of those realms. On the shore of the dusky Whippoorwill Pool; in the great Throne Room with its canopied chair of state and its graded seats for nobles and for thralls; or, yon side of Fat Man's Misery, in the low-roofed Room of the Fountains, with its cold, crystal streams flowing over the fluted lips of the terraced basins — through all these, the torch-bearer was our seer, our interpreter, making the near mysteries revelations and the distant secrets lures.

Once, twice, we tarried behind, and were left in pitch blackness, scarcely daring to move foot for fear of disaster. All about us, doubtless, were wonders: columns and arches, moldings and frescoes of brown and gray and white, marvels of nature's art; but they were all hidden to our eyes. To us they did not exist until the torch again flooded the recesses of our station, and brought them to life.

The pine-knot boys were racing and leaping and halloing from rock to rock and room to room, crying out splendid discoveries, breaking off trophies of crystal-studded treasures of the cave, and with their torches making great strips of blackboard whereon to write their names. But to us they were only will-o'-the-wisps, and their unrestrained vandalism but the regrettable excesses of an alien enterprise.

Once they came in touch with our torch-bearer. At one end of "the Cathedral," where the high roof stooped toward the floor, rose the great pipe-organ, its columns of stalactites reaching down their slender arms to touch the sturdier forms of the stalagmites below. The white light of the electric torch streamed upon the snowy surface, from spreading base to arching top, and made it indeed all that fancy called it. The hush of sacred thought and feeling came upon us, and in some hearts there rose the strains that echo what the angels sing.

Then through the stillness rang the shout of a pine-knot boy, as he clambered behind the organ. Through the holes and the screen of the thin stone connecting the pipes his torch shone out redly; and suddenly all the mystic beauty of the structure vanished, and we stood gazing upon the fiery mouths and the glowing eyes of a monster, one of those metal-eating monsters that devour the mountains, the heat of its inward fires glaring through its belly and the smoke pouring forth from its nostrils. And then all the air was filled with the clamor of the multitude, shouting. But the clear white light in the hands of our torch-bearer led us away and on.

For hours we wandered through the mazes of the cavern, till it seemed we must be miles away from our starting point. Then at last we climbed into the dry atmosphere of the "Saltpetre Room," whose crumbly dusty floor was ridged and furrowed by trenches and excavations. Our leader paused, while the company, weary for the most part, and anxious for the end, gathered around him. The pine-knot torches had burned to the last of their lives, and now but two or three pieces remained to be thrown, spluttering and fuming, upon the floor. Of the oil lamps, all had burned out except little Emmy's faithful big black lantern. She lifted it now to look at its yellow flame, and her little fingers carefully, anxiously turned the wick a trifle higher.

"Teacher," she said, "when will we get to the end?"

"Do you know where we are?" he asked. Some of the older boys knew; but a depression, mystically born, perhaps, with the dying of their torches, sat upon them, and their grimy faces remained stolid as they fixed their eyes on the teacher.

"Do you know where we are?" he said.

"I should say," replied one whose lantern light had lasted till a few moments before, "I should say we are about ten miles from daylight."

"We have traveled a long way," said the teacher, "and our lights have shown us many things, the things, I suppose, that we each were most interested in. And now we have no light but this one and Emmy's. But we shall not need them long. We are in the "Saltpetre Room," where long ago that substance was mined to make gunpowder for the war. And this room itself has seen more than one fight; for this ground was sought by all the warring factions. It is very close to the surface; and we are very near daylight now."

So, turning to the right, he led us down a little bank and forward. And then, at another quick turn, we saw, just a little ahead, the white patch that meant the day.

There are torch-bearers in the darkness today, leading the leaderless, lighting the benighted, revealing the treasures that may be monuments or that may be plunder. Some of them are pine-knot boys, bearing the cloudy light of material science, careless of foot and hand and eye, prodigal of beauty, who rush among the treasures revealed by their torches, showering their smoke and sparks, shouting their gainful discoveries, and leaving behind in their vandal track a ruined realm.

Others there are, like gentle Emmy, whose quiet

little amber flame throws no great splashes of light upon a wide or distant field, but with quiet illumination brings out in pleasing distinction the features of a life close at hand. They are safe guides, and they live long.

And to others is given the greater duty and the greater joy to throw that pure and strong and steady light that reveals the beauty and the grandeur and the glory of a world in which these things are greatest, but where they yet lie hidden in the darkness. He who carries the undying torch of truth has need not to think of himself, his own aggrandizement, his repute, his pleasure. He is made an interpreter to those who follow him or who may find him. He may not boast to others or to his secret self of his superior light or of the favor its possession accords him. He may not use it for his pleasure alone, forgetting the slow or the weak or even the careless. He is a guardian against dangers, a portrayer of wonders, a revealer of secrets. He may not clamor against vulgarity, lest he be vulgar; nor fret at waywardness, lest he estrange the wayward; nor be impatient at sluggishness, lest he lose his following. And if, in patience and in peace, he lead his people through the mazes of the dark land he lightens, teach them the wonders and the joys of the way they tread until they forget their weariness, and bring them at last about him — yes, even, perhaps, the smutty stragglers that have lost their torches — in the battle-scarred vestibule to the great new earth, he may happily be able to say to them, "We are very near the daylight now."

The mountains of the South will not much longer be in any great degree an unknown land. Their great valleys, always the center of a broad life, have become the bases of assault from all the forces of the age upon the mountain world. Capitalism has seized it in its grasp; philanthropy is casting its mantle over it. To the west of the Appalachian Valley, the capitalist at work is exploiting its great oil and coal and iron and timber treasures; to the east, the capitalist at play is raiding its

"Land of the Sky." The state is pushing its program of education farther and higher in the mountain land, and the forces of religion and religious education are making an earnest effort to keep pace.

Today the mountaineer of the accessible regions is being lock-stepped with the rest of the country in its march of civilization — comrade not merely in knowledge and power, but in recession of virtue as well. Tomorrow the remote hills will echo to the tread of this same civilization; and it may not be long till we shall have only the nooks and crannies of the mountain land to match, in some sort of kinship, with the shanty towns of the North, the hardscrabble farms of the East, and the slums of the great cities. In what ranks the mountaineer will then march depends upon the course made clearest for him today.

And so far the broadest open road is the road to the new Americanism, paved with dollars, decorated with display, and ending in dissipation. The mountaineer of old was dependent on his own efforts. If he was "forethoughted and fore-handed," he lived well if plainly by his industry and his providence. He knew he must make his own crop and fat his own meat before the winter, or he should go hungry. His wife knew she must spin and weave and fit, or her family would shiver. There was little exchange of labor for cash, little cash to be expended, and in consequence there was self-dependence rather than a trust in easy money to be made somehow when the need came.

But today, cheap though mountain labor may be, it has a market; and, deceived by the sight of a silver dollar every new day, the dollar that once went so far around the circle of the year, the mountaineer is apt to forget his fields and let other people grow his stock, while he spends his strength for other men's dollars and his dollars for other men's cunning. And the exchange is not equal, as he soon discovers, both because his common needs require more money than he thought, and because uncommon needs and luxuries have been born with the advent of the new life. Fashions of diet and dress and adornment must be copied from the world. The sunbonnet gives way to the flower-decked hat, that lasts half as long and costs ten times as much. Homespun that knew no age is discarded for bright calicoes that live but a year. Rent eats big holes in the weekly pay-roll; and food, even if stinted in desperation, takes more than the laborer ever dreamed food could cost. The vices get a new foothold in the camps and the towns, or under the fostering indulgence of millionaires at play.

If it is to the cotton factory the mountaineer has been lured, he finds, with his large family of children, a rare chance for evil development of his cupidity. Child labor is popular at the looms, and the father can put his children and his wife to work at a combined wage sufficient to support him in leisure, and this he very frequently does, sometimes conniving with conscienceless mill-owners at the admittance of children below the legal age.

If it is to the mines he goes, he takes his oldest boy and works tremendously at first, perhaps, until he is able to earn five dollars a day underground — and not a cent out under the sun. Then, perhaps, he discovers that it is not necessary to work every day or all day, and his leisure time is spent at the grog shop or the "blind tiger," while his easy money goes for whatever he may cast his eyes upon, until the pinch of necessity drives him underground again.

But if he has the somewhat more fortunate lot of living in the play-ground land of the tourist and pleasure-seeker, he may not be torn from his farm, but he nevertheless neglects it to minister to the pleasures of the wealthy. He and his sons discover that the possession of a span of horses and a smart rig, or perhaps a second-hand automobile bought on time, is the open sesame to a life of rolling leisure, with easy money, driving from mountain top to laurel-lined glen with parties whose fashions of dress he copies, and whose fashions of morals he as yet may only wonder at. His wife more strenuously, but with the same thought of easy money, keeps boarders, finding at the close of the season big receipts and some small gain. And then everything dies till the opening of the next season.

Through all this life of change and excitement and flowing money, there runs little thought of betterment of mind and soul. The children are likely to be kept from school for any slight advantage of money earning. Religion, under the blighting influence of outsiders' neglect and light scorn, is shamefacedly abandoned, and the easy tolerance and thoughtless skepticism of America's great godless majority takes its place. The mill-hands and the miners become a migrant class, wandering from place to place in ostensible search of better wage or living conditions, but in reality for sheer weariness of life's monotony and a craving for change and excitement. Their lands have been sold, perhaps, to the great corporation seeking mineral rights, or to the agent of the wealthy pleasure-seeker who wants a summer residence; and the stability, the solid force, of the free land-holder have gone with their sale.

Their neighbors who remain, refusing to be parted from their homes, are perhaps the select remnant, and to them must we look for a maintenance of the worth of the mountaineer. And yet they do not wholly escape the influence of new standards and opportunities. The mountaineer is inevitably changing. His resources are being taken by the exploiter, for the benefit of the nation, perhaps, as well as the capitalist, but not to the net profit of the mountaineer. For these new forces, so far, are against his development. His ancient arts, suited only to the needs of a primitive, isolated society, are useless in the new era of divided labor and mechanical substitutes, and he forgets them. His religion is too old-fashioned for a formal Christianity and a material-

By courtesy of Berea College.

A Family Reunion.

"God has been training in his mountain strongholds a picked guard." Page 310.

istic philosophy, while his culture is laughed out of existence by a society that runs from board-walk loungings to Argentine tangoes. In this sudden awakening from the sedate life of our great-great-grandfathers, to the feverish, ceaseless movement of this crazed age, the shock to the mountaineer unanchored by a prime hope in God and unhelped by a training for a broader life, is likely to prove fatal. Wrenched from his moorings as an independent, self-reliant, God-fearing American freeholder, he drifts to swell the restless, discontented, terrible array of America's employed and unemployed. Whether he shall be saved from this is a question that waits on the action of America's forces of conservation.

Over against this trend is set the influence of the school and the true church of Christ. The defect in their program is that they have chiefly followed rather than preceded the economic invasion. But where they are, they are more than gathering salvage; they are saving crews that may bring the fleet into harbor.

The state (which means the community under the guidance of some great-souled leaders) is pushing hard to extend the term and improve the efficiency of the public school. It is beginning to introduce the study and practise of hygiene and to create a love for country life and agricultural science. The more colorful life typified by the boys' corn clubs and the girls' tomato clubs is becoming known in the mountains, though as yet only on their outer edges. And a community spirit is being fostered, more, perhaps, by the school than by any other agency.

The handicap of the school is the scarcity of well trained and devoted teachers. And, beyond all local problems, comes the query whether that which the public school has failed to accomplish in the great world outside, where it has not succeeded in stemming the tide of materialism, it can accomplish here. It can train the intellect, it can sharpen the wits for the fight over material things, but it cannot shape the soul.

To the church, that true church of God which stands by the Bible, resists the aggressions of clerical and scholarly agnosticism, believes in the law, trusts in the gospel, preaches salvation through Christ alone, and holds up the hope of a returning Saviour who shall restore all things, to that church belongs the greatest responsibility and the greatest opportunity of the age in the saving of the mountaineer. This is the religion yet popular in the mountains; unknown in its fulness, perhaps, not all its bearings recognized, not all its obligations observed, but yet in substance treasured in the hearts of the mountain people.

To them let men and women come as unassuming Christian friends, settling among them as farmers, or mechanics, or nurses, or housewives, holding up the steady light that illumines and wins. To them also is due to come the torch-bearers who can throw the broad, clear light of flaming truth upon the uneven path, the dark abysses, and the splendid walls and domes.

Who has more light has more responsibility. He to whom has been entrusted so great a power must seek for wisdom to use it righteously and well. Not in boasting, not in self-gratulation, not in stupid arrogance, but with earnest thought for the slightest and the greatest good he may do others—in this spirit must the light-bearer come. And for him the mountains hold a reward that he may not fully realize until he is about to lead his people into the great day of a new heavens and a new earth.

XXVII

A CHOSEN PEOPLE

THERE have been many peoples chosen of God through time's history, and never once from among the mighty of earth. They have done great deeds, they have preached great messages, they have endured great trials, they have won great victories. They have seen a world drowned in overwhelming flood, they have turned their backs upon a crumbling Babel to found an empire of souls, they have trod through deserts and camped beneath mountains where wonders of earth matched wonders of the heavens, they have turned from the shadow of a Cross to become the ambassadors of a Kingdom. In the dungeon and at the stake they have triumphantly assaulted the gates of hell; through jungles and deserts, through witchcrafts and tyrannies, through stripes and imprisonments, through perils of land and sea and wrestlings with the princes of the powers of darkness they have carried the banner of their King — a chosen people, but not from the great of earth.

They have heard the great apostle say: "God hath chosen the foolish things of the world to confound the wise; and God hath chosen the weak things of the world to confound the things which are mighty; and base things of the world, and things which are despised, hath God chosen, yea, and things which are not, to bring to nought things that are." They have heard the great prophet say: "The Lord did not set his love upon you, nor choose you, because ye were more in number than any people; for ye were the fewest of all people." And they have learned to repeat the humble avowal put into Israel's mouth: "A Syrian ready to perish was my father, and he went down into Egypt, and sojourned there with a few . . . and the Egyptians evil entreated us, and afflicted us, and laid upon us hard bondage . . . And the Lord brought us forth out of Egypt with a mighty hand, and with an outstretched arm, and with great terribleness, and with signs, and with wonders." And thus they hear his purpose: "Ye are a chosen generation, a royal priesthood, an holy nation, a peculiar people; that ye should show forth the praises of him who hath called you out of darkness into his marvelous light." "I the Lord have called thee in righteousness, and will hold thine hand, and will keep thee, and give thee for a covenant of the people, for a light of the Gentiles; to open the blind eyes, to bring out the prisoners from the prison, and them that sit in darkness out of the prison house."

For this purpose God has called, not men from king's houses, not men clothed in soft raiment, not men shaken like reeds in the wind. He has called men who worked with their hands, like Noah; men who turned their faces away from the city, like Abraham; men whom he snatched from prospective thrones, like Moses, to learn patience in the wilderness; men who learned patience and trust and joy in the fields, like David; men who despised effeminacy, like Elijah; abstemious men, like Daniel; and single-minded men, like John the Baptist. The life of plain living and single aim that made these men the chosen of God, is bounded by laws far too strict to invite the majority of men. When God would try the experiment of embracing within the ranks of his chosen people a whole nation, heirs of the promise made their fathers, he gave them in great detail the laws whose essence their fathers had known and kept. They were

A Chosen People

laws that would distinguish them for temperance, patience, justice, loyalty, and devotion. If they could keep that code, it should be their wisdom and understanding "in the sight of the nations, which shall hear all these statutes, and say, Surely this great nation is a wise and understanding people."

Seldom, however, were all this chosen people true to their God; and from among them he must again and again take, to do his work, his true chosen ones, like Gideon's band in the valley of Jezreel and Jonathan at Michmash, like Elijah's scattered seven thousand and the three worthies on the plain of Dura. But in every case the chosen ones were noble souls who had had training, by fate or will, in hard and simple living. And thus has it been in all succeeding ages.

Moreover, this distinction has not been a legacy, kept by one people from age to age. It is a spiritual, not a natural, birthright. The fathers that should rightly train their sons did indeed pass on to them in some measure the precious heritage; but few were the sons who could be soul-proof against worldly prosperity. So, then, the honor has passed from people to people, each one of which came forth from a life of simplicity and industry to meet the tests.

Who were the fathers of those vine-dressers and herdsmen of Italy's Alps that through the midnight of Europe defied and defeated the armies of Rome? Who were the followers of Ziska and Procopius but breakers of clods and threshers of grain, when they were called to swing their iron flails against Austria's priest-ridden power? Who had heard of the prowess of the Lowlanders, except as builders of dikes and makers of meadows, when they rose against the barbarism of Catholic Spain, and established a home for freedom? Who prophesied, when a little band of persecuted men found refuge on the estates of a German count, that from feeble Hernhutt was to go forth the greatest missionary crusade since the days of the apostles, that from that feeble, flickering light should flame forth a glory through the frozen North and the wild wilderness of the West, through the dank jungles of the tropics, through deserts, and to the isles of the sea?

God is no respecter of persons, and in every land he has those that serve him. Whosoever will may make one of the chosen. Philistine and Canaanite, Ethiopian and Gaul, Chinese and Kanaka, have furnished recruits for the army of the Lord — rare souls who revolted from their surroundings and their training, and by overcoming gained power as warriors of God. Yet their lives are also proof of the fact that privation, whether chosen or forced, is the armorer of heroes. And it is from among those who as a people are accustomed to this privation that the most recruits are gained.

It has come now to the time when God is enlisting his last legion. The long war against sin and Satan is drawing to a close. The last defense of God's positions must be the most courageous, and the last assaults upon the devil's trenches must be the most determined and heroic. Is it too much to expect of our King that, while receiving volunteers from every land, he has also been training in his mountain strongholds a picked guard for a special service, the spiritual sons and successors of Gideon and Elijah, of Maccabeus and Gianavello, of Zwingle and Knox? For this position and this service are the mountaineers of Appalachia fit. Do any question their fitness? — Listen to the testimony of those who know them best.

In their souls lives the mystic beauty of the hills that inspired God's prophets of old: "Only a superficial observer could fail to understand that the mountain people really love their wilderness — love it for its beauty, for its freedom. Their intimacy with it dates from a babyhood when the thrill of clean wet sand was good to little feet; when 'frog houses' were built and little tracks were printed in rows all over the shore of the creek; when the beginning of esthetic feeling found expression in necklaces of scarlet haws and headdresses pinned and braided together of oak leaves, cardinal flowers, and fern; when bear-grass in spring, 'sarvices' and berries in summer, and muscadines in autumn were first sought after and prized most for the 'wild flavor,' the peculiar tang of the woods which they contain.

"I once rode up the Side with a grandmother from Sawyer's Springs, who cried out as the overhanging curve of the bluff, crowned with pines, came into view: 'Now ain't that finer than any picter you ever seed in your life?—and they call us pore mountaineers! We git more out o' life than anybody.'

"The charm and mystery of by-gone days broods over the mountain country — the charm of pioneer hardihood, of primitive peace, of the fatalism of ancient peoples, of the rites and legends of the aborigines. To one who understands these high solitudes it is no marvel that the inhabitants should be mystics, dreamers given to fancies often absurd but often wildly sweet.

"Nothing less than the charm of their stern motherland could hold them here. They know well enough that elsewhere they might sit by the flesh-pots. Occasionally a whole starved-out family will emigrate westward, and, having settled, will spend years in simply waiting for a chance to sell out and move back again. All alike cling to the ungracious acres they have so patiently and hardly won, because of the wide world that lies outside their puny fences, because of the dream vistas, blue and violet, that lead their eyes afar among the hills."[1]

They have the poverty, the bare living, that has made the more than Spartan heroes of the church: "This poverty of natural resources makes the mountaineer's fight for life a hard one. At the same time, it gives him vigor, hardihood, and endurance of body; it saves him from the comforts and dainties that weaken; and

---

[1] Emma B. Miles, *The Spirit of the Mountains*, pp. 17-19.

it makes him a formidable competitor when it forces him to come down into the plains, as it often does."[1]

Will there be need today, in foreign lands or in the hard places of the home field, for such endurance as was shown by the circuit-riders of 1800?— Behold it still living in the mountaineer heirs of those fathers: "As a class, they have great and restless physical energy. Considering the quantity and quality of what they eat, there is no people who can beat them in endurance of strain and privation. They are great walkers and carriers of burdens. . . . One of our women, known as 'Long Goody' (I measured her; six feet three inches she stood) walked eighteen miles across the Smokies into Tennessee, crossing at an elevation of five thousand feet, merely to shop more advantageously than she could at home. The next day she shouldered fifty pounds of flour and some other groceries and bore them home before nightfall. Uncle Jimmy Crawford, in his seventy-second year, came to join a party of us on a bear-hunt. He walked twelve miles across the mountain, carrying his equipment and four days' rations for himself and dogs. Finding that we had gone on ahead of him, he followed to our camp on Siler's Bald, twelve more miles, climbing another three thousand feet, much of it by bad trail, finishing the twenty-four-mile trip in seven hours — and then wanted to turn in and help cut the night wood. Young mountaineers afoot easily outstrip a horse on a day's journey by road and trail.

"In a climate where it showers about two days out of three, through spring and summer, the women go about, like the men, unshielded from the wet. If you expostulate, one will laugh and reply: 'I ain't sugar, nor salt, nor nobody's honey.' Slickers are worn only on horseback — and two-thirds of our people had no horses."

"In bear-hunting, our parties usually camped at about five thousand feet above sea level. At this ele-

---
[1] John Fox, Jr., *Blue-grass and Rhododendron*, p. 17.

vation, in the long nights before Christmas the cold often was bitter, and the wind might blow a gale. Sometimes the native hunters would lie out in the open all night without a sign of a blanket or an ax. They would say: 'La! Many's the night I've been out when the frost was spewed up so high (measuring three or four inches with the hand), and that right around the fire, too.' Cattle hunters in the mountains never carry a blanket or a shelter-cloth, and they sleep out wherever night finds them, often in pouring rain or flying snow. . . . Such nurture from childhood makes white men as indifferent to the elements as Fuegians."[1]

Some even of the mountaineer's faults are born of his virtues. Is he quick to resent injury and apt to strike hard in revenge?— it is a trait derived from his regard for justice and schooled by his sense of personal responsibility and clan loyalty: "Consider for a moment the mental attitude of the Elizabethan gentleman who carried a sword, or the Southern gentleman who carries a revolver. He has not yet entrusted himself in all things to the protection of his government. He looks upon the state as an organization for carrying on foreign wars, but feels that it is his own prerogative to defend his property, his household, and his honor with his own right arm.

"This temper, still strong in all the South, is naturally strongest in the mountains, where as a matter of fact the government has not always been able to inspire either confidence or fear. The conditions which sometimes justified arming for self-defense on the frontier are likely to be present more or less in many parts of the South, and particularly in the mountains.

"The operations of the government are weakened by the fact that it has never had the thorough-going efficiency known in some other places, and the further fact that mountains furnish convenient refuges for those who defy the law. Furthermore, in Southern commu-

---
[1] Kephart, *Our Southern Highlanders*, pp. 216, 217, 219.

nities which have received no foreign influx and sent out few settlers to the West, everybody is related by ties of blood to everybody else. In rural life this counts for much. Family loyalty requires that one support his kindred in court and quarrel to the last traceable degree. . . . [Yet] there is probably no mountain country in which ten per cent of the population have ever been engaged in these lawless proceedings. The mass of the people is made up of simple, primitive people, showing the strong traits of their race — independence, respect for religion, family affection, patriotism."[1]

Undaunted before difficulties, daring and resourceful, able to make the farthest use of the most limited opportunities, is the best type of the mountaineer: "Where the struggle with nature has not too deeply depressed the body and mind, all the splendid homely virtues of the pioneer survive, and often take on rare attractiveness in the sons and daughters of the mounttains. Their delayed development conserves much that this age lacks of unspoiled elemental manhood and simplicity of spirit — both profoundly urgent moral needs of today. Beneath a reckless individualism and ignorant conceit, one discerns resources of sturdy independence. The mountaineer faces his hard circumstances with a heart at once undaunted and resigned. A saving sense of humor breaks every fall and turns defeat into more than half victory. Having shrewdly fathomed human nature as it exists in his narrow range, he finds his judgments surprizingly just and accurate when opportunity comes to apply them to the larger world. He undertakes unwonted responsibility with a certain honorable largeness and perspective; thus showing that wisdom is born of insight rather than of mere multiplication of experiences. Lincoln was such a man and had such wisdom. 'He that is faithful in that which is least is faithful also in much.' Training in the school of adversity often develops in the mountaineer a practical capacity

---

[1] William Goodell Frost, in *Independent*, 1912, pp. 709, 711.

for making small resources count which spells marvelous success when once the instruments of modern life are put into his hands. Recently I watched a mountain student's first inspection of the newly installed hot-air furnace in a mission school dormitory. The mountaineer, like the Indian, studiously refrains from confessing surprize at the unaccustomed; but this boy's curiosity and interest got the better of him. Soon he was freely speculating on the operation and success of the innovation; yet not for a moment did he admit to the world or to himself that he was not its potential master. He seemed to me typical of the mountaineer facing modern civilization. The mood of the forward-looking among them is the mood of conquest. Put it to the test, by furnishing it an opportunity, and it will justify itself as it has done ten thousand times."[1]

These traits and powers, admirable and useful as they are, might yet miss their chief value if ununited and uninspired by the power of religion. But, reinforced by them, and binding them together for service, is the predominant religious nature of the mountaineer: "The mountaineer lives 'the simple life' in close touch with nature in its varied manifestations. From nature, but more yet from the Scriptures, and perhaps principally from strong heredity, he has acquired an absolute faith in a personal, omnipotent, omniscient, and omnipresent God, who has to do with him in 'all the good and ill that checker life.' He believes in the substitutionary sacrifice of Jesus as the Saviour of the world. He has no doubt that Jesus will 'come to judge the quick and the dead'; while 'the forgiveness of sins, the resurrection of the body, and the life everlasting' are unquestioned tenets of his creed.

"His faith is not merely intellectual or theoretical, but it takes strong hold of his thinking and, in many cases, of his life and conduct. The Southern mountaineers are grave by nature. The few native ballads that

---

[1] H. Paul Douglass, *Christian Reconstruction in the South*, pp. 331, 332.

they have are, like those of most mountain dwellers, somewhat weird and are written in the minor key. The native character is a serious one. Nothing interests a mountain audience so much as does a debate on some question of Biblical interpretation or doctrinal dispute; and where the Spirit of God is moving upon hearts, nothing holds the attention more fixedly than does a discussion of some point of Christian duty. The one book that is read in the Appalachians more than are all others combined is the Bible; and many readers have an intimate acquaintance with its contents.

"As has been said of the race of Shem, it may be affirmed of the mountain race, 'It has a genius for religion.' Too often, as everywhere else, this religious nature is dwarfed and misshapen by environment and natural depravity; but though stunted and deformed, it often, by many a token that is recognized by the quick vision of sympathetic lovers of souls, proclaims its latent strength and future possibilities. There is always something responsive to appeal to, in the man of the mountains."[1]

To see a promise of this power, you have but to step into the mountains and witness the earnest evangelism of such preachers as "Proctor Bill": "I shall never forget his manner, or his matter. Both were peculiar and unique. He spoke with tremendous earnestness and energy. He was Boanerges, in action. No one could doubt his sincerity, nor his courage, yet his language was as simple as a child's, for he knew no other, being an unlearned man. It was the speech of the common people, who heard Jesus gladly. It was largely the language of the Bible.

"It was in the summer-time, but he had on a suit of winter clothes, and the effort of speaking covered him with perspiration. He was profoundly moved, and he moved the people as few college men could have done.

---

[1] Samuel T. Wilson, *The Southern Mountaineers*, pp. 154-156.

"As to the matter of his discourse, I was as much surprized. It was largely scriptural and entirely evangelical. His quotations were apt and correct, and the wonder grew when I learned how and where he was reared.

"I shall never forget his introduction. As near as I can recollect it, he said: 'My friends, you know me. I was born and bred in this country. On this very spot where this schoolhouse stands I once sold and drank whiskey. Left an orphan by a good father, I had no one to teach me to do right. My mother was a godless woman. I never heard her pray in my life. When a boy, I tried to kill Bob Hill for striking a smaller boy. As I grew older and larger I grew more wicked and desperate. In drinking, gambling, and fighting I was a leader. Just over this hill I tried to kill a man for an insult. I was tried and sent to the penitentiary for three years. I had never learned to read, and I never owned a Bible. I neither feared God nor regarded man.

"In the penitentiary, I was compelled to attend the prison worship on the Sabbath day. A Mr. Morrison preached, and God sent his words to my heart. I felt I was a lost sinner, and for twelve days I could neither eat nor sleep. I lay in my cell, the most miserable of men, and cried to God for pardon. Blessed be his name, he heard my cry and pardoned my sins and saved my soul. I rose up a new man, and determined to read God's Word. I was then thirty-nine years old, but, by hard work, I learned to read, and determined to tell others what he had done for my soul. This is why I am here today.' This is only a bare outline of what he said.

"It was a remarkable discourse and produced a profound impression. Men knew he was honest and earnest, and not afraid to say what he believed. Since the day he left the penitentiary, he has been trying to preach the gospel in the very country which knew his sin and shame. Men hear him and wonder at the wonderful change. Many have been led to Christ through his ministry.

"Having no horse, he walks across the mountains to his appointments. Having no money, he has no books nor clerical clothes. His only possessions consist of a wife and four little girls and a boy, on a rented mountain farm. This he works through the week; and walks to his appointments on Sundays, sometimes fifteen miles."[1]

It is the faith of the mountaineer's helpers that from the seed sown there will come a more bounteous harvest, a wider husbandry, than from an equal labor anywhere else bestowed: "I make the statement more as a hope than as a prophecy, but I feel sure of my ground in saying that these North American Highlanders will yet become a grand race; a race that shall stand for freedom political and industrial; a race that can no more endure unjust rule than it can thrive in the tainted air of the low country. Types come and pass in nature's scheme of economy, but not until their usefulness is ended. The mountaineers are a young people, not ready to pass away; their strength lies dormant, awaiting its hour. To the mountains, in time to come, we may look for great men, thinkers as well as workers, leaders of religious and poetic thought, and statesmen above all. So much passionate loyalty cannot be lost to the government, must find expression in redeemers of practical politics as well as in military service. From the mountains will yet arise a quickening of American ideals and American life."[2]

"If we enter into this field merely to denude the hills of timber and to penetrate them for coal, our work degenerates into a selfish enterprise, and the mountain people may become a positive menace to our country. If the mountaineers are to be given up entirely to the tender mercies of commercialism, we might as well

---

[1] Edward O. Guerrant, *The Galax Gatherers*, pp. 69-71.
[2] Emma B. Miles, *The Spirit of the Mountains*, pp. 199, 200.

give up all hope of ever recruiting our strength from theirs. They must be given financial aid in their educational struggle, so that they can reach a knowledge of themselves and their capabilities. They need to become acquainted with the best elements of modern civilization, and they need to be left in profound ignorance of all else. Their individuality must not be merged into the monotonous life of our own communities. Their vigorous traits of character must be preserved intact. The native shrewdness that is shown in escaping the vigilance of revenue officers and the courage displayed in the management of the feuds, should be turned to higher uses. Their contempt of physical harm and their devotion to principle may be of inestimable value in the maintenance and propagation of spiritual truth. Their only need of others is to aid in helping them to know themselves, and after that aid has been given, 'let us lift our eyes to the mountains, from whence cometh our help.'

"Again, it is a mistake to suppose that mission work in the mountains is a work of charity, or a one-sided philanthropy, where much is given and nothing is received in return. The returns are immediate, and of far greater value than the investment. As it is, the whole country might, with profit, take lessons from these hardy mountaineers in love of home and country, in hospitality, in unwavering friendship, in adherence to conviction and in reverence to God. They need no master come from abroad to teach them patience under difficulties, or endurance under adversities. In the homely virtues they are our peers, and in the matter of strength and courage they are the masters of all."[1]

The optimism that sees in man's history a natural evolution from base to noble, that hopes therefrom a development of the race into demi-gods, and that looks to the upbuilding of any people as a factor in that apotheosis, is doomed to a disappointment as certain as the

---
[1] Professor McDiarmid, in leaflet of the Soul Winners' Society.

Judgment Day. But the optimism that is based upon the regenerating power of the religion of Jesus Christ; that, while seeking the elevation of all men, disappoints itself with no hope of a universal salvation; that, above all, is inspired with the certainty of an early and complete triumph of good over evil, through the advent of our Lord Jesus Christ — that optimism is true, and sure, and unconquerable. In that spirit of optimism the Christian world may look with confidence into the swiftly coming clouds of battle; and, instructed by the Word of God, may expect the reinforcement necessary for victory. And for such a reinforcement we may on earth, as well as toward heaven, lift up our eyes to the hills, whence cometh our help. For "the God of the hills" whom the Syrians feared has kept in reserve in the mountains a chosen people who shall have a mighty part in the closing of the wars of the Lord.

The End

TEACH Services, Inc.
P U B L I S H I N G

We invite you to view the complete
selection of titles we publish at:
www.TEACHServices.com

We encourage you to write us
with your thoughts about this,
or any other book we publish at:
info@TEACHServices.com

TEACH Services' titles may be purchased in
bulk quantities for educational, fund-raising,
business, or promotional use.
bulksales@TEACHServices.com

Finally, if you are interested in seeing
your own book in print, please contact us at:
publishing@TEACHServices.com

We are happy to review your manuscript at no charge.

www.ingramcontent.com/pod-product-compliance
Lightning Source LLC
Chambersburg PA
CBHW052049230426
43671CB00011B/1847